On My Own

On My Own

The Challenge and Promise of Building Equitable STEM Transfer Pathways

XUELI WANG

Harvard Education Press
Cambridge, Massachusetts

Copyright © 2020 by the President and Fellows of Harvard College

All rights reserved. No part of this publication may be reproduced or transmitted in any form or by any means, electronic or mechanical, including photocopy, recording, or any information storage and retrieval systems, without permission in writing from the publisher.

Paperback ISBN 978-1-68253-489-2
Library Edition ISBN 978-1-68253-490-8

Library of Congress Cataloging-in-Publication Data is on file.

Published by Harvard Education Press,
an imprint of the Harvard Education Publishing Group

Harvard Education Press
8 Story Street
Cambridge, MA 02138

Cover Design: Ciano Design

The typefaces used in this book are Carrara, Gotham, and Bradley Hand.

*To the students
who participated
in this study.*

CONTENTS

Preface ix

Introduction: Same Aspirations, Different Trajectories 1

1 The Contradictory Promise of Math and Active Learning 27

2 Left to Their Own Devices 43

3 Coping, Hoping, and Diverted Dreams: Women on the Road Less Traveled 59

4 Resilience, Despite All: Students of Color Navigating Transfer 77

5 Waiting to Be Seen: More Student Faces 91

6 Tempered Aspirations 107

7 Momentum Trajectories and Embedded Inequities 121

8 Reducing Friction to Level the Playing Field 137

9 Toward Equitable Access to Transfer 155

Appendix A: Methodological Notes 171

Appendix B: Annotation for Data Sources 207

Notes	209
Acknowledgments	231
About the Author	235
Index	237

PREFACE

But many of us didn't make it here.
—Kimberly

I REMEMBER EVERYTHING that I felt when meeting Kimberly on that crisp September day in 2005 at The Ohio State University. Kimberly had just transferred from Columbus State Community College to work toward her bachelor's degree in the College of Engineering. I was starting my second year as a doctoral student in the College of Education and was a research assistant at the Office of Student Affairs Assessment, working on a project about transfer student experiences at the university. Our paths crossed at the Oval, the enormous quad at the campus center, where Kimberly asked me for directions to the bookstore. I offered to walk with her as that's where I was headed too, and we struck up a conversation as we went. We quickly connected through our shared experience of transitioning into a new campus environment, hers as a transfer and mine as an international student, and laughed around a few "culture shocks." And of course, the second I found out that Kimberly was a new transfer, I couldn't help but start to eagerly share resources at Ohio State that my limited knowledge could offer. When we hit the bookstore, there was a long line as usual for the start of the quarter. "See? You might end up spending an hour here just to purchase your textbooks," I said, heaving a big sigh.

"No worries," Kimberly replied. "I ordered all my books from the store's new online system, and I am just picking them up." She proceeded to the information desk and located her preordered books in no time. I watched, wondering where I had been all this time, totally unaware of such an obvious service, while assuming that my academic standing and greater experience with the university meant I was the one holding the knowledge.

Connected, self-reflective, and inspired was how I felt meeting Kimberly that day. It was about experiencing the brilliance, grace, and savviness of transfer students firsthand. It brought life and texture to my then evolving exposure to the community college[1] and transfer literature, and fueled my growing interest in studying transfer for my dissertation research. In short, my encounter with Kimberly coincided with and further solidified my decision to pursue a research career focusing on community college transfer. As an international student coming from a highly structured and closed education system with little to no possibility for student mobility across institutions, my introduction to the American community college, particularly its upward transfer function, was both eye-opening and uplifting. Coupling that with my personal interactions with Kimberly and the many savvy, successful, and kind transfer students whom I have met since, I internalized the idea that any postsecondary education path that was structurally set to be "terminal" was beyond unacceptable. Therefore, as I delved deeper into any topic on community colleges that fall quarter and onward, any missing thread about two-year colleges' transfer function, which allows students to achieve a baccalaureate degree and beyond, if they so desire, was remarkably troublesome. And this omission is especially pervasive in the narrative around the shortage of talent in science, technology, engineering, and mathematics (STEM) fields of study, as I discuss later in this book.

I didn't know at the time that my initial fascination with transfer as a democratizing function was to be complicated when I saw Kimberly again—and for years to come. Later that winter, I helped conduct a series of focus groups with transfer students at Ohio State, and to my delight, Kimberly participated in one of them. The focus group conversations helped confirm and contextualize what I found on the survey that had been sent out earlier: transfer students were as engaged and successful academically as their counterparts who started as university freshmen. As Kimberly and I left that focus group, we fondly recalled our fall encounter and teased each other about textbook purchases. When I told Kimberly how inspiring I found her experience and those of other transfer students, she said something that has stuck with me since: "But many of us didn't make it here."

Fast forward to fall 2018, during a class session of my doctoral seminar on community colleges at the University of Wisconsin–Madison (where I am a faculty member), when I previewed some of the findings from the research undergirding this book. The story of Katy, whom you will soon meet, struck a particular chord among my students. Katy was a community college transfer-aspiring student who ended up not transferring or earning any credential. As my students discussed what went wrong and what could have been done differently to change Katy's course for a more positive outcome, LaShawn, one of our doctoral students who attended a community college as an undergraduate, spoke in a somber voice uncharacteristic of her typical upbeat style: "I feel so sad. I've always loved my community college and I am a proud transfer, but it is just sad to think that I made it and others didn't."

With well over a decade between their experiences, Kimberly and LaShawn, both successful transfer students, both identifying as women of color, spoke of the perennially elusive nature of transfer and the disconnect between aspired and realized goals among transfer-aspiring students. Startlingly enough, although 70 to 80 percent of students who enter two-year colleges aspire to transfer to a four-year institution, only around 20 percent actually do so. And this pair of statistics did not change much from when Kimberly voiced her sentiment to when LaShawn realized that she had beaten the odds.[2] This is especially disheartening when considering that success rates for community college students who make it through the transfer process are on par with those who originally started at four-year institutions.[3] To think that only a fraction of those motivated students ever transfer, which means the post-transfer success is enjoyed by that same small fraction. As this book will show, the disconnect between aspired and realized goals among transfer-aspiring students permeates all areas of study but is particularly pronounced in STEM. In a similar fashion, the structural and institutional barriers inequitably experienced by transfer-aspiring students manifest across all fields but are noticeably magnified in STEM. It begs the question: Why do students with the same desire to transfer end up on different trajectories, and what can we do to reduce the gap between what students aspire to and what they actually attain?

My book set out to answer this question from the vantage point of how students experience and negotiate a path to or away from transfer. It portrays the unfolding educational journeys of roughly 1,670 beginning two-year college students over the course of four years.[4] But first I want you to meet four remarkable students among this group: Jordan, Seamus, Kanda, and Katy, whom I was privileged to get to know, interview, and learn from through the research underlying this book. Their experiences and the trajectories each represents are previewed in the introduction and further unpacked throughout the book. Individually and collectively, their stories epitomize this book's title, *On My Own*, along with all the depth, complexity, and paradox that come with it.

INTRODUCTION

Same Aspirations, Different Trajectories

" *You do have to search for it yourself."*

—Jordan (linear upward trajectory)

In the fall semester of 2014, eighteen-year-old Jordan started his college career full-time at Great Lakes College, a local two-year school, with a firm intent to transfer into the College of Engineering at Capital University, the state's flagship university.[1] A white male, Jordan came from a single-parent household with a modest income.[2] His mom held a bachelor's degree and was determined to offer Jordan a great deal of support for his plan to transfer, including financially. He was taking math, English, and other general education courses—transferable courses to pave his way. Jordan was in the so-called guaranteed transfer program—an arrangement made between his two-year college, Great Lakes, and Capital, which were part of the same state university system.

Guaranteed transfer programs are not new. They are the types of program through which a two-year college student will, in theory, attain junior status (which equals to about sixty credits), upon fulfilling certain credit and grade point average requirements.[3] Jordan's school website notes: "After meeting... requirements, you will transfer with the same rights and privileges as those who begin their education at the baccalaureate institutions." This promise appealed to Jordan. Speaking of why he chose to start at Great Lakes College and his transfer prospect, Jordan was confident: "I'm just getting my general education out of the way. And then I think I'm going to transfer to Capital. It is easy to transfer from Great Lakes College to Capital because they're part of the same system." (I1)[4]

What Jordan did not see coming was how vague these requirements could be in reality. He would learn the hard way that it was almost completely up to the students to figure out these requirements. How and where did they apply? To which specific schools? To which specific majors? And some aspects were hard to predict—what exactly was needed to meet the requirements set by specific majors at a given four-year college? By the time I saw Jordan again during the summer of 2016, he was deeper into the process of exploring how to transfer in engineering, searching for information on a website brought to his attention by an advisor. When I inquired about additional supports and resources from the school to help him figure out the nitty-gritty of transfer, Jordan took a long pause and then said:

> I don't really know. I guess there isn't. Some of the advisors here kind of helped me, but ultimately, it's kind of hard to find. There's only a few routes you can really use to figure out the information you need for transferring. Unless you dig for it, you're not really going to run into it very easily, so I do think that that's something that the college itself could work on, is helping kids discover that information to help them transfer, I guess. It is a little... you do have to search for it yourself. (I2)

In 2017, three years after his initial enrollment at Great Lakes, Jordan successfully transferred into Capital's College of Engineering. Looking back, Jordan had little he would have changed except one thing:

I didn't really know exactly the specific classes I should be taking at Great Lakes that were going to be helping me at Capital. But I guess, in some sense, making it very easy to find a website that shows you—for these majors, you want to take these courses. Have that more apparent and out in the open. Because that stuff is definitely up there, but you have to search. And if you don't even know what you're searching for, you're not going to find it. Yeah, make it more apparent what classes would be very helpful for these particular majors. (I3)

> " *I've already wasted the last six years trying to figure out what I want to do."*
>
> —SEAMUS (detoured trajectory)

Seamus was in her early twenties when she enrolled full-time in the biotechnology program at Centerville College, the state's second-largest comprehensive two-year college. Like Jordan, she too was raised by a single mom who holds a bachelor's degree. Early on, when we first talked to Seamus, her family income was higher than most—over $90,000. However, increasing financial hardships reduced this, and starting in 2016 her family income was low enough to allow her to qualify for a Pell grant. Based on its website description, the program Seamus was in prepares students for both jobs and transfer. Her enrollment at Centerville College was not her first encounter with postsecondary education. A few years earlier when she was eighteen, Seamus had begun college as a freshman in Capital's School of Engineering. Her admittance into Capital seemed a perfectly natural outcome of her participation in an engineering summer camp program there when she was a junior in high school. This six-week, fully funded program is designed to immerse "academically talented women and students from historically underrepresented groups" in the field of engineering, something perfectly suited for Seamus, who identifies as a multiracial Black woman, and who has been into science and technology since she was a kid. Seamus thought the experience was "super fun." She stayed with some twenty peers on campus and enjoyed the guest lectures, industry site visits, field trips, and faculty mentoring that the program provided. By the end of the program, Seamus was in love with the place and decided to apply. She was admitted to Capital on a competitive scholarship program that shared its mission with the summer program in which she had participated.

Until then, Seamus's story had been a success story, one that adds more anecdotes to the research base on summer bridge programs as an effective tool for recruiting underrepresented students in science and engineering, young people whose participation in these programs appears to garner a greater likelihood of eventual college completion.[5] In particular, the summer program exposure rekindled Seamus's longstanding interest in math and science, and paved her access to a baccalaureate engineering program.

Unfortunately, Seamus's evolving career in engineering took a sharp turn the minute she set foot on the university campus again, this time as a college freshman. She found her first-semester classes to be completely irrelevant and boring, so uninteresting that she often skipped the classes entirely. She did not know how to better engage with her coursework. During this transition, advising was glaringly missing. Recalling that experience, Seamus was appreciably frustrated and disappointed with both her advisor and herself: "I came up here, and my advisor personally sucked. She was not helpful at all. When I was like failing classes, like this was not the best thing, but you could've dropped a class; you could've. You can do other things than just fail a class and like she wasn't really helpful with that at all, and like I mean, I wasn't really proactive in seeking her help either, so it kind of goes both ways." (I1)

Seamus got kicked out of the university. After working as a cocktail server for two years, it dawned on her: "This is not what I want to do with the rest of my life. I need to figure something out." (I1) Still determined to get her bachelor's degree, she had to take a detour. She turned to Centerville and was proactive in finding her program fit. "So I literally went on Centerville College's website and went through almost every single science, technology, engineering, and mathematics (STEM) program that they had, and the description for this one [biotechnology] really stood out to me, and I was like, 'This is what I want to do. I want to be in a lab working with, like, cells and, you know, different organisms.' After my first year here, I was like, 'Wow, this is like exactly what I want to do.' So I kept continuing on with it." (I1) While the technical component of the program greatly interested Seamus, her real goal was to transfer and earn a baccalaureate and beyond. Speaking of her next steps: "But it [the biotechnology program] can only take me so far. If you want to be like a research scientist, you need to have all those nice little letters behind your name—PhD, BS." (I2)

By now, Seamus had navigated multiple paths into, through, out of, and back to college. She started at Capital, flunked out, and eventually enrolled at Centerville, all the while with a firm desire to earn a bachelor's degree and beyond. Seamus is one of the many students who follow a swirling pattern of postsecondary attendance.[6] This sort of back-and-forth enrollment can happen at different institutions or a mix of attending more than one institution and stopping out. Although it has not been quite clear in the extant, quantitative-heavy research base why students swirl, Seamus's telling trajectory offers rich insight into the causes and prompts behind the kinds of swirl and detour that students like her have experienced. It was not lack of academic preparation, interest, or family support. On the contrary, Seamus had plenty in each domain, as clearly indicated in her interviews, surveys, and transcripts. If anything, her story showed us that finding the right fit—a place that engages her and where she feels that she belongs, intellectually and otherwise—is the single biggest factor behind her swirl. Reflecting on the winding path that she had taken and was still on toward a baccalaureate degree, Seamus wished she could have chosen a more linear route: "If I could do it all over again, I would have definitely picked a two-year college, saved money, saved time, saved stress, and then gone to Capital ... I can see now why I didn't do well there [Capital], and why I'm doing well here [Centerville College], and when I go back next time, just being actively involved with your advisors and your teachers, like, you can do well and still be in a three-hundred-person lecture. You just have to actually talk to your teachers, which I did not do. And your advisors." (I2)

Seamus appeared to have found her fit at Centerville College. However, as you will learn, although her perceived fit kept her enrolled at Centerville this time around, it continued to derail her from a straightforward transfer path.

> *I have to get a job first."*
> —Kanda (deferred trajectory)

In the same fall semester of 2014, Kanda, an eighteen-year-old Native American woman, started as a full-time student in the information technology (IT) programmer analyst program at Metroshore College, the state's largest comprehensive two-year institution. Kanda is from a family of five with an annual income of around $90,000. Besides her parents, she has two brothers, both disabled and in need of long-term support. Kanda's entry into the IT program was far from predetermined. In her high school senior year, she took a programming class as a random, purposeless choice, but ended up liking it. She stuck with programming when exploring college and chose the IT program at Metroshore.

The road was a bit bumpy in the beginning. She struggled academically, citing her lack of IT experience. At one point, she even considered switching fields of study, doubting her "talent." But a chain of interesting events toward the end of Kanda's first term kept her from doing so. As the new course schedules were released for the following term, Kanda found out that several important program courses were offered in inconvenient places and at inconvenient times. Apart from her own difficulties, Kanda was deeply concerned about the challenges this might pose to other students, who "are either there because they've been laid off or because they are trying to get jobs to help benefit their kids and stuff, so they have obligations with family and all that." (I1) So she created a petition to have the courses offered at the downtown location, making them more accessible. After much back and forth, to her own amazement, the petition succeeded. "By that time I had invested so much time and effort into it I had decided, I think I'm going to stay in my program, and I decided to stay in it and my grades improved." (I1) Kanda completed the program with an almost perfect academic record. Soon after graduation, she landed a job as a software engineer with a financial services organization near her home city.

Picture-perfect as Kanda's trajectory might seem, she did not realize her educational goal, which was to transfer to earn a bachelor's degree in software engineering or information systems, something she ever persistently had been telling us, whenever we asked our students whether they intended to transfer. Kanda's actions spoke even louder of her keen interest in transferring. During her time at Metroshore, she literally exhausted all sources of information on transfer, and accumulated quite a wealth of knowledge on where and how her IT program would transfer. Across all three interviews, Kanda clearly described the names of the programs and universities that would accept transfers from her program. In many cases, she was able to name the exact courses that would or would not transfer and to which programs or institutions. But the numbers and information of which Kanda was most cognizant were related to money. The financial implications that came with transfer emerged as her biggest barrier: "So far the only school that has decent plans for transferring is Wering University [a private four-year institution in the state], but I don't have fifty grand a year to spend on education. So I think what I'm going to do is I'll probably try to get a job first and then finally transfer so that way I can actually have some funding before school, and once I gain those skills then I can probably strive for more." (I2)

College affordability is a major issue for community college students.[7] Education researchers Lorelle Espinosa, Frankie Santos Laanan, Soko Starobin, and Latrice Eggleston all found that women and students of color, more so than others, experience financial concerns related to transfer.[8] These students are often in severe need of supports such as scholarships and transportation, and Kanda was no exception.[9] Although finances had always weighed on her mind as a huge obstacle to transfer, it was not until her final semester that she decided to put transfer on a temporary hold. When I asked Kanda whether there was a moment when she knew for sure that she would stop pursuing transfer and get a job instead, she paused a while and said:

> It was around the final semester I had at Metroshore College. It was basically, I was still living at home. I didn't have a job. I was very—it's like, I didn't have a whole lot of money so I was still very dependent on my mom and dad. And I was, like, I had kind of felt like a burden. So I was like, "Oh, I really want to do all these things, but they cost money that I don't have." And it was like, my parents were absolutely super supportive of me. They were like, "If you want to go, you can go and get on that degree." But for me, what was really important was just being able to have some degree of financial independence. It was that final semester, I was like, "I have to get a job first. I'm going to finish this up and then I'm going to see if I can get a job within these next couple of months." And then kind of save up some money and go back to school once I have the funds to do so. (I3)

Kanda still had a lot of support for transfer from her parents. She was only twenty-three and was working a decent job, doing a lot of community work that she was passionate about. Although her dream to transfer was temporarily delayed, she was committed to getting her baccalaureate degree someday soon:

> So, I still definitely will work towards getting that bachelor's degree. One of the big reasons why I didn't end up getting that bachelor's was financial. It was a lot of student loan debt I would have to take on. Plus, my major wouldn't exactly transfer the way I wanted to at the

universities I was looking at. So I was like, "Well, let me work a few years. Build up a savings. Build up the things that I need. And then go in and get my bachelor's once I have some stability." (I3)

" *I can't make this decision on my own."*

—Katy (taking a break trajectory)

Other than identifying as white, Katy could not be more different from Jordan. When she started at Centerville College in the fall of 2014, she was in her early thirties and a single mom with two young children, earning less than $30,000 a year across multiple low-paying jobs. Katy was attending school part-time and exploring her options for a major program of study, potentially something in a scientific field. Although not as certain of her path as Jordan, Katy, too, initially intended to transfer into a four-year program one day, but she had little support for transfer financially and otherwise. Her first course was a general chemistry class. Katy described it as challenging and overwhelming in a double-layered way. First, there was a lot of memorizing, which was hard for her. To make things worse, due to her attention deficit disorder (ADD) along with challenges associated with her mental and physical health issues, she was in over her head with the lab as well:

> I couldn't concentrate on what I needed to do for the lab itself because everybody around me was doing things and like visually and auditorially? Is that a word? It was just, it was too much input for me to focus on what I needed to do. So I had a lot of trouble grasping those experimental kinds of platforms. Like how do I, how do I do this again? Like what are the directions? I'd go back to the directions too many times and got frustrated. So I think for me that was one of the more frustrating places. (I1)

Katy tried once to discuss her struggles with the instructor, whom Katy described as "kind and accommodating." This conversation did not really go anywhere, and the instructor reassured Katy, telling her, "I feel like you're doing fine. Like I don't feel concerned about your progress. I think you're doing okay." So Katy thought to herself, "Well, I must not appear to be struggling." Katy appreciated her instructor's belief in her and came away with the understanding that she would have to solve her own issue, like using earplugs in the lab. This did not fix the problem. Katy never completed that chemistry class and her STEM transfer prospect never moved beyond that point. Looking back, Katy wished she had communicated her issues much more forcefully before she realized she was completely overwhelmed by the chemistry class: "I don't think I had the awareness to say anything about it, like, 'I don't get the lab. I don't understand how to work with other people when there's noise and movement and fire and chemicals and all.' I just don't know what I'm doing." (I1)

Katy is not alone in her struggles with introductory math and science courses. There is a reason why these courses are commonly referred to as "gatekeepers," due to their remarkably low pass rates hovering around 50 percent as highlighted by education researchers Linda Hagedorn and Daniel DuBray.[10] Unfortunately, Katy was among the other, nonpassing 50 percent. Although these types of courses are supposed to be introductory and are necessary for choosing a major and for eventual program completion and transfer, ironically, due to their lower pass rates, they stand in the way of entering and completing a program, let alone transfer. Katy's flunking out of the chemistry class set in motion a series of failed attempts at a number of possible academic paths over the next four years.

In chapter 1, I discuss in detail students' learning experiences within these introductory courses. Indeed, the way they were largely taught essentially turned them into a gatekeeper instead of a gateway for Katy and many other students. In Katy's case, the mentality that everything had to be done on her own, compounded by her chemistry instructor's well-intended dismissal of her concerns, exacerbated the problem, driving her further and further away from a baccalaureate path despite her early intention to transfer. As we left our final interview in the summer of 2018, Katy teared up and told me, "I hope that somehow, through my story, the research that you're doing will be able to positively impact other students. And that they'll be able to figure out how to find the support that they need to follow what it is that they want. If I could only give myself the advice and hear it. Some of us live obscured for a while. But if we can continue to cultivate clarity—that's really beautiful." (I3) Katy did not transfer. She was no longer enrolled at Centerville, nor did she leave Centerville with any credentials. She was unemployed and was part of a band that performed occasionally at the local farmer's market.

Jordan, Seamus, Kanda, and Katy are among the many transfer-aspiring students who are part of a longitudinal study that I initiated in the fall of 2014. Each represents one of the four trajectories on which the students landed by the close of our project. As this book will show, they are a group of "typical" two-year college beginning students who encountered, endured, and every now and then thrived on some extraordinary circumstances to get where they ended up four years later. While none of these transfer-intending students traveled a smooth road, they arrived at very different places, and the important differences that set their paths apart cannot be ignored. This book unpacks those differences in detail, with the hope to illuminate much clearer, more equitable pathways toward transfer in STEM fields and more broadly. But before I tell their full story, where did all this start?

THE STEM SHORTAGE NARRATIVE

For well over a decade, federal agencies and the media have engaged in the much contended issue around the shortage of individuals in STEM education and the STEM workforce. According to *Rising Above the Gathering Storm: Energizing and Employing America for a Brighter Economic Future*, published in 2007 by the National Academy of Sciences, National

Academy of Engineering, and Institute of Medicine: "Although many people assume that the United States will always be a world leader in science and technology, this may not continue to be the case inasmuch as great minds and ideas exist throughout the world. We fear the abruptness with which a lead in science and technology can be lost—and the difficulty of recovering a lead once lost, if indeed it can be regained at all."[11] The issue was presented as even more dire and critical in the follow-up report, *Rising Above the Gathering Storm, Revisited: Rapidly Approaching Category 5*, published in 2010.[12] This shortage discourse presents STEM education, particularly at the postsecondary level, as a solution to feeding the STEM workforce. But even this sector of education has its share of trouble: "The United States has increased the proportion of its college-age population earning first university degrees in the natural sciences and engineering over the last quarter-century, but it has still lost ground, now ranking twentieth globally on this indicator."[13] The need to increase completion rates in STEM education, including at the baccalaureate and graduate levels, has been repeatedly promoted as a national policy priority.

I was first exposed to this STEM shortage narrative back in 2008 when completing my dissertation on community college transfer student success. The ways in which two-year colleges were portrayed both fascinated and bothered me. To be clear, two-year community and technical colleges have their fair share of attention in these discussions. However, when taking a closer look at the narratives, the focus at the time was keenly on STEM workforce preparation and participation at the "sub-baccalaureate" level for "mid-skilled" jobs, whereas upward transfer as a prominent role of two-year colleges was largely, if not entirely, invisible. Other than a brief recommendation by the National Academy of Sciences, National Academy of Engineering, and Institute of Medicine for funding expansion for STEM programs at the two-year level, along with access to courses and resources to prepare students for advanced STEM coursework, the role of these institutions as a contributor to STEM bachelor's degrees was barely acknowledged. While not necessarily the intended goal, narrowing STEM education at community colleges exclusively to job preparation at the subbaccalaureate level runs the risk of tracking in a metaphorical sense—by limiting choices of highly motivated students to a more terminal goal, thus blocking their upward mobility in education and careers. This is particularly ironic in light of the repeated calls for enriching the diversity of the talent participating in baccalaureate STEM education, when at least a partial response can be found in two-year colleges, the very institutions that enroll more students of color, women, students from low-income families, and first-generation students than their four-year counterparts.[14]

TRANSFER AS A POTENTIAL YET TO FULFILL

Both the potential of the community college STEM transfer pathway and the problem of ignoring it have stuck with me since. As soon as I landed my faculty job at the University of Wisconsin–Madison, my first few research projects dug into existing national databases on these issues. Indeed, my analysis confirmed the community college promise in broadening access to baccalaureate programs in STEM for historically underserved students through their upward transfer function. Drilling into STEM enrollment nationally, I found that, among students who started at a public two-year institution in 2003–2004, with a declared major and intent to transfer, nearly 40 percent of them were in STEM fields of study, and among these STEM majors, 36 percent were students of color underrepresented in the STEM workforce.[15] This potential becomes even more tenable in light of the strong empirical proof by education researchers Tatiana Melguizo, Gregory Kienzl, and Mariana Alfonso, as well as Di Xu and colleagues, that once students transfer to a four-year institution, their odds of completing a bachelor's degree and enrolling in graduate school are as strong as those of their four-year beginning counterparts.[16]

However, my work as well as that of others also found that there is a troublesome disconnect between the rich supply of STEM talent provided by the community college and the comparable rates of post-transfer success. Echoing the gap between transfer aspirations and attainment that I described in the preface, this picture is even bleaker for students in STEM who aspire to transfer. A mere 12 percent of all transfer-intending students who majored in STEM fields at community colleges ever transferred over a six-year window.[17] Indeed, the distressing reality is that the two-year college STEM transfer promise is far from being fully realized.

To be fair, this unfulfilled promise of community college STEM transfer has not gone unnoticed. For instance, in 2012, the President's Council of Advisors on Science and Technology called for nationally funded STEM initiatives to develop and expand transfer pathways from two-year to four-year institutions.[18] To achieve this goal, there has since been a growing number of national and local initiatives.[19] However, these efforts are often not closely guided by rigorous research. The numbers I showed earlier about STEM participation, transfer, and completion do not look good, and neither do two-year college students' chances of completing a STEM bachelor's degree. Yet we know very little about how students experience STEM learning, curriculum, and the actual pathway to or away from transfer. Further complicating the problem is that these initiatives tend to assume homogeneity in the backgrounds and experiences of transfer-aspiring students, often leaving unaddressed the disparities that exist in STEM learning and attainment, largely based on student sociodemographic and cultural backgrounds, as demonstrated by education researcher Becky Wai-Ling Packard and her colleagues.[20]

THE STUDY—TRANSFER IN AND BEYOND STEM

On My Own is a response to these issues and gaps. In this book, I discuss work from my longitudinal, mixed methods research project that follows a cohort of 1,670 students beginning in STEM programs and courses at three large two-year institutions in a Midwestern state in fall 2014, spanning four years until fall 2018. During those years, I worked with a brilliant team to gather data from these students through multiple waves of surveys, in-person interviews, and college transcripts in documenting their educational and life experiences as they moved toward or away from transfer to a four-year college. A study of this nature and scope requires substantial resources, and I was fortunate to receive a major award from the National Science Foundation (NSF) that allowed me to carry out this work. Equally if not more important, as a then pretenure faculty member and new principal investigator to the NSF, I particularly appreciated the autonomy and freedom I was given to execute the research in honest, careful, and yet nonprescriptive and sometimes "forgiving" ways.

This is an important point because it helps set the context for the research undergirding my book and what its findings mean. Anyone who studies community college students would admit that there is no perfect way to measure students' educational intent. Some say that survey items on intent are unreliable because intent evolves and changes over time, and even students themselves simply may not have enough clarity to report it accurately. This is further complicated by the multiple missions and functions of two-year colleges. Some argue that genuine intent lies in the very coursework students are taking. For example, if we want to know if students' intent is to transfer, we should look at whether they are enrolled in liberal arts transfer programs instead of what they self-report, say, on a survey instrument asking about intent.

While these arguments all have merit, the truth of the matter is that research on a given educational outcome—transfer in this case—has to start somewhere that can hopefully capture all this good fluidity and messiness in a reasonably fair manner. And that is what I strived to do with this project. I included all students who were enrolled in STEM programs and courses as first-year students at the three institutions that participated in the study, and asked about their educational intent multiple times in multiple ways through the surveys and interviews. This approach has two major implications: For one, I worked with a large enough student pool of roughly 1,670 students that allowed me to account for and tease out the inherent messiness around intent to transfer and transfer in STEM. For example, this overall study sample size enabled me and my team to conduct quantitative analysis using multiple measures to determine if our findings were sensitive to different ways of asking about intent.[21] Second, as a result of that, the students included in the study comprise those with initial exposure to STEM programs or courses, but who did not end up focusing on STEM, or who did not necessarily intend to transfer, as their interest may have been outside of STEM subjects or transfer. What this means is that I ended up doing a study that has a fair concentration on STEM and potential transfer in STEM, but the study is also broadly relevant to transfer in general in both its findings and implications. In my methodological appendix, I provide more in-depth details of the study design and its implications.

Defining the Undefinable: STEM and Transfer in STEM

Within the world of education, STEM is a widely used and widely contested acronym. Taken literally, it stands for science, technology, engineering, and mathematics. However, what specific fields of study constitute STEM, or even each letter of STEM, varies across national agencies as well as research and policy contexts. For example, the National Science Foundation defines STEM fields as biological and agricultural sciences, physical sciences (like chemistry, physics, astronomy, and earth/ocean/atmospheric sciences), computer sciences, mathematics and statistics, engineering, psychology, and social sciences but excludes health sciences.[22] American College Testing (ACT), on the other hand, considers medical and health fields as part of STEM, but not psychology or the social sciences.[23] Although the critique is warranted that this broad-stroke approach does not attend to heterogeneities within STEM fields, this loose reference does have value in offering a comprehensive, skills-based definition.[24]

In this book, my use of the term *STEM* aligns mostly with the NSF definition but also mirrors each institution's local context.[25] This wide inclusion reflects the fluidity and broad schemes within students' educational pathways and experiences. By and large, the contemporary two-year college does not provide, and their students do not follow, highly prescribed curriculum and programs within each specific letter of "STEM." Many subject-matter courses in math and science serve as foundational coursework across a significant number of STEM majors. A case in point: calculus is not only for math majors, just as organic chemistry is not only for chemistry majors. Calculus is needed for essentially all engineering degrees and many science degrees. A major in biology—as well as environmental sciences and food science, among others—either outright requires or offers organic chemistry as an optional degree requirement. Thus, students intending to transfer in STEM are not confined to a singular discipline; they are exposed to all of STEM. As a result, students interested in STEM subjects and the potential to transfer to earn a baccalaureate degree are often dispersed across a wide spectrum of subject matter and general education courses. To gather experiences shaping transfer in STEM, then, means to cast a wider net that captures the intersected and muddy realities in the educational and life domains of students.

Where the Study Occurred

The study behind this book is situated within a Midwestern state and includes three large two-year institutions in the state that have transfer as a distinct mission and that offer a broad spectrum of STEM curricula. Enrolling nearly 14,000 students, Great Lakes College's primary mission is to prepare students of all backgrounds to transfer into baccalaureate programs. Centerville College (enrolling around 33,000 postsecondary students) and Metroshore College (also enrolling about 33,000 postsecondary students) are both comprehensive in their mission, with a dual focus on workforce participation and upward transfer. Well over 50 percent of the students enrolled in these colleges are first-generation students. Enrollment of students of color ranges from 13 to 47 percent, and female students constitute slightly over 50 percent of the student body. What the book portrays is not meant to be completely generalizable to state and institutional settings outside of the state under study. However, it does offer relevant implications for similar students and institutions, as well as for researchers and policy makers grappling with similar issues elsewhere in the nation, for the reasons noted below.

The kinds of questions we asked our students pertain to factors that are common in educational settings across different two-year and four-year institutions, including learning experiences in STEM courses or programs, student motivation, transfer knowledge and resources, student supports and services, and more. These are elements that can easily be adapted and examined across a variety of colleges, programs, and state contexts. In addition, the three institutions that were a part of the study are similar to a fair number of institutions outside of the state and have comparable peer institutions in a wide range of states, such as Ohio, Texas, Oregon, Missouri, New York, and North Carolina, among others. Including two-year institutions with varying degrees of focus on transfer also mirrors the realities of the diverse transfer pathways available through community colleges nationally and thus involves settings and student groups that are sufficiently diverse to make the findings broadly relevant.[26]

OVERVIEW OF THE STUDENTS AND KEY FINDINGS

The total number of students included in the larger longitudinal project is approximately 1,670. These students started in STEM programs or courses at the three two-year institutions in the fall of 2014. Table I.1 summarizes some general background characteristics of these students. Among them, 1,170 (70 percent) had the initial intent of transferring into a four-year program.[27] This statistic may seem high to some, but is in fact quite on par with estimates across the country. The National Center for Educational Statistics' (NCES) 2004/2009 Beginning Postsecondary Students (BPS: 04/09) Longitudinal Study reports that 68 percent of all

TABLE I.1 Study participants' background characteristics

BACKGROUND CHARACTERISTICS		FULL STUDY SAMPLE (n=1,670)	TRANSFER-INTENDING (n=1,170)
Sex	Female	700 (42%)	525 (45%)
	Male	970 (58%)	645 (55%)
Race/ ethnicity	American Indian / Native American	20 (1%)	15 (1%)
	Black/African American	130 (8%)	80 (7%)
	Hispanic/Latinx	175 (10%)	130 (11%)
	Asian/Pacific Islander/ Southeast Asian	120 (8%)	90 (8%)
	Multiracial/ Race unknown	135 (8%)	80 (7%)
	White	1,090 (65%)	770 (66%)
Age	18 to 19	890 (54%)	755 (65%)
	20 to 23	275 (16%)	185 (16%)
	24 to 29	215 (13%)	115 (10%)
	30 and older	280 (17%)	115 (10%)
Employment	Full-time	350 (21%)	195 (17%)
	Part-time	895 (54%)	700 (60%)
	Not employed	420 (25%)	275 (24%)
Income	Less than $30,000	585 (36%)	370 (32%)
	$30,000 to $59,999	410 (25%)	295 (25%)
	$60,000 to $89,999	340 (21%)	255 (22%)
	$90,000 to $119,999	205 (13%)	150 (13%)
	$120,000 and above	110 (7%)	80 (7%)
First-generation student	Yes	895 (57%)	680 (58%)
	No	665 (43%)	490 (42%)
Full-time student	Yes	1,160 (70%)	890 (76%)
	No	510 (30%)	280 (24%)
Single parent	Yes	85 (5%)	55 (5%)
	No	1,580 (95%)	1,115 (95%)

Note: Sample and subsample sizes rounded to the nearest five. Column counts and percentages may not sum to totals due to rounding or missing values. Reported percentages are unweighted.

students starting in STEM at two-year colleges have goals of obtaining a bachelor's degree.[28] This percentage is even higher among students specifically in science and engineering programs, with 81 percent intending to transfer.

Fully recognizing these initial high transfer aspirations has important implications. Plenty of federal STEM initiatives have focused on what have been labeled "subbaccalaureate" degrees, career pathways, workforce preparation, or occupational education, among other terms.[29] This is not to say that these efforts are not useful or helpful. On the contrary, they can assist students looking to get into college without breaking the bank and get them quickly on track toward a career. Yet, should students have to stop there? By and large, the types of programs under these labels do not necessarily guarantee that students can build on those credentials or eventually transfer if they decide they want to continue toward a baccalaureate degree or higher. This can present a problematic scenario when a large share of transfer-intending students later find that the programs they started in cannot go up but only out. How can two-year colleges fulfill their multiple missions if they cannot provide the multiple paths their students with high educational aspirations may need?

Mirroring the community college student body nationally, our students as a whole are more diverse and heterogeneous than students who start immediately at a four-year institution. Our students also have many characteristics that are distinct from those of the traditional four-year college student. To get a better sense of these students, consider these few important descriptors: overall, a little over one-third are students of color, close to one-third are twenty-four or older, nearly two-thirds fall under the two lowest income categories, well over half are first-generation students, and three-quarters work part-time or full-time. As for our students who intend to transfer, the proportions are fairly similar, with the exception of students over the age of twenty-four, with one-fifth of these students intending to transfer.[30]

Family Income

One of the most important characteristics to note is that, as they began their enrollment in fall 2014, 36 percent of our students had a total family income of less than $30,000, and 60 percent of the entire cohort reported a total family income of less than $60,000. Indeed, when students spoke with us about what drove them to the two-year colleges, finding affordable options was among the most prominent. Kirsten, a white female student starting in engineering at Great Lakes College, considered cost as a huge decision point, and the two-year college she was attending offered a potentially good return: "I think that the fact that the economic cost is great, like obviously Great Lakes College is such a great deal." (I1)

The issue of affordability was even more salient when transfer factored into the picture. Shinichi, an Asian male student aspiring to major in biology at Centerville College, viewed his two-year college enrollment as a cost saver for the same kinds of courses that would potentially count toward a baccalaureate degree assuming successful transfer: "I'm going to take some courses at Centerville College and transfer over because well, yeah, it's much cheaper first of all, and you still get the same level of education." (I1) Shinichi was far from the only transfer-aspiring student who saw starting at a two-year college as a key cost-saving mechanism. Kevin, a Native American male looking to pursue an engineering program at Great Lakes College, believed that his courses would all eventually be a part of his four-year degree: "I'll have enough accumulated where I can be pretty well off when I go over there [four-year institution]." (I1)

Parental Education

Closely tied to family income is whether our students had college-educated parents. Well over 50 percent of our students were the first in their families to go to college. For many of these first-generation students, parental encouragement was often missing in their pursuit of college. Nelkowicz, a white male at Centerville College, described the lack of parental guidance and support regarding his college choices: "I didn't really have a father around. My stepfather wasn't much into schooling and doesn't really talk. I mean he said yeah, everybody should go to college, but then the actions didn't meet what he would talk about, so I was never discouraged from going to school, but it wasn't something that was... I didn't see much of it. It wasn't, I don't know, promoted." (I1)

On the contrary, for students with college-educated parents, college as a priority was often the default. This was especially pertinent as our students contemplated demanding STEM majors. The pathway that a parent may have taken often factored into what students chose. Elizabeth, an Asian female student at Great Lakes College, described her dad as a main influence on her choice of college major: "My dad has a bachelor's in general sciences... So he—and he still has an interest in a variety of fields and stuff. So this is what I'm thinking... this is what I'm leaning towards [a science major]." (I1) Similarly, Scott, a white male student at Great Lakes, has multiple close family members with engineering backgrounds, which made it an appealing option: "My dad was an engineer— well, he *is* an engineer... that's what my dad does, and my uncle's an engineer too. So, I guess the kind of work they do is kind of interesting, so that's what I want to try so far." (I1)

Life Circumstances

Only slightly over 50 percent of our students represented the traditional, eighteen- to nineteen-year-old freshmen, with the other near half being less traditional in terms of age when starting college. When we first got in touch with them in fall 2014, roughly 30 percent of our students were twenty-four or older and 17 percent of the cohort was thirty and older. These adult learners often negotiate complexities caused by combining life and work in multifaceted ways. James, a Black male enrolled in an information technology (IT) program at Metroshore College, had to put off going to college multiple times to care for his ailing mom: "My mother was sick and stuff like that. I couldn't go to school this time so I had to take care of my mom... My family comes first so I had to let school go. I really hated to, but it is what it is." (I1)

Many of our students are primary care providers serving multiple roles. Over 15 percent of them had children who lived with them, and 5 percent were single parents. Callan, a Black man who started at Metroshore and was interested in agricultural engineering, said that he was "still raising a couple of kids at home, that ain't out yet, and they always got problems. So, yes, sometimes I got time to go out to the school, but sometimes I got these little bitty kids at home that I've still got to watch out for." (I1) To compound these worries, Callan also had children for whom he was concerned about providing child support. This issue was even more prevalent among our female students who were parents and constantly worried about childcare. Jasmine, a white woman pursuing a degree in IT at Centerville College, spoke of the way in which classes were structured that helped her persevere: "Our classes are always during the week during the day, so we never have night classes; we never have weekend classes. It's really great for, like, people like me who have to worry about daycare. I can't do daycare on the weekends. I just can't. I can't figure that out. That's too expensive." (I1)

Some students have caretaker and primary breadwinner roles in addition to school. Gwyneth, a white woman starting in the chemical technician program at Metroshore College, told of how she wanted to take care of herself and her husband, who was enduring a major health issue: "I'm married and my husband can't work full-time anymore, so that's been a big influence for me. Going back to school and saying that I gotta do something more and be able to take care of myself and provide for myself and us." (I1)

Like community college students across the country, our students worked while attending college. About 75 percent of our student cohort worked at least part-time. About 21 percent worked full-time, and on average, across all the working students, they devoted twenty-five hours a week to employment. The significant amount of time our students put into work restricted their class schedules. "I've got to take all my classes in the morning. We get busy and we start working ten hours a day; then it gets kind of hard because you've got to . . . I work until midnight, then I sit up until two, and then I'd have to get up at seven and come in here, then go back to work. Sometimes it gets kind of stressful," said Gertrude, a Native American man interested in a mathematics or computer science program at Great Lakes College (I1). The competition between work and school often meant that students were faced with narrowed prospects of taking the right classes at the right time to ensure a seamless progression to the next academic stage, a major concern weighing on Gertrude's mind: "And with work at second shift they have most of their labs at this time of day, so it's gonna be hard to do. I'm going to either have to miss work or try to see if I can get an online course or something." (I1)

These students were juggling to keep all the balls in the air and their lives going. James described how he struggled with the hectic schedule while trying to complete his math courses at Metroshore College: "At that time I was working second shift so I would come in and then I have to go to work, get ready for work now. So I switched to third shift . . . I just have to balance it I guess." (I1) Often, for financial reasons, this was done without a choice, just like in Gwyneth's case: "And also not being able to work as much while I'm in school. I have a lot lower income." (I1)

Four Years Later: Four Different Momentum Trajectories

Over the course of four years, our 1,170 transfer-intending students followed four distinct pathways, or what I call momentum trajectories. The first was *linear upward* (40 percent). This trajectory was not completely smooth, as you may have gleaned from the preface, but overall Jordan and other students on this trajectory made their way to a four-year institution in a fairly straightforward fashion. The second trajectory was *detoured* (13 percent), on which Seamus and others had to assemble and reassemble various institutions and programs in order to transfer upward. The third trajectory was *deferred* (9 percent), where students originally set to transfer, such as Kanda, let go of that goal in hopes of more immediate returns to their education. The fourth and final trajectory for transfer-aspiring students was *taking a break* (38 percent), which describes Katy and her peers who, as of fall 2018, had left the institution without any credentials.

I discuss at length in chapter 7 the notable inequities that both shaped and further maintained these trajectories. But take this book as a journey to unpack the profoundly distinct and disparate factors, spaces, and mechanisms through which students both chose and were forced into these different trajectories. Focusing on learning experiences within the classroom, chapter 1 depicts the prominent yet nuanced, almost contradictory role of math and active learning in shaping whether students stayed on the transfer path. Chapter 2 details how students went about figuring out a potential path to transfer and documents the very individual, isolated, and isolating ways in which they negotiated the process.

Chapters 3, 4, and 5 highlight the experiences of several subgroups of students who have been historically underrepresented and underserved in STEM fields. Chapter 3 depicts the multiple identities and life responsibilities that women reconciled, along with biases they encountered and their coping mechanisms. Chapter 4 centers on the experiences of students of color in STEM and documents how they maintained remarkable resilience despite countless intersecting barriers. Chapter 5 brings to light the experiences among several other and often overlooked groups, including adult learners and students with mental health issues and learning disabilities.

Chapters 6 and 7 portray the progression of students' educational journeys as they unfolded over four years. Chapter 6 describes the dwindling of transfer aspirations as the participants' educational journeys evolved over time. The chapter discusses how students' educational goals and plans fit or did not fit within the broader scheme of their life circumstances, as well as how this dynamic was further influenced by how educational opportunities were and continued to be constructed. Chapter 7 presents the four momentum trajectories on which students ended up four years later. The chapter reveals that these trajectories were deeply seated within the quality and quantity of the resources and experiences that students had.

Chapters 8 and 9 conclude the book by providing a synthesis of this longitudinal project around the importance of naming and eliminating the friction that thwarts student momentum. Chapter 8 describes the kinds of counter-momentum friction embedded within several key domains that disadvantage students from minoritized backgrounds, hence further maintaining and intensifying inequities already in place. Chapter 9 engages in a discussion of overarching future policy directions to guide our collective efforts toward a new way of conceptualizing equitable transfer in STEM and beyond, and concludes with a set of reflection questions to inform immediate action.

1

The Contradictory Promise of Math and Active Learning

TWO DECADES AGO, Seymour and Hewitt's book *Talking About Leaving: Why Undergraduates Leave the Sciences* portrayed how disengagement and dissatisfaction with their experiences within science, technology, engineering, and mathematics (STEM) classrooms drove students away and toward non-STEM fields. They concluded that "the most effective way to improve retention among women and students of color, and to build their numbers over the longer term, is to improve the quality of the learning experience for all students."[1] This landmark book on why undergraduate students leave STEM majors set the foundation for decades of debate and research on reforming the way STEM courses are developed and delivered.[2] Nonetheless, the STEM pipeline continues to leak, with the recent follow-up study *"Talking About Leaving* Revisited" largely confirming earlier results, and pointing to deep problems with students' classroom learning experiences that continue to push students out of STEM majors.[3]

CENTRALITY OF THE TWO-YEAR COLLEGE STEM CLASSROOM

What happens within and as a result of STEM courses clearly makes a difference in whether or not students stay in STEM, and this issue is even thornier in the two-year college context. Nationally, 33 percent of STEM students starting at two-year colleges switched to non-STEM pathways and 37 percent dropped out altogether; the primary factors leading students toward the exit door centered on STEM courses.[4] Obviously, building smooth transfer pathways in STEM to begin with hinges upon a positive classroom experience that supports and hopefully boosts transfer-aspiring students' interest in the subjects instead of discouraging them. But even more important, given the limited time two-year college students have to engage with the campus community in the same ways as their four-year counterparts, the classroom is almost the sole scene in which they interact with the college they are attending. In this sense, the classroom experience is as central, if not heightened, as it is in the four-year undergraduate STEM context. This knowledge was not my only motivation to embed an in-depth investigation of our students' classroom learning experiences. I had a more intimate reason to do so, based on research I conducted with researcher and practitioner colleagues on developmental math at a two-year college in the Midwest in 2013. What we learned from classroom observations, as well as from interviews with students and instructors, was how high-stakes a single class can be (in this case a developmental math course) for an aspiring STEM student. It can be *"one of the most complicated things"* and a roadblock leading a student to either follow a long road of additional developmental courses or drop out altogether.[5]

The central role of the two-year college STEM classroom venue is well recognized. Back in 2012, the National Research Council and the Carnegie Academy for Science Education hosted a summit, Community Colleges in the Evolving STEM Education Landscape, that emphasized how crucial it was to reform STEM education to enhance student persistence and success. Suggested actions included research on teaching and learning as well as in-depth exploration of students' course experiences.[6] Yet the research that ensued has remained limited, but for a few notable exceptions, including work by education researchers Elvira Abrica, Erin Doran, and Anupma Singh.[7] This chapter extends the small but important body of work on the inner workings of the two-year college STEM classroom, especially in connection to students' transfer path. It illustrates how students' classroom learning experiences shape their transfer trajectories in complex and nuanced ways. Two main findings cut across the study's various data sources, the first highlighting the prominent role of math and related perceptions in the making or breaking of an academic career in STEM, and the second elucidating how pedagogies intended to foster active learning can be both a push and a pull factor in whether students stay on the STEM transfer path. This chapter does not, however, complete the full picture of what we have learned about our students' classroom experiences, especially among women, which deserves its own chapter (chapter 3).

DO MATH IN ORDER TO DO STEM

" *Math should be a gateway, not a gatekeeper.*"

In a 2010 *Chronicle of Higher Education* article, Anthony Bryk, president of the Carnegie Foundation for the Advancement of Teaching, and Uri Treisman, executive director of University of Texas–Austin's Charles A. Dana Center, a research unit in the College of Natural Sciences, rightfully argued that "math should be a gateway, not a gatekeeper."[8] Their statement should strike a nerve within the large community of STEM education, as the depicted reality of math as a gatekeeper is sorely applicable to almost all introductory STEM courses. Indeed, if we were to build robust

STEM transfer pathways for students that include a solid foundation in math, there is work to be done.

Coming into this research, I already knew that math matters in charting a STEM education and career path based on the rich body of research in this vein.[9] Math matters not only because it is foundational to many STEM subjects in the intellectual sense. It matters also for a dire reason: so few students successfully complete foundational math to progress further in their education. A National Center for Education Statistics report shows that 59 percent of two-year college students are not ready for college-level math right away and need to take a developmental math course first. Only half of these students actually complete their developmental math sequence.[10] For those students who are deemed math ready and immediately enroll in college-level math, the outlook isn't rosy either, with a course completion rate of only 48 percent. Underneath these well-known trends, what remained unclear is how math manifests its influence within the core of students' learning, and that motivated our research to take this issue head on.

Math indeed emerges as a pervasive theme at the very core of our students' experiences with learning and identities as STEM learners. The exchange below occurred during my second interview with Jordan in 2016, nearly two academic years after he initially enrolled at Great Lakes College. I was asking Jordan about things or people that would help him to progress further toward his goal of transfer in engineering:

> JORDAN: Maybe a mentor at times, somebody that's been through the ropes and can show me a route to how they did it. Yeah, I guess that would probably be the most beneficial. Besides that, it's all going to be on me.
>
> XUELI: What would an ideal mentor be like?
>
> JORDAN: Somebody that likes *mathematics* [emphasis added]. (I2)

There is no denying that math is important, and like Jordan, our students came into their STEM programs or classes well aware of that.

Three-quarters of our students felt that knowing math was very or extremely important to succeed at college, and that they would at least "somewhat" need math for their future career.[11] Students we spoke with mentioned the inseparability of math in relation to their STEM curriculum and the importance of their ability to handle math. However, recognizing math's importance is one thing; believing that one can do math is quite another. Well over half of our students indicated at least once across the three surveys that they were not able to master math or do well on math exams. In particular, the interviews with our students delved into this paradoxical relationship between the high value attached to math on the one hand, and fear and self-doubt on the other.

Students' self-perceptions and prior experiences in math remain areas of struggle for community colleges, as noted by education researcher Valerie Lundy-Wagner, and our students were no exception.[12] Numerous students expressed either math-related anxiety or poor self-image, which posed a major roadblock requiring extra effort when students were trying to envision transfer and a career in STEM. Case in point: unlike Jordan, Katy never really entertained an engineering major. In fact, Katy never got to explore the engineering prospect at all, as her fear of math and her justified perception of the math-dense nature of engineering perpetually closed the door for her before it was even open: "So I think the idea of, of being an engineer myself, getting through a dense, like you know a math-dense program, that's terrifying. Like it makes my heart beat faster just thinking about it. And on the idea of, of being on this treadmill that's going faster than I can walk, it is just terrifying. Yeah. That's me. I feel terrified." (I1)

Many of our students, even those who had already embarked on a STEM path, said that at least sometimes, they had a poor self-image of their ability to learn and master math, and they had to work extra hard at it to stay in STEM. Take Gwyneth, for example. She described how, to make her way through her environmental science program, she needed to work at math: "Math isn't one of my strongest points, which is also a bit challenging for going into something science-related because there's a lot of math. I just have to try a little bit harder." (I1)

Serving as the main point of reference when viewing themselves as learners in STEM, students' math-related attitudes and beliefs extended their influence beyond the psychological domain. The negative self-beliefs and self-doubts related to math were incredibly detrimental to our students, as they could literally pause or delay students' academic progress. Nelkowicz, a student enrolled in an industrial maintenance technician program, shared the same long-standing self-doubt in regard to conquering math: "For a long time I just had a poor self-image of myself, not being very good at math or not being very good at school the first few times around." (I1) Having struggled academically both in high school and when he first started college over a decade ago, Nelkowicz internalized a persistent self-doubt of his ever succeeding in a STEM field. Four years later when I interviewed him for the third time, he still acknowledged that he did not really enjoy math and had to "really struggle at it." Because of this long-harbored anxiety, Nelkowicz had been putting off the required math course for as long as he could because he really did not like doing it. His graduation timeline kept being pushed out because of this indefinite hold—a math course he must fulfill to graduate, and one that, as he put it, he "should have just done" during his first year.

Further inquiry into our students' prior learning experiences revealed that those with negative self-beliefs in math often suffered from poor math instruction in the past and disparaging remarks about their math abilities from teachers. Take Jennipher, a white female student studying animation—when asked to describe her initial experiences with her first-semester courses, she named the understanding of math and community as an important highlight. She also commented on the high attrition rate in math: "My math class went from a full house to like 25 percent." (I1) Because Jennipher used to have a very low self-assessment as a math learner, being able to pull off that difficult math class, one so many students quit, with an A was a huge deal for her. It was a big deal not only because she was able to earn a good grade. It mattered in a much larger, symbolic sense as Jennipher recalled the root causes for her past self-perceptions as a poor math learner: "When I was in high school, my math teacher said I would never accomplish anything in math because I was so bad at it, but she didn't realize, like, other people also suffered under her reign. But now I'm an A student in math and I can't believe it, but it also helps to have encouragement and not saying you'll never succeed at anything like that. And also a little bit of proving her wrong goes a long way for that." (I1) For many students, the issue was not their math abilities in and of themselves as much as their beliefs in their abilities. With proper mentoring and support, students are often surprised at what they can accomplish.

Exposure to college preparatory math and science courses in high school can also scaffold the path for college coursework.[13] Greer, a white female engineering student at Great Lakes College, is a case in point: "Math was pretty easy [for precalculus] because I had that in high school. Calc was a little bit harder because it was new to me but I kind of got the hang of it towards the end." (I1) Elizabeth, enrolled in a guaranteed transfer program at Great Lakes College, took AP-level coursework in math: "My last math course in high school was AP Calc, and I didn't pass the exam, but it gave me a foundation." (I1) High school preparation in math pays off, even for students like Gertrude as a returning adult whose high school learning was years back: "In high school I made it through college math, which is calc, precalc, so right now most of these math classes I'm taking are trying to refresh what I used to know, 'cause it's been so long since I've been in school." (I1)

These more encouraging stories of coming in ready to take on math were only incidental cases among more advantaged students. As discussed, most of our students had internalized math anxiety through prior negative exposure, resulting in a low math self-efficacy that was more of a barrier than their math ability itself. The rare few who arrived at two-year college STEM classrooms feeling confident in their math ability and excited about learning math tended to be from backgrounds with notable differences from their peers'; namely, they attended better-quality high schools and had taken higher levels of math in high school, such as precalculus or calculus. For example, of our students who indicated that they were extremely confident in their ability to master math, 45 percent had completed calculus and 29 percent precalculus as their highest level math during high school, compared with 18 percent who had completed algebra II and 16 percent algebra I as their highest level math. There is a yet more complex layer to who gets access to higher-level math courses before college. A noticeable difference existed based on race and ethnicity among our students, with 47 percent white but only 34 percent students of color having completed precalculus or calculus during high school. This speaks to larger issues of inequity that permeate schools and society, and are further exacerbated in college to impact students' STEM paths; I further disentangle these in chapter 7.

Since students' affective traits pertaining to math squarely draw on their learning experiences, and the college STEM classroom is now an entirely new learning environment, there should be many ways in which instructors can help students overcome their fear of math. Actually, many of our students did experience a transformation of their math self-image to the positive, especially if they were exposed to classroom practices that centered their role as active instead of passive learners; but as I am going to describe below, this process panned out in a highly intricate and somewhat unexpected way.

ACTIVE LEARNING—A CONFIDENCE BOOSTER THAT "DIVERGES"

Part of the remedy to potentially transforming students' math learning experiences and self-efficacy beliefs appears to lie in effective pedagogical practices. It was crucial that we dig further into the classroom and students' learning experiences to get a glimpse of the impacts of structures and activities characterizing the STEM classroom learning experience.

To do this, we asked students to reflect on certain kinds of experiences within their STEM courses over several years, and how often they had such experiences. Some of these questions included how often they had to gather information from multiple sources, draw conclusions based on the description of a situation, present what they learned to the instructor or their peers, think and discuss questions before the instructor gives an answer, apply what they learned to real-life situations, integrate skills and knowledge learned to solve problems, and work in groups to solve complex and realistic problems.

These questions speak to teaching strategies that fall under the larger umbrella of active learning—approaches meant to purposefully turn students from passive recipients of knowledge into key inquirers in the learning process.[14] Strategies aimed at facilitating active learning may allow students to see parallels and build explicit connections between the content and what they may deal with in their lives and careers. These practices have been lauded for fostering STEM learning and outcomes, including critical thinking, higher-order thinking, and better information retention and transfer. The 2012 President's Council of Advisors on Science and Technology report abounds with research revealing that students exposed to these types of practices time and again learn more and do better on homework and exams or other pre- and posttest assessment instruments compared to other traditional approaches, like lectures.[15] An emerging body of research has demonstrated that active learning helps enhance students' performance in STEM.[16] In particular, a contextualized approach is critical in fostering knowledge transfer, academic performance, and career readiness.[17] In our own research, we have found that a contextualized approach, as a key component of strategies to promote active learning and one that complements other strategic elements, played a great role in students' learning experiences and self-efficacy around their abilities and later success.[18] Gauging the extent to which such practices exist lends an important and unique window through which we learned about our students' classroom experiences.

Further, our students described in detail their experiences in classes that may fall anywhere across the wide spectrum of how these practices are operationalized, giving us a better idea of which approaches tended to predominate in the two-year college STEM context.

Active Learning Experiences as a Confidence Booster

Active learning experiences, such as contextualized instruction that situates math concepts within real-life settings, help alter students' initial self-perceptions as poor math learners toward more positive ones. We believe this positive link between active learning and math self-efficacy is attributed to this often hands-on, applied approach. For instance, when Nelkowicz described his blueprint class, he commented on the positive influence such an approach helped with his self-belief: " [The instructors] took me under their wing, like showing me stuff, like I've gotten more hands-on training than I ever would have like working a job for a year or more, so it's been invaluable ... It's been extremely helpful and has shown me that I can do a lot more than I thought I could ... I've always thought my math skills would hold me back." (I1) A similar surge in math self-efficacy was experienced by Kooks, a Latino electrical engineering student, through a more hands-on approach to teaching and learning math: "I definitely felt, you know, by this time I learned a lot more in math. I felt like I was stronger in my understanding of the concepts in the basic mathematics. But also I saw how certain concepts could link with other things in other classes." (I1)

It is clear that active learning practices resulted in an increase in students' math-related self-beliefs, but what about their impact beyond math, on students' aspirations to transfer? We found that the more exposure students had to active learning, the more confident they were in their ability to transfer upward into both STEM and non-STEM fields of study. This positive influence on students' beliefs in their ability to transfer in turn translates into students' intent to transfer in general.[19] Figure 1.1 graphically summarizes this analysis.

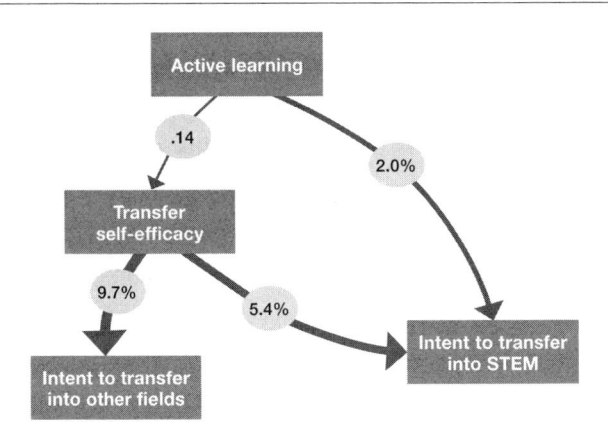

THE CONTRADICTORY PROMISE OF MATH AND ACTIVE LEARNING 37

FIGURE 1.1 Relationship between active learning, transfer self-efficacy, and intent to transfer

[Diagram: Active learning → (.14) → Transfer self-efficacy; Active learning → (2.0%) → Intent to transfer into STEM; Transfer self-efficacy → (9.7%) → Intent to transfer into other fields; Transfer self-efficacy → (5.4%) → Intent to transfer into STEM]

.14 — The more active learning students are involved in, the higher their transfer self-efficacy. A 1-point increase in students' active learning scale (a 5-point scale with 5 indicating the highest amount of active learning) is associated with a .14 point increase in their transfer self-efficacy scale (a 5-point scale with 5 indicating the highest level of self-efficacy).

9.7% — The higher self-efficacy students have about their ability to handle the transfer process, the stronger their intent to transfer into a non-STEM field at a four-year institution. A 1-point increase above the mean in a student's transfer self-efficacy scale (a 5-point scale with 5 indicating the strongest transfer self-efficacy) is associated with a 9.7 percent increase in the probability of the student having the intent to transfer into a non-STEM field at a four-year institution, as opposed to not intending to transfer.

5.4% — The higher self-efficacy students have about their ability to handle the transfer process, the stronger their intent to transfer into a STEM field at a four-year institution. A 1-point increase above the mean in a student's transfer self-efficacy scale (a 5-point scale with 5 indicating the strongest transfer self-efficacy) is associated with a 5.4 percent increase in the probability of the student having the intent to transfer into a STEM field at a four-year institution, as opposed to not intending to transfer.

2.0% — The more active learning students are involved in, the higher their intent to transfer into a STEM field at a four-year institution. A 1-point increase in a student's active learning scale (a 5-point scale with 5 indicating the highest amount of active learning) is associated with a 2.0 percent increase in the probability of the student having the intent to transfer into a STEM field at a four-year institution, as opposed to not intending to transfer.

This connection between active learning and transfer intent extended into the larger motivational environment of student experiences in that, when students were exposed to more active learning experiences, they became more self-confident not only as learners in math and other STEM fields, but also about their future education and life in general. Citing the importance of getting math in this much larger sense, Nelkowicz commented:

> Like I kind of viewed myself as sort of like poor, lower class, you know. That's it. That's where I would stay. But I don't think that's the case anymore. The sky is definitely the limit, so I'm just going to keep going. I mean it was just a couple years ago, I was just playing in bands around town playing music, had no future and no real desire to think about a future. But things change. People get older. So, time to grow up, I think. Just lucky that I found something that I can do. (I1)

The Push and Pull of Active Learning

This boost in motivation, however, did not automatically result in students setting foot on the transfer path. In an almost ironic way, a close examination of students' course-taking records showed that students reporting more engagement with active learning were more inclined to persist in coursework that focused on vocational training and did not bear much transferability. More active learning within students' classrooms during the first semester made them more likely to move away from the transfer track and to a vocational track. Similarly, among students who were exploring college without a declared major during the first term, those who had experienced more active learning were more likely to transition into a vocational track than into a transfer track.[20] A finer look at students' exposure to active learning across transferable and nontransferable STEM courses they took was telling of where active learning experiences tended to occur.

As shown in figure 1.2, students whose completed STEM courses included more than 50 percent "terminal" STEM courses reported more active learning activities (higher active learning factor scores) than their counterparts whose completed STEM courses contained less than 50 percent "terminal" ones. In other words, those students whose completed coursework featured 50 percent or more transferable courses reported

FIGURE 1.2 Students' exposure to active learning across STEM courses

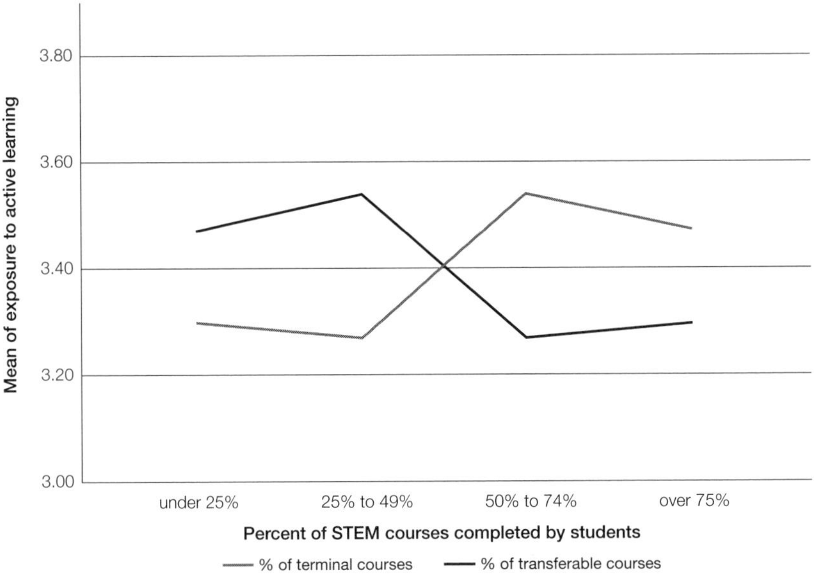

Note: We constructed this plot based on analysis using students' first wave of survey data and administrative data that included student transcripts. STEM courses were classified into transferable and "terminal" based on whether courses were accepted by four-year institutions for credit. For each type of STEM courses, we calculated the proportion of their completion relative to all completed STEM courses, using students' transcript records. We then plotted proportions of course completion by the two types of STEM courses against the active learning factor score, which ranges from 1 to 5.

less active learning activities than their counterparts. It suggests that active learning experiences occurred more often in STEM courses not designed to transfer.

When we talked to students, we learned that it was indeed within the vocationally oriented courses that students experienced the most active learning and an applied and collaborative learning environment. Often, the students exposed to these programs described their highly interactive nature and a heavy focus on hands-on and applied activities that frequently occurred in a workshop or laboratory setting, be it a computer lab, a chemistry or biology lab, or a manufacturing workshop. Instructors in vocational courses tended to incorporate teaching and learning experiences that allowed students to acquire and practice skills. Temperance, a white female student, described her instructor for her Solid Works course, which counted toward the Mechanical Design Technology program but was not transferable: "She takes us through step-by-step, showing us different things up on the screen because her computer is projected in front of the class. And so we're working along with her on our computers... my instructor was very good at coming around and making sure everybody was still staying on base and catching up with things. And then we would learn the new skill." (I1)

On the other hand, interviews with those students initially enrolled in transfer programs were replete with descriptions of boring lecture-based classes, little hands-on work, and few examples of how to apply the content of the course. Instead, these transferable classes served as counterexamples of active learning, dominated by abstract presentation that required memorization rather than connection. These hallmarks of passive learning and decontextualization appeared to prevail in the transfer programs. Kevin described his Chemistry 1 class: "In lecture basically [the teacher] would start the class and he would turn on the projector and then he would start writing down notes and just explaining a lot of things and we copied the notes... That was basically the lecture, just copying notes, listening to what he's saying and taking quizzes occasionally to see if we actually understand what we're doing. And then there would be the occasional homework from the book." (I1) While chemistry lectures were often linked to labs and discussion sections, connections seemed to be missing in Kevin's description of his experience. He reported similar experiences with his math courses: "[In trigonometry class] there wasn't really a lot of activities. It was just mostly come to class, write down the notes, answering questions, do the quiz or the final, and then doing the homework." (I1)

Some students even mentioned the lack of periodic quizzing or testing for knowledge, which would provide students with an opportunity to practice using the knowledge they were responsible for learning. When describing her calculus class, Elizabeth said, "The professor, he would lecture and stuff. And I feel like in our calc class what he would do, he would have quizzes and then there was the final exam at the end. And that was the only test that we had—the final." (I1) Constrained by the course offerings and their schedules, most students did not have the luxury of choosing a different section or instructor of the same course, and had to stick with the instructor they got regardless of whether the teaching style matched their learning style. Bethany, a white female in the biotechnology program at Centerville College, recalled, "I had Math Analysis the next semester and the teacher, his style just didn't really work for me and it was like going so fast I couldn't keep up with it." (I1)

It is clear that the more applied and collaborative learning environments made available within vocationally oriented courses subsequently opened up an appealing window to explore an educational pathway with a stronger vocational and technical component, even rerouting transfer-aspiring students away from transfer. In the end, though active learning holds reasonable promise in cultivating self-efficacy in math and in advancing one's education in STEM and potentially transfer, such experiences were largely absent from transferable STEM courses, and students were drawn more to "terminal" courses with a strong vocational and technical orientation. Thus, where and how active learning occurs in today's two-year college STEM curriculum created a conundrum in that our students, highly involved with active learning, could be so motivated to transfer, yet were steered onto a path that took them further away from transfer.

Our students' experiences with regard to math and active learning serve as a wake-up call for two-year college instructors to abandon the idea that math needs to be abstract to be appreciated and to create a safe space that allows students to build their confidence and identities as learners in STEM. Further, active learning pedagogies and practices should extend far beyond vocational training and into the wide spectrum of two-year college offerings, including transfer courses, so that their promise as a motivational booster is fully realized instead of acting as a diversion from the transfer pathway.

2

Left to Their Own Devices

RECALL THE STORIES of Jordan, Seamus, Kanda, and Katy. Distinct as their trajectories may look, there is one striking common element woven across their experiences: *They felt that they were on their own.* One to two years after they enrolled, we asked them how they went about figuring out school and transfer. This is what they had to say:

> I met with a Capital advisor. She gave me the website that they're kind of using to help transfer students, so I kind of just searched around that website she gave me, and she didn't give me a ton of information. Most of it was on my own searching through this website, but I was able to find most of the information on this website. (Jordan, I2)
>
> So it's like, those Capital courses, either you take them, or you don't. You can't make it work with other things that you have going on, which kind of sucks because then it kind of prolongs the transfer process. But, otherwise, I haven't really talked to anyone in the transfer program here yet. I haven't talked to anyone in the transfer program at Capital either. (Seamus, I1)

All I just know is that online they have a thing that will tell you whether your credits transfer to any of the four-year public schools, and then if it's not at any of the public schools, you pretty much have to figure out on your own what to do. (Kanda, I1)

So when I registered for classes at Centerville College, I don't even remember how I figured out what I was taking, other than to go to their website, figure out what the program was, figure out what order the courses needed to be taken, and sign up for them. And I think it was the way that Centerville is, for some reason the way they're formatted as a school, you don't kind of get routed through some of those channels. (Katy, I2)

ON MY OWN: AGENCY BY DEFAULT

The fact that these four students, along with their transfer-aspiring peers, all largely resorted to their own initiative may not come as a surprise. After all, community college students are known to be a resilient, agentic, and self-reliant group of individuals. They demonstrate a strong sense of purpose, autonomy, and motivation.[1] They desire efficient course or program options, and often rely on themselves to seek out the information and resources to find them.[2]

However, self-initiative and agency can only go so far, as clearly, the transfer path is one that is filled with intricacies and convolutions in need of illuminating guidance from someone equipped with accurate information and knowledge. The experiences of these four students illustrate this problem in distinct ways, each unveiling systemic issues permeating the current ways in which transfer is negotiated. This includes a lack of clear articulation in courses that apply to specific major areas of study. Also, there are no clear course pathways that accommodate students' scheduling needs in light of external responsibilities as well as other academic requirements. Furthermore, financial support through affordable transfer options is sorely missing, an issue compounded by a lack of articulation between public institutions, which may limit students to expensive, private institutions to transfer most credits and courses. The resulting unsystematic, uncoordinated communication and vague articulation of program requirements can be particularly difficult for students to navigate as they explore the transfer process. All these concerns cannot be resolved by student agency alone. But ironically, by their nature, these issues left students muddling through the process using solely their own initiative, without much choice.

In Jordan's case, he had to meet with two transfer advisors from Capital to gain further clarity about transfer in engineering. In fact, although the website brought to his attention was helpful, Jordan did not feel that he got much information at his meeting with the first advisor. This motivated him to meet with another advisor from Capital. He got a lot more out of this second meeting, but still left the experience wanting a bit more: "Those meetings that I had with those advisors, they're helpful, but I feel like if they knew a little more about each of the programs it would be even more helpful, because sometimes they don't know exactly what to say with some of your questions, I guess." (I2)

What Jordan described exemplifies a significant tension in the transfer system—transfer into an institution as opposed to transfer into students' desired majors. General transfer rates into a four-year institution are already low, and more problematically, it is incredibly rare that students are able to transfer into their desired major. Over the course of four years, among our students aspiring to transfer in STEM, almost 34 percent transferred to a four-year institution, but only 15 percent transferred into a STEM field of study.[3] As Jordan and other students described to us, navigating transfer into specific majors was not an easy feat, especially when it came to matching up the right courses with program requirements. No wonder the transfer process is often described as a "maze" due to the vague and inconsistent alignment between course and major requirements.[4] As a result, students often have to settle for a block of credits to transfer, picking up the pieces after they get to a four-year college.[5]

Although Jordan eventually transferred into his dream major, he ended up with many extra credits that didn't count toward his major, and he wished he had had much clearer guidance rather than having to find the needed information on his own:

> I didn't really know exactly the specific classes I should be taking at Great Lakes that were going to be helping me at Capital. But I guess, in some sense, making it very easy to find a website that shows you—for these majors, you want to take these courses. Have that more apparent and out in the open. Because that stuff is definitely up there, but you have to search. And if you don't even know what you're searching for, you're not going to find it. Yeah, make it more apparent what classes would be very helpful for these particular majors. (I3)

For Seamus, not being able to coordinate transferable courses with other school and life obligations had preoccupied her mind. However, she had neither sought nor received help from anyone in an advising capacity. During the first interview, she expressed her desire to talk to an advisor soon. However, when I saw her a year later, things had not changed. Her transfer process was indeed prolonged, and so was her plan to complete the associate degree program. When I asked about the reasons behind this delay, Seamus said, "I think that was mostly on me. I have been like registering and like enrolling in classes at my own free will... The program schedule and the transferable class schedule conflict sometimes, so certain classes had to get pushed into certain semesters, you know. So like I didn't realize that not taking this one class [organic chemistry] would push me back a whole year." (I2) When I inquired why she tended to navigate this process without seeking out her academic advisors, Seamus immediately reminded me of her first year at Capital: "It was like your academic advisors did not really help you. Yeah, it was like you do it on your own and you know what I'm saying?"

While Seamus recognized the difficulty of getting her transferable courses in accord with her other options, the long-range impact of how such a reality inhibited transfer did not hit her acutely until after the fact. Community college students often juggle a multitude of educational and life commitments and responsibilities, which restricts their schedules in taking courses. This, compounded by the fact that not all programs and courses are created equal, with some courses more "transferable" than others, deeply complicates the process of selecting and taking courses for transfer-aspiring students.[6] It is an especially concerning and distinct problem for transfer in science, technology, engineering, and mathematics (STEM), because unlike liberal arts courses, which are often intentionally set up for transfer and offered fairly regularly year round, many STEM subject courses are highly linear and sequenced.[7] These courses are offered at very specific times, with unexamined and unquestioned expectations that students will complete the corresponding STEM program within a certain time frame. This works against students who need greater flexibility in course options and availability, especially if they wish to keep moving forward toward transfer. Seamus shared her frustration over credit transfer in the system: "You can take chem 1, you can chem this, chem that, chem this, or chem that. They have four options, but only one of them will transfer to Capital, and the one they usually transfer to Capital is always at a time where it conflicts with, like, two or three other different classes." (I2) Consequently, for Seamus and students like her, access to transferable courses becomes a very high-stakes game because one missed offering can throw off the entire sequence and either prolong a student's STEM transfer path or completely derail it.

Kanda, like Jordan, was introduced to the online transfer module early on. Unlike Jordan, however, that was the beginning of the end of her immediate transfer outlook, even before she realized it. Going through the online transfer options, Kanda found that none of the credits she had taken in the information technology (IT) program transferred to any of the public universities in the state, which were relatively affordable options. Kanda also found out that "the only schools that really have something are the very expensive private schools like Wering University and Freistadt University, and it's nice that they have schools that take the program; it's just not nice that they cost like more than a house." (I2) During this awakening to the severe financial burden that transfer in IT might impose on her and her parents, Kanda did reach out to her advisor, the only full-time academic advisor for IT. However, she found her advisor pushing Freistadt University, a local, private four-year college, not because it might possibly interest Kanda, but because it was her advisor's alma mater. Kanda also mentioned that, as the sole person who managed all the academic counseling, her advisor had almost five hundred students to help out, which perhaps explained why Kanda had since figured out, all by herself, what transferred in her major and how much the different options would cost.

Kanda had also looked into any financial aid that could help her offset the costs associated with transferring, but in vain. Taking stock of all her transfer knowledge and disheartened at the costs, Kanda said:

> If we could work on possibly teaching some of the state university system schools: Hey, we got this program, this could help a lot of people get jobs, this could solve a huge STEM problem that we don't have enough people in STEM fields. If you guys could see that these students are very talented, very skilled, they know what they're doing—if you guys see that, take their credits. They can actually go on to get their bachelor's degree and it would make them more money, so I don't see why they're not taking it, but they should! (I2)

The costs to transfer in STEM remain a significant challenge for community college students. They are faced with the difficult choice of forgoing potential employment opportunities and wages to focus on the intensity and perceived rigor frequently associated with STEM disciplines.[8] Add in the fact that they have to concentrate on their studies full-time long enough to get a bachelor's degree. Although the rewards for a STEM bachelor's degree are high, because so many community college students come from low-income backgrounds and are working, the long-term economic benefits are almost an illusion that does nothing to address their immediate needs and pay the current bills.[9] This sensitivity to costs deters talented and interested students, such as Kanda, from enjoying the benefits that STEM baccalaureate degrees may bring, which makes the calls for broadening the STEM transfer path a rather ironic and disingenuous commitment.

As a first-generation student and single parent, Katy has a tendency to figure things out on her own and attribute any challenges she encounters to herself alone. Across my three interviews with her over four years, Katy did not express a single negative remark about Centerville, except that figuring out courses and programs was difficult. Describing her time there, Katy clearly defaulted to blaming herself for any stumbles along the way despite the immense challenges she faced: "I haven't really been adept at managing, 'cause I have like four jobs, and so like figuring out the jobs and the academics and the kids, and I don't have access to internet, and so it makes it really challenging. I should be a little more structured about my time and go to the library, but sometimes I just get really tired and I don't want to leave my apartment anymore." (I1)

The way Katy approached school was similar to the approach taken by many of her first-generation college student peers. They tended to navigate college almost entirely on their own for a host of reasons, including a lack of parental support or a fear of the stigma associated with being first-generation.[10] Although these students might be deeply driven to navigate college successfully, often on their own, this situation is complicated by the "cafeteria-style" course selection and registration prevalent at many community colleges, the lack of both systemic and coordinated communication, and unclear articulation of courses and programs.[11] These issues can be especially problematic for first-generation students to discern and navigate as they consider transfer. When there are too many options and the path is not structured or clear, these students can quickly become confused, discouraged, and ultimately pulled away from transfer.

Where Is Advising?

Katy, Kanda, Seamus, and Jordan all largely relied on their own initiative. All expressed frustration, confusion, or in some cases, a sense of hopelessness. The severe need for stronger and more effective advising is not a new issue for students starting at community colleges. Sadly, it continues to plague two-year and four-year institutions alike in their attempts to improve student progress, transfer, and completion, and was a salient theme echoed by numerous students.[12] One student put the following words in the final follow-up survey about advising at Centerville:

> As far as transfer advising, you can ask different people about transferring and everyone will tell you a different thing. I think the advisors should all be on the same page and knowledgeable about transferring and its requirements. Same goes with the regular counselors. When I first came to Centerville College, I was told many different things by a handful of counselors regarding classes and such. It can be a bit confusing because you don't know who to listen to. (white female, first-generation, low-income family background, taking a break trajectory, S3)

Another survey response from a student attending Great Lakes College:

> My biggest hang-up with the transfer thing is it's hard to navigate. I have been led down the wrong path by advisors, and that has caused me a lot of wasted time (taking classes that I don't need, NOT taking the classes that I DO need, etc.). There is a large amount of fluff between you and what you want to accomplish. Not one single process or protocol set up by the system is concise. Most of the processes and protocols are incoherent and often lead to dead-ends in which everybody has already redirected your request to somebody else. (Black male, first-generation, low-income family background, taking a break trajectory, S3)

These students' words illustrate the common concerns with advising and a desire for clarity, accuracy, and consistency in advising. Here in particular, I want to stress that these conclusions are not meant to place fault on individual advisors, who are often overworked and trying to meet the needs of a diverse student population faced with so many options. Rather, what I am highlighting here is a set of systemic issues that pose some real challenges that constrain advisors from fulfilling their role in sustainable ways. One of the major problems has to do with advising loads, which at community colleges have typically ranged from 800 to 1,200 students per one advisor.[13] Even when institutions are more intentional about reducing these numbers, like in California, the ratio of community college students to advisors was still 615:1.[14] These numbers are not helpful to our students, who either found it difficult to access advisors, or for those who did have access, came away with very few or contradictory answers. This can leave colleges struggling to keep students on track and students feeling consistently lost and unsupported. Yet, the blame should not fall at the steps of community colleges; this is a larger systemic issue that goes back to state and federal support for these institutions. Essentially, the underfunded, underresourced advising system contributes to the inevitable fact that the students are left to their own devices, and only perpetuates a hopeless cycle of inefficiencies and students dropping out before they can complete a credential or transfer.[15]

HOW PREVALENT IS "ON MY OWN"?

The experiences of Jordan, Seamus, Kanda, and Katy are not isolated anecdotes. By and large, our transfer-aspiring students only occasionally sought out institutional services designed to support transfer, such as transfer advising, transfer credit assistance, and published transfer information. As figure 2.1 shows, half of our transfer-intending students never or rarely used these services.

When it came to interactions with others for transfer-related issues, 66 percent of transfer-intending students never or rarely discussed transfer with instructors, and this number was 48 percent for academic advisors

52 ON MY OWN

FIGURE 2.1 Percentage of transfer-intending students who never or rarely used institutional services designed to support transfer, by type of services

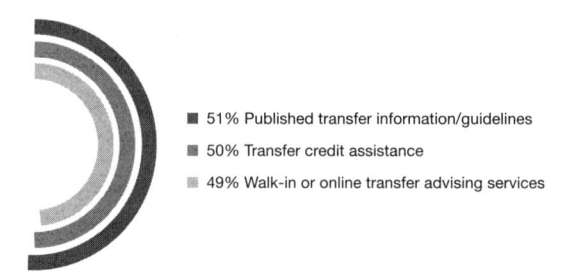

- 51% Published transfer information/guidelines
- 50% Transfer credit assistance
- 49% Walk-in or online transfer advising services

Note: Percent estimates are based on the first wave of the longitudinal survey among transfer-intending students only.

or counselors, 52 percent for fellow students, and 34 percent for family members or friends (see figure 2.2).

As shown in figures 2.3 and 2.4, the patterns were largely similar across all four momentum trajectories, pointing to "on my own" as a dominant theme among our students.[16] Our interviews further illuminated the

FIGURE 2.2 Percentage of transfer-intending students who never or rarely discussed transfer, by groups of contact

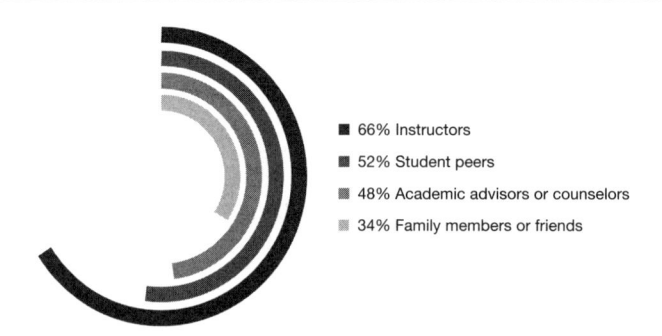

- 66% Instructors
- 52% Student peers
- 48% Academic advisors or counselors
- 34% Family members or friends

Note: Percent estimates are based on the first wave of the longitudinal survey among transfer-intending students only.

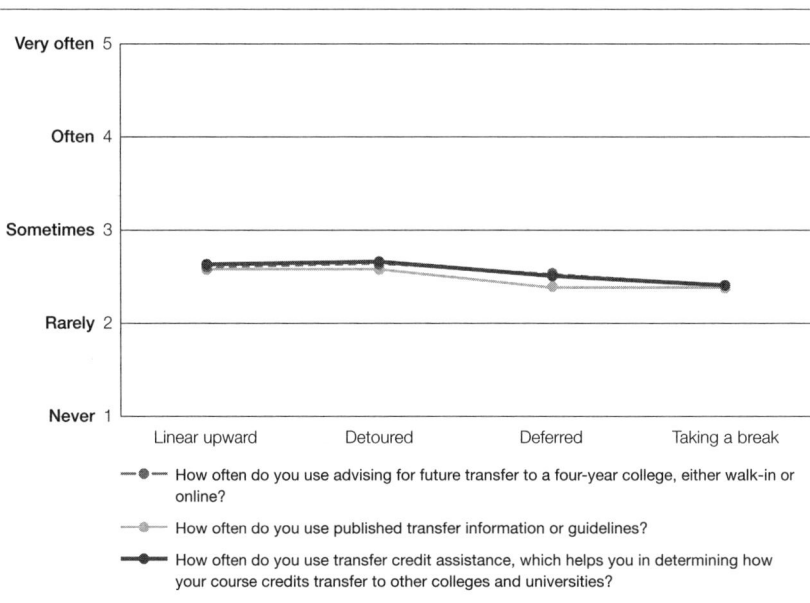

FIGURE 2.3 Mean frequency of student usage of institutional services designed to support transfer, by type of services and trajectory

```
Very often 5
Often      4
Sometimes  3
Rarely     2
Never      1
              Linear upward    Detoured    Deferred    Taking a break
```

—●— How often do you use advising for future transfer to a four-year college, either walk-in or online?

——— How often do you use published transfer information or guidelines?

—●— How often do you use transfer credit assistance, which helps you in determining how your course credits transfer to other colleges and universities?

prevalence of this pattern. While individual stories were different, one central theme wove through all of them—students felt that they were on their own, often harboring many doubts and uncertainties when contemplating, visualizing, and clearing the path to transfer.

Among these four groups of individuals students could turn to, family members or friends rose to the top, but even when participants turned to them, their support could carry students only so far. Our first-generation students especially, although friends and family offered support and positive feedback from a broader standpoint, ultimately found themselves relying on their own motivation to persist on their transfer path. Jennifer, a first-generation white woman initially pursuing a chemistry major, had plenty of family encouragement and support for going to college. However, her parents never attended college, and while her siblings were in college, they pursued different areas of study. Therefore, she felt

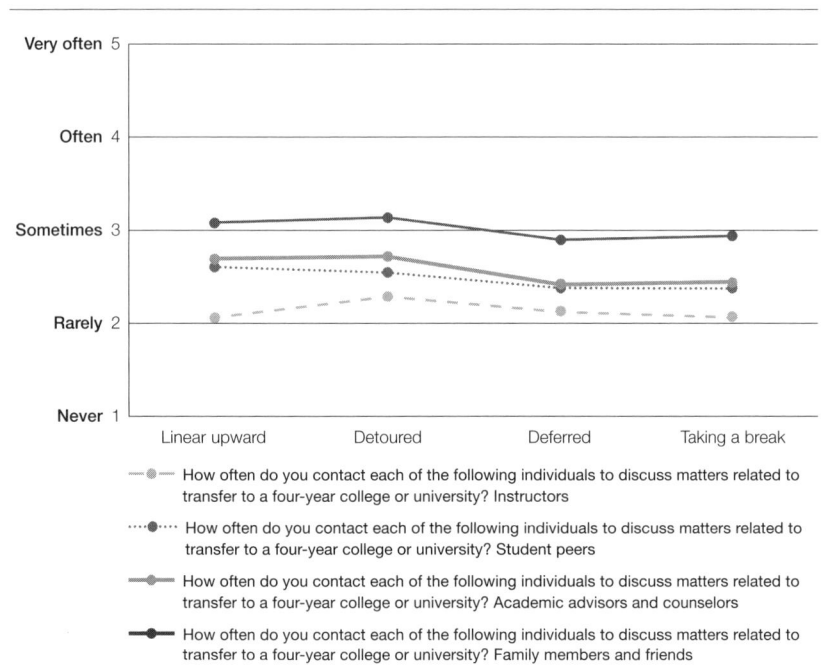

FIGURE 2.4 Mean frequency of students' discussion of transfer, by group of contact and trajectory

- — ● — How often do you contact each of the following individuals to discuss matters related to transfer to a four-year college or university? Instructors
- ···●··· How often do you contact each of the following individuals to discuss matters related to transfer to a four-year college or university? Student peers
- —— How often do you contact each of the following individuals to discuss matters related to transfer to a four-year college or university? Academic advisors and counselors
- —●— How often do you contact each of the following individuals to discuss matters related to transfer to a four-year college or university? Family members and friends

she was the only one into the "sciencey stuff," limiting the depth of her discussions regarding college and transfer: "Mostly it's just on me. I can have help, you know, I can talk to my family about it, but none of them are really where I'm at." (I1)

Similarly, Gwyneth was lost in the prospect of transfer and tried to sift through where to begin:

> I guess figuring out how the credits would transfer because I don't want to have to start all over again. And then finding out how to talk to someone. I guess I'm a little unsure of the, you know, reaction I'm going to get; if I can just go talk to someone or if I have to fill out the application and pay the application fee first and then I can talk to someone...

have heard that from a couple of people, yeah. But they weren't real happy with what the advisors told them or that they heard their credits were going to transfer when they wouldn't or didn't. Or there was some loophole that, you know, it should have transferred, but for this reason the school doesn't have to accept it kind of thing. (I1)

Gwyneth tried to talk to people she knew who transferred, thinking it might help her understand the process, which ended up only adding more noise. Indeed, students may turn to those they know and trust to gain honest insight. However, this can leave students with conflicting information, and once again on their own to figure out transfer. This is not to say that students never receive useful information or support from instructors, advisors, services, and resources; they do. However, such support exists and occurs in such incidental and unstructured ways that not all students have equal access to an equally stable and robust institutional web of support beyond their own family and friends. The consequence is that one either has to come with plenty of know-how to locate institutional supports and resources, such as in Jordan's case, or occasionally, rely on pure luck, as what one student described in her survey response:

> I have huge respect for my teacher, who is unfortunately retiring. He is probably the sole reason I am still in school after all the hardships I went through just to get enrolled and get things moving. As a worker full-time and having a part-time job solely to pay for school, it is hard for me to get to campus early or on weekdays to talk to advisors about transferring in the future, or which classes to take at which semesters. My teacher so far has been so much more helpful than my "advisors," who just send mass emails. I am unsure of what to do once my main instructor retires, as I do not know where or who I will go to for advice anymore. (Latina, first-generation, low-income family background, deferred trajectory, S3)

ON MY OWN: SIMILAR BUT NOT SO EQUAL

Indeed, although students were largely left to their own devices to negotiate their path to transfer, not every student had equal access to the same "devices," and the "devices" available to students were not of equal quality and utility. In fact, while it appeared that everyone relied on their own initiative to figure out transfer, the resources that students had at their disposal and could potentially tap into varied widely. On one end of the continuum were students who came in with a considerable amount of resources and know-how, and on the other were those with little to none. The large majority, though, fell in the middle, with a reasonable level of access to support systems. However, the kinds of advice and information they acquired from these systems often fell short of providing clear and on-point guidance that was truly conducive to advancing their transfer path. Accordingly, while students may have appeared to rely on their own initiative, the quantity and quality of the informational resources they sought out were uneven and unequal, and were largely shaped by preexisting social advantages or lack thereof.

As seen throughout this book, opportunities to advance in transfer were structured in a restrictive manner, granting more access to the types of students who fit the traditional image of a college-going student. Jordan described some of the transfer resources students could use. However, because of limited time and space, along with a lack of awareness of services, only small pockets of students were able to take advantage of them, including himself: "Yeah, but it's like first-come, first-serve, and you have to go down to the Academic Success Center here to actually sign up for the advisor meeting, because they're only here for like two days, and for only a couple of hours each day, so there's a limited amount of space." (I2) If students did not know about these meetings ahead of time, they could quickly lose out on crucial information and resources. Compounding this issue was availability or students' ability to be on campus to sign up for those appointments. First-come, first-served unfortunately became a first-to-lose-out on transfer for many students.

Jordan, Seamus, Kanda, and Katy, along with their transfer-aspiring peers whose experiences I describe throughout this book, chose to attend community colleges and looked upon them as a gateway to a four-year degree, as often expressed in the mission statements of their programs or institutions. However, during much of their time attending college, the institutional side of the story was largely missing from students' narratives of how transfer was being configured and figured out. This chapter shows that, perhaps unintentionally, the transfer function was institutionally constructed in a convoluted manner that was inherently challenging to communicate to students, let alone for them to navigate. Transfer is a complicated artifact of each institution and its inner workings, and because each program is constructed differently, there are inherent challenges associated with creating effective communication about what students need to do to transfer. At the bare minimum, our students' stories suggest that there must be a more present and clearly structured flow of information and resources through ties and networks that are formally set up within the student experience and engagement with college. As I discuss further in chapter 7, access to transfer was also shaped by inherent and perpetuated inequities that seeped into students' prior social capital and contexts of which students took advantage. This creates room for a reflective reexamination of students' preconceived notions of transfer that may or may not be true. While students' own initiative is critical, it should never be the sole item in students' toolbox on their quest to transfer.

3

Coping, Hoping, and Diverted Dreams
Women on the Road Less Traveled

My parents are burdened because my twin brother recently started college as well. Two of my brothers are disabled. There is some financial difficulty with the idea of having them pay.

—Kanda (I2)

THIS CHAPTER IS DEVOTED to the female students we have come to know, learn from, and admire through working on this project. The topic of women in science, technology, engineering, and mathematics (STEM) is a hot one. National policy proposals and the media are replete with urgent calls to improve the opportunity, experiences, and outcomes for women in STEM.[1] Yet, despite their talent and interest, women continue to face an uphill climb in their pursuit of STEM degrees and careers. National statistics show that, upon entering college, female students are less likely to major in STEM: approximately 15 percent of women intend to declare a major in STEM areas compared with one-third of men.[2] Female students who do choose STEM majors are much more prone to leave these fields of study than men. Of all students entering STEM programs, 32 percent of women left STEM for a non-STEM field in contrast to 26 percent of men.[3] Among men and women earning a bachelor's degree in a science or engineering field, barely two-fifths are women.[4] Although women make up 47 percent of the overall workforce, only 28 percent of them are employed in science and engineering fields.[5]

Much of what we know about women in STEM education, though, is situated within the four-year college context and concerns those who directly enrolled at a baccalaureate institution instead of a community college. Prior to our work, there was evidence by several education researchers, including Dimitra Lynette Jackson, Frankie Santos Laanan, Soko Starobin, Becky Wai-Ling Packard, and others, showing that community colleges offer uniquely encouraging, inclusive, and supportive environments for women in STEM fields, who attributed their inspiration, motivation, and persistence in STEM to community college faculty, advisors, and peers.[6] What we did not know, or knew very little about, was how community college women's experiences across the various domains of their life and identity play out over time, and why they persisted on or left their path toward transfer in STEM. Thus, we came into this work wanting to learn the rich individual contexts, identities, and experiences women bring with them, and how they affect women's pursuit of transfer. Through that understanding, we hoped to identify elements and mechanisms that make a strong STEM transfer pathway for women, thereby supporting the female talent in progressing further toward a bachelor's degree and a career in STEM.

Given what we already knew—and all we still wanted to know—about community college women in STEM, we came in with a keen interest in pinpointing what exactly shapes the unique experiences and transfer process for the women who constituted 43 percent of our transfer-aspiring students. Over the course of four years, we learned about these women's dreams and hopes, trials and triumphs, and in some cases, talked with them over an extended period of time and got to know them as individuals. After spending these years learning from and about these women, we found that there was not a clear and simple answer to whether and how women persisted in their STEM pursuit; similarly, the solution to resolving the challenges experienced by women on the STEM transfer path was within reach but complicated.

Across the board, when trying to make college work, whether this meant pursuing STEM fields, deciding to transfer, or exploring other options, our female students had to reconcile their multiple roles and identities, which could either give them the strength to persevere or force them to revisit their choices and priorities. Earlier in this book, I offered a general account of the trajectories of Kanda and Katy. In this chapter, their more detailed experiences and stories help illustrate the push and pull arising from this complex conundrum women faced when navigating transfer in STEM. From the get-go of her program, Kanda was deeply committed to helping others and giving back to the community. Trying to support other students, she led the petition that advocated for more course options so her peers with competing life demands could progress and graduate in a timely manner. The success of this effort not only resulted in having the courses offered at times and locations that accommodated the needs of many of her peers, but was also a major source of motivation for Kanda to persist in her program. Years later, Kanda described how she engaged in community work with her current employer, including a Women in Technology group: "I'm a part of the communications committee for Women in Tech. I got involved with a lot of opportunities to pitch new ideas to my company. And I've gotten involved with getting that opportunity to teach others. Like, we do Tech Thursdays where we discuss new trends in tech, and how to apply them to the work we're doing." (I3)

A community-oriented helper, Kanda was also an aspiring information technology (IT) professional with a strong desire to earn a bachelor's degree. Her budding IT identity grew throughout her program, going from "almost zero background," to developing apps for faculty and students at her college, to becoming an associate's degree graduate with a near-perfect academic record, and to landing a job as a software engineer. Although she enjoys her job, she still has a deep desire and concrete goal to get her bachelor's degree. This has led her to leverage her IT professional identity toward that end, by gaining valuable work experience and establishing herself at her job. In doing so, she hopes to eventually obtain tuition reimbursement through her employer to actualize her transfer aspirations.

Kanda is a daughter and sister as well. Financially, she was not entirely independent, so she was motivated to move through college with expediency and as little financial burden on her parents as possible. Yet, she was conflicted: "And it was like, my parents were absolutely super supportive of me. They were like, 'If you want to go, you can go and get on that degree.'" (I3) Considering her family's constraining circumstances, it would be too expensive to ask her parents to contribute financially to more education: transfer to a four-year institution. Her baccalaureate prospects were already costly, and also limited if she wanted her associate's program to closely align with a bachelor's degree program and transfer with minimal credit transfer issues: Wering University and City University. Perhaps Kanda's community orientation supported and drove both her sense of familial obligations and her longer-term desires for her education and career. As a daughter and a sister, Kanda deferred upward transfer for the moment. As an aspiring IT professional, Kanda's baccalaureate prospect lives on.

Katy, too, is a helper, a server to people: "I think the bottom line for me is helping people somehow." (I1) This desire to help others led her to the STEM path in the first place and guided her educational choices, including transfer:

> What's an environment I think I can work in, both academically and professionally? Where I'm gonna be helping people.... So, I think

with the occupational therapy assisting, the initial kind of drive that I had for getting into Centerville College in the first place, I could see myself down the road using the creative engineering parts of my brain to support people recovering from pain, from injury. Which I deeply identify with.... And, I mean, I think there was probably a part of me that thought, okay, so, the good news about the occupational therapy assisting program was that those two years that you put into school will transfer if you go on to a four-year degree. And they'll transfer if you go on to further education. (I3)

At the same time, Katy is an artist, creator, and entrepreneur. She comes "from a family of makers.... So you know I just come from people who are like that. Like they see something, they want to know how it works, they figure it out, they draw it, and then they make it." She is constantly inspired to make and mold: "I like creating things. Like creating to me is huge." (I1) Katy tapped into her creative identity to develop various products throughout her life, including a device to improve productivity for a local florist. This artist and creator identity also led her to explore the field of design, with the possibility of transfer still at the back of her mind if that was where her path led. Also within that creative identity is musician. Katy has been passionate about music all her life: "I wanted to write, record, and perform music." (I1) She currently performs with a musical group. However, Katy questions whether her creative identity would give her a sustainable education and career, as she is responsible for people other than herself.

Especially her children. Katy is a mom, initially staying at home with her children to care for them while her spouse supported the family. She eventually divorced, leading to an identity shift to a single mom. This development presented her with a new situation of having to independently provide for both herself and her children, which often meant taking on numerous jobs and transitioning among various living arrangements to seek stability and stay financially afloat. For Katy, being a single mom presented her with numerous hard decisions around caring for her children while potentially pursuing STEM transfer, leaving her with a sense of hopelessness and disappointment: "So a motivated single mom is probably gonna do what she can. So had I been able to pick a program that I thought I could complete and then transfer to Centerville . . . I mean, I'd like to have degrees. I would love to have an impressive resume for people. But I don't. I certainly would've loved to achieve those things if I could." (I1) Katy tried to stay motivated, exploring multiple educational and career prospects as a helper and creator that might lead her to a transfer path. As a single mom, she ultimately took a break in the hope that she could eventually get a job and provide for her family.

MULTIPLE IDENTITIES, GENDERED EXPERIENCES

The stories of Kanda and Katy illustrate some core experiences commonly shared by our female students. To more fully understand how these experiences were shaped by women's multiple identities, let's first take a closer look at our women's backgrounds. About two-thirds of the women come from the two lowest income categories, and one-third are first-generation students. They have high aspirations, with over three-quarters aiming to transfer. The women we talked to also assume multiple identities and life responsibilities: Just like Katy, many of our female students are mothers and/or the main provider for their children and sometimes spouse. Similar to Kanda, they also hold a strong sense of obligation to support their family as daughters and sisters. Almost all of them work part-time or full-time while attending school.

Inevitably then, these deeply intertwined identities and experiences shaped whether and how women pursued transfer. For example, Katy brought up her colliding identities as an employee, student, and single parent: "I have like four jobs and so like figuring out, you know, the jobs and the academics and the kids . . ." (I1) Balancing these identities exhausted Katy and made it difficult for her to keep up with all of them simultaneously. She was not always able to be on top of things, including applying for grants and financial aid late one semester. She was well aware how important it was to do these things, but working and being a parent could make it difficult to leave the house to fill out college paperwork at the end of the day.

Gwyneth, who was profiled in the introduction, highlighted her role as an employee: "I didn't feel like I was going anywhere... I have been kind of stuck in this loop of jobs that are not really getting anywhere and I don't have that much of an income; I'm not really getting ahead." (I1) Although her employee identity shaped her decision to embark on the STEM transfer path, this identity also presented challenges as she navigated her STEM courses:

> I had three part-time jobs in the fall and school full-time, so I was tired a lot... and running around and busy and crazy and I still managed to get a 4.0, which I was pretty impressed with. This last semester I did give up one of the jobs, and I feel like I was starting to get a little, a little exhausted with trying to keep up with everything... I don't think my grades were as good this semester, but I think having the summer off and having time to kind of get things back together, I'll be ready again to, to jump into it in the fall. (I1)

Gwyneth tried to temper her employee identity in order to stay on track, eventually dropping a job and regrouping so she would be ready for her STEM courses the following semester.

Many of these women's experiences were compounded by other identities, particularly their family roles. Like Katy, Jasmine was also a single mom, which influenced her journey in STEM: "I had had a rough semester... and the little guy had been sick, so I missed school, and I had missed a decent amount of classes... And I came in and I spent a ton of time in the lab, and I started catching on really fast and catching up really quick. ... I came in and what the students learned in four weeks I learned in five hours, which I don't think is necessarily, completely accurate, but I learned enough to get an A on the exam." (I2) While Jasmine's single-parent identity could present challenges for advancement in her courses, she was determined to persist and succeed.

Gwyneth described her caretaker identity: "I'm married and my husband can't work full-time anymore, so that's been a big influence for me—going back to school and saying that I gotta do something more and be able to take care of myself and provide for myself and us." (I1) Gwyneth was compelled to follow the transfer path for others who depended on her for care and support. However, being a caretaker at times would conflict with her courses: "I did miss a couple classes, when I would have to take him to the hospital, or just stay home with him a couple times when he really wasn't doing well." (I2) Yet Gwyneth did not let her caretaking identity limit her from progressing toward STEM transfer.

Finally, a key identity of our female students is simply and prominently that: being a woman in STEM programs and courses. This was never a smooth journey, not only because it was often infiltrated by taxing demands from the other roles they played, but our female students also endured severe biases imposed on them as they navigated classroom learning and figured out transfer. In our conversations with these women, they often described the chilly environment they or their female peers and instructors were exposed to. When we asked Gwyneth about any barriers she might encounter in realizing a career in STEM, she pointed to classroom environments and her own appearance as a small woman:

> I think just being who I am makes a difference. Being a girl and being kind of small and whatever I think makes a big difference; I don't think people always take me very seriously. I have gotten some condescending comments just from, even from the classmates that I like in the program, that I'm kind of friends with, have made references that, you know, I'm not as smart as them, you know. There's only, there are only

three girls in the program, and the rest are guys. So there's already—
I can already see the difference there and then. I know there's some
people that give the instructor a hard time, I think just because she's a
woman. I can kind of see a difference between the classes also, so that
definitely sticks out in my mind as a barrier. (I1)

Echoing Gwyneth's experience, Greer, majoring in mechanical engineering, explained that, while she enjoyed her STEM courses, being a woman in a male-dominated field had its challenges. She often felt there was male suspicion of whether she could handle STEM courses and a major in engineering. Their eyes were on her, watching and scrutinizing her every action or response, which often led her to be silent, as that was safer than to risk making a mistake. Greer recounted how she had to put up with this severe gender stereotype threat:

I feel like they're always watching me, almost just because I am a girl . . .
In like the video classes, I wouldn't really say too much. I just don't
want like people or guys necessarily to look down upon me for any like
little things that I say, because I feel like they wouldn't let it go. Like,
even if they like make a mistake, like everybody has to let it go, because
everybody's a guy and they just kind of joke around about it. But if I
would, they would kind of think I'm not kind of smart as them almost.
And that makes me kind of mad so I just, I don't really say too much
besides the guys that I had every class with. (I1)

Similar gender stereotypes may well extend beyond STEM classrooms into women's experiences figuring out transfer. Digging into the longitudinal survey data we collected from the students, we found that male students were more likely to sustain their aspirations to transfer in STEM if they used transfer services more frequently. In contrast, the likelihood that female students would persist in their STEM transfer aspirations was in fact negatively related to their transfer service usage.[7] Connecting back to what Gwyneth and Greer shared with us, this alarming discovery may mean that women's experiences with transfer services were qualitatively different from men's. Women may have felt less at home, or may have been exposed to a more unwelcoming context that discouraged their STEM transfer aspirations. They may have felt more pressure to make it seem like they knew what they were doing and hesitated to ask specific questions or say anything, even when such questions or information would have been most helpful, in case it might have reflected poorly on them as a woman figuring out STEM transfer.

Gendered experiences, biases, and stereotypes left women feeling apprehensive about their future education and career. When asked to reflect on the potential challenges of pursuing STEM, Greer worried that "when I get a job [in engineering] I feel like they're going to look down on me kind of because I am a girl and they're not going to take me as seriously. That's what kind of scares me." (I1) Our surveys showed that women reported lower levels of self-efficacy in transfer compared with their male counterparts. They struggled to believe in their ability to do STEM courses, transfer in STEM, and so on. They battled the pressures of competing and performing well in STEM, and wrestled with feeling capable of succeeding in STEM compared with men.[8]

With this in mind, community colleges have to revisit the environments they cultivate for and behaviors they exhibit toward women interested in transfer in STEM. Implicit bias toward women in STEM is real and pervasive. Faculty, staff, and students continue to hold implicit bias, tending to favor male students over females.[9] Along the same lines, stereotype threat can also keep many women from pursuing the STEM transfer route. Many of these stereotypes center around STEM fields being masculine, very independent, and requiring an extremely high level of "intelligence" and "achievement."[10] Moreover, these stereotypes embody the blatantly wrong and damaging message that women are inferior to men in these fields.[11] Women enduring these biases and threats struggle to cultivate a strong sense of belonging and capacity to succeed in STEM, as poignantly shown through the stories of our women.[12]

COPING MECHANISMS

Grappling with competing identities and enduring or combating gender biases, our female students clearly had their moments of self-doubt and intimidation. On the other hand, they also developed coping mechanisms to keep moving forward. Our transfer-aspiring women, especially, came up with two main ways to cope with these challenges, hoping to keep alive their prospects of transfer and a career in STEM. The first focused on using what happened outside of college as inspiration, and the second concentrated on turning what happened inside of college, especially those less-than-pleasant experiences, into a resistance driver.

In regard to the first coping mechanism, it was remarkable to observe that, regardless of how exhausting it might be to maintain their other roles beyond that of a student, these women tended to view their identities and life responsibilities outside of school as major sources of motivation to persist in their educational trajectory. Instead of viewing these multiple roles and obligations as barriers holding them back, these women turned them into fuel to realize their educational and career goals. It was their way of trying to reconcile their numerous competing demands, to inspire and support one other, rather than view their situation as an insurmountable and unsustainable whole.

As we heard from Gwyneth earlier, she was driven to pursue STEM transfer because of the need to break a cycle of dead-end jobs and to do better not only for herself, but for her husband. However, her goal was not just to provide for her husband financially; she was also inspired to better understand and hopefully improve her husband's medical condition: "There's a lot of chemistry involved that [is] affecting animals and people's overall health and neurologically damaging, having all these effects. And I also know several people now, including my husband, who have some kind of neurological problem, so that's very interesting and frustrating and motivating for me to want to do more with that and learn more about it and try to be able to help if I can." (I1)

Yet Gwyneth also recognized the need to stay close to family. To make it all work, she considered four-year institutions geographically close to her: "City University would probably end up working out better since my family is in this area and I live in this area. As much as I would love to go to Capital University, that would probably be pretty difficult to move up there or commute." (I2) Gwyneth explored multiple options in a variety of locations across the state, including those near where she lived. She found several possible programs near her that would accept her credits for transfer, giving her hope to continue toward transfer.

Although Elizabeth developed an interest in psychiatry along with the nervous system and brain function during high school and through exposure to STEM coursework in college, her family also inspired her fascination with neurobiology and the desire to follow the STEM transfer pathway: "I've been kind of exposed to it because my little sister, she has a neurological syndrome and stuff. So like from a young age I was exposed to it and then I guess just the way like how the brain is the control center of your body." (I2)

At the same time, Elizabeth had her own health condition to contend with: "I'm diabetic, so with that comes good exercise, good diet, that type of thing and during college you don't—sometimes you have to choose between one or the other." However, she did not let it stand in her way of moving forward on her transfer path: "So it's just juggling that.... Eat this time, I'm going to study this time, and that type of stuff, and not just go, like, whatever type of thing. Just planning stuff out and then doing all the diabetic stuff I'm supposed to do like exercise, diet, blood check, medicine, that type of thing." (I2)

As for the second major coping mechanism, while women we spoke with often alluded to the chilly environment they encountered in STEM classrooms, where their intellects and belonging were questioned, they defiantly turned the negative remarks and attitudes against them into a stronger drive to achieve. For instance, Gwyneth took the pressure of having to act "super smart" as a motivating force that kept her going:

So, I try to show up and do what I have to do. I don't want to be a showoff, but when people, when some of the guys try to compare their test scores and their grades with me, I say, "Yeah, you know I got an A too," or I—there was one time that one of the guys said, you know, "Oh, I got 102 on this test, what did you get?" And I said, "I got 106," *[laughs]* and it felt pretty good. So, yeah ... sometimes it feels a little bit like a game, like playing a game, but I think as long as I stay focused to do what I have to do and stay on top of things and not look stupid and not look like I'm falling apart and can't handle it, that I'll get respect from the rest of the class and get ... everything that I need to do done, get where I want to go. (I2)

Kirsten was also very aware of the smaller number of female students in her STEM courses. Instead of seeing this as problematic, she considered it an opportunity to make a difference: "I actually really enjoy the gender gap in STEM because you kind of feel like you're doing something for the female community, I guess. That you're elevating those numbers. . . . I felt like I had a purpose bumping up that male-to-female ratio. . . . It's different than sitting on the sidelines and complaining how there's a gender disparity and actually doing something about it." (I3) Although a lack of female presence may seem intimidating, many of the women we spoke with refused to dwell on it and instead focused on staying on track and moving along their STEM path. These women approached their learning experiences with tenacity and a determination to prove they had the ability to handle STEM subjects and, just like the guys, deserved to be in the same learning space.

It was quite extraordinary to observe that the women coped with these two different types of deterrents in strikingly similar ways, with both involving the translation of what appeared to be a demand, a distractor, or a challenge into fuel for further learning, transfer, and education in general. Underneath this similarity was women's remarkable resilience in the face of adversities. However, these two coping mechanisms played out very differently over the course of women's STEM transfer trajectories. Toward the end, the educational outcomes and prospects of these women were not entirely compromised, but became rather complicated. Conceivably as a testament to their resilience, we found that women completed a credential and transfer at a higher rate than men four years after they initially enrolled. Among all students, regardless of their transfer intent, 52 percent of all women as opposed to 45 percent of all men earned a credential. When looking at transfer-intending students only, 44 percent of all women transferred to a four-year institution relative to 36 percent of all men.[13] However, when it comes to transfer in STEM specifically, while the women seemed to have survived the male-dominant learning environments by demonstrating that they were the same, if not better, STEM caliber through good grades and growing expertise, the broader set of their life circumstances outside of school eventually took a heavy toll. Significantly more women than men (30 percent versus 16 percent) initially aspiring to transfer in STEM diverted to other majors, put their initial STEM transfer goal on an indefinite hold, or left school altogether for the immediacy of getting a job that would pay. Like Kanda, Katy, Gwyneth, and other women in this book, they faced hard choices that took priority over transfer, leaving many women with a hazy and uncertain view of the STEM baccalaureate pathway through community colleges.

(NO MORE) DIVERTED DREAMS

The women we interviewed gave us a glimpse into the multifaceted identities, experiences, strengths, and vulnerabilities they negotiated and reconciled throughout their journey in STEM. Their stories richly extended what we knew about female students in STEM at community colleges. Although we came in with an awareness that community colleges could present encouraging and supportive environments for women, we discovered that gendered attitudes, behaviors, and less-than-warm environments continued to plague spaces in these institutions, as reinforced by education researchers Xiaodan Hu and Justin Ortagus.[14]

What can be done? While not a panacea, implicit bias training, which has shown some potential to mitigate implicit bias toward women in STEM, could serve as a starting point to help faculty, advisors, and other college staff to be more cognizant of their actions and behaviors.[15] Do college faculty and staff regard men as protective or dominating rather than viewing women as equal if not superior participants in classroom activities, projects, labs, or assignments? Are they expressly pointing out the unique perspectives that women bring to STEM issues and solutions? By looking inward and questioning bias, various community college actors can work toward demonstrating explicit actions that cultivate a more inviting and equitable STEM classroom environment for women.

Focusing more specifically on transfer, institutions must carefully consider how transfer services may be experienced by women and what transfer information and materials look like for women. Does the transfer advising staff mirror and, more importantly, fully support the complex set of interests, identities, and experiences of its female students? Are transfer services designed in ways that women feel they can easily access to freely explore and inquire about transfer? Are women pictured in transfer information and materials? Does this material appeal to women without stereotyping them? Do transfer advisors help women chart educational goals that affirm and inspire their sense of self in relation to their experiences, contexts, and role in society? This is just a simple start of the many hard questions community colleges can ask when assessing, revisiting, or potentially revamping their efforts to support transfer for women in STEM.

In addition, community colleges can consider a few support mechanisms for women in STEM that are vital yet underimplemented. For instance, mentorship is a promising but overlooked support mechanism in the community college. In fact, we know that role modeling and mentorship opportunities are available for women in STEM post-transfer, with positive reports by female students.[16] These mentorship relations can occur between faculty and students, among peers, or through partnerships with local organizations. Having these women serve as role models, sharing their experiences and offering insight, can help female students strengthen their belief in themselves and keep them motivated to pursue a STEM degree and career. These are just a few of the many ways in which institutions can think about boosting and supporting community college women's beliefs in their ability to succeed and transfer in STEM.

Other general institutional structures to support women in STEM would involve childcare options, targeted grants, and adequate course options to enable female students to better integrate and address their multiple identities and responsibilities. We spoke with several single moms who made the challenges they faced very apparent. Yet there was very little if any mention of daycare offered by the community colleges to help them manage their family responsibilities and STEM path. Although community colleges have been known to offer daycare services for adult students, these opportunities are actually quite limited.[17] This signals a need for many institutions to revisit the types of services they provide women in STEM, as they may be missing the mark on what female students need the most. This similarly applies to grant opportunities and course options so women are not faced with choosing between work and school when they have dependents to support.

Women in STEM at community colleges, both the ones we met and nationally, begin with an immense amount of promise and motivation, but as our female students' stories showed, the narrative can complicate and shift. To prevent women's pursuit of a STEM transfer path or a STEM career from being perpetually thwarted, higher education institutions must give full consideration to the relationships, experiences, and environments external to college that often dominate women's decisions and trajectories. Transfer should be situated as part of the larger scheme of students' lives—something much bigger than just an academic matter. Helping women to envision transfer as a tenable and viable part of their many ways of being will continue to be a main task and challenge toward a more gender-equitable STEM education pathway.

4

Resilience, Despite All

Students of Color Navigating Transfer

> *There were so many things that got in the way of success for persons of color.*
>
> —Kanda (I3)

BEFORE GETTING TO this and the following chapter in detail, it is worth noting that the sheer diversity within the student body, in many different forms, touched our students across different backgrounds in meaningful ways. In particular, our students described their two-year college campuses as "diverse" and "open," which in turn helped prepare them for a diverse workplace, especially in science, technology, engineering, and mathematics (STEM) areas, even among those who did not transfer or earn a credential. For example, although Kanda did not see a lot of women, especially women of color, in her information technology (IT) program, her exposure to individuals who either shared her racial identity or were from other minoritized backgrounds at Metroshore as a whole made a difference:

> But when I got to Metroshore, I met other students who were Native American and other minority groups, and it really helped me build a cultural understanding and gain some knowledge about other cultures and other perspectives and other walks of life. And that really helped me, especially professionally because I learned to work with people that I had never interacted with as often as maybe a high schooler, as a kid in the K–12 system. But these were gonna be people that were gonna be my future coworkers. And learning their different backgrounds helped me understand their style of working, their motivations, and seeing where mine are and finding some common ground in working together. (I3)

This exposure to diversity appealed to Kanda's preexisting tendencies to serve the community and paved the way for her longer-term engagement with community work and capacity to work in, with, and for a diverse workforce. Similarly, Chad, a Black man who graduated with a physical therapist assistant degree from Metroshore, singled out the diversity in his classes as a highlight of his experience:

> You have a diverse class—diverse class group. And your patient population is diverse there. So that applies. What they teach, they teach you about all that—you know, cultural awareness and things. And sometimes there's no better way to learn that than to experience it. So there's a big diverse group of people studying there in different fields, and it makes you develop a respect for everybody's field as well. Even though sometimes we did, as a class, get a little boisterous. You know, we'd be proud of PTA—our PT program. But at the same time, we still knew everybody was important. So, in the hospital, you know that everybody plays a role. And without them, the place falls apart. The cleaning people don't do their job and stuff—they're equally as important as we are. It really makes you kind of aware that everybody needs to do their role, and you need to respect people. (I3)

For white students, such exposure can be an initial shock that leads to an understanding of diversity, particularly for those coming from a predominantly white, rural background. When asked what stood out over her entire experience at Metroshore College, Jennipher, who was pursuing an animation program, said, "It was overwhelming when I first came here because it's just five thousand white people come here. It's 75 percent all different races and I was just like, what is this? But it was good to see that because it broadened my horizons and gave me more insight into, like, people are more open and welcomed than in my little town, so it's very nice to see that." (I1)

WHAT CAMPUS DIVERSITY DOES AND DOESN'T DO

It appeared that all students, regardless of their racial, ethnic, and other backgrounds, had something positive to say about the diverse makeup they saw among their peers, especially in terms of the range of racial and ethnic backgrounds. However, the sheer presence of structural diversity—meaning the numbers of different groups of students of color that make up the student population of an institution—does not automatically translate into a deeply, culturally inclusive environment that engenders a positive impact on the experiences and outcomes of many minoritized and historically underserved populations in our education system.[1] While it does seem that the structural diversity that our students saw helped them visualize, or perhaps even idealize, a diverse and vibrant STEM workforce and audience, structural diversity alone does not do it.

Over the years, there have been many arguments in support of structural diversity and its purported impacts on students and their learning in college and beyond. The appeal and simplicity of this idea quickly drove the priorities of federal education and research funding where the initial goal was to increase the numbers of underrepresented students with a focus on racial and ethnic diversity. However, we would be naïve to think that simple increases in the numbers alone would lead to real change. The quality of interactions and relationships among diverse groups holds much greater weight and is more impactful than the mere quantity of structural diversity.[2] While an environment may appear diverse and integrated on the surface, the actual qualitative experiences and interactions may remain unequal. In reality, many of the positive impacts as a result of structural diversity focus on what it can do for white students and not what the implications are for students of color. Interacting with students from different racial and ethnic backgrounds and developing close interracial friendships and relationships have shown to benefit students; however, it seems that this benefit accrues more for white students than students of color.[3]

The same carries over into STEM programs and classes, where many students of color as a whole and female students of color may not fully enjoy the benefits that may come from interracial interactions, as found in work by education researchers Marie-Elena Reyes and Isis Settles.[4] In short, structural diversity does not address the deeply seated and intersected racial and gender stereotypes and biases, explicit or implicit; nor does it guarantee equitable STEM educational and career outcomes. Much of what we know about what structural diversity does or doesn't do focuses on four-year institutional settings, while community colleges remain overlooked. In particular, the potential and pitfalls of structural diversity may play out differently in the STEM context at community colleges, some of which is illuminated through the lived experiences of students of color, which I discuss next.

Our students of color—those who identify as Black, Latinx/Hispanic, Asian, or Native American—came to their two-year colleges with high educational aspirations, and although these aspirations plummeted a bit over the course of our study, they remained relatively high four years later.[5] During the more in-depth interviews we had with each of the nineteen students of color (four Native American, three Asian, five Black, and seven Latinx/Hispanic), they commended their two-year colleges for providing them with educational opportunities in ways that four-year institutions would not and for supporting them in general. For example, when Elizabeth, interested in medicine and neurobiology, described her overall experience at Great Lakes, the people there came to mind first: "I guess the people here are—I've heard of friends who've gone off to different colleges, and they're kind of met with some sort of racism and stuff like that. I feel like here the people are really open-minded and welcoming, so I haven't had to deal with any of that type of stuff, so that's kind of made me enjoy my time more here." (I1)

However, when digging further into their experiences sifting through the transfer process, what we found was not as heartening; instead, it was perplexing, and in some cases, troublesome. When we looked at the students' progress toward earning a credential or transfer, we saw a steep gap between their aspired and realized goals, especially in contrast to their white counterparts. Among students whose primary goal was to transfer, 31 percent of students of color transferred to a four-year institution, compared with 46 percent of white students. Even for those who did not attend the two-year colleges for transfer but primarily for earning a credential, four years later 64 percent of white students obtained a credential as opposed to 55 percent of students of color.[6] Underneath this large disparity was a profoundly concerning finding that students of color who perceived that they had more support from family and friends for transfer were in fact less likely to maintain momentum toward transfer.[7] Why did students of color who initially felt that they received more support for transfer actually get derailed from the STEM transfer track? Some of our students' stories may shed light on this puzzling issue.

Shinichi is an Asian American male student keenly interested in transferring in biology. His parents, sister, and peers were all a big part of the support crowd cheering him on. Having this great network of support should have set him on a sure path to success. However, when I asked him about transfer advising, he at first hesitated to say anything negative, but then opened up more: "So my advisor actually, she gave me a bit of helpful review, but at the same time, it wasn't much help at all. She sort of told me just to take general studies, and just go on from there. . . . She helped me with my classes a little, but she mostly said, 'Once you are confident enough to transfer over, come back and talk and we can go through steps.' So I find that unhelpful, because well, I mean, she didn't really give me any insight about like what to do." (I2) While Shinichi did not reveal anything further about the "confident" comment, his advisor's impatience and assumption that he was *not* confident despite his proactivity, coupled with the lack of concrete steps for transfer he so desperately needed and was ready for, left him with utter confusion and frustration.

So he mainly resorted to his family and friends. However, while his family undoubtedly supported transfer, they were steering him toward something not aligned with his genuine interest: "Medical science is what my sister is going to. And my family also hopes for me to go into; that's a predominant thing in Asian cultures—Asian things. They want, like, a medical kind of family background. But to me, medical was never my liking. 'Cause that dealt with a lot of memorization of bodies and, like, small compounds. Which, for me, I can't do. My sister's going to do that. I'm very proud of her. But to me, that's just not my go-to—my 'cup of tea' I guess." (I3)

Shinichi then turned to his friends to figure out more about the transfer process and what courses to take in preparation:

> I'm also asking my friends for their personal experience and how they transferred over, because this year, once spring ended, some of my friends transferred or graduated from here, and transferred over to Capital University, and I've asked them, "How have you transferred? And what did you guys do?" I've talked with them about what classes did they take, and what seemed more valuable to me, so I can just take it, instead of taking miscellaneous [courses] that don't have credit that

can't transfer over, so yeah, I'm relying mostly on my friends' experiences and seeing how I can benefit off of that. (I2)

Shinichi's story illuminates several racialized tensions and contexts, both those unique to his racial identity as an Asian American and those common among our students of color. As an Asian American, the model minority myth was imposed upon him in multiple layers, and to some extent including the ways in which his family internalized it.[8] The almost dismissive manner in which his advisor talked to him was likely an exhibition of her stereotypes, checked or unchecked, of Asians being socially introverted, obedient, and submissive.[9] The intense family expectation that he should go on to be a doctor, a stereotyped notion but one embraced by many Asian parents, acted as a burden that went against his true interest. Shinichi's experience illustrates the pressing need to debunk the model minority myth as it communicates sweeping misconceptions that all Asian Americans are the same.[10] Not only are there inequities in educational attainment across numerous Asian subgroups, but as Shinichi's story shows, we have reason to believe that there are wide variations within a specific Asian group, especially in the community college context that accommodates diverse goals and interests.[11]

Adding to the complexity, as a first-generation student, Shinichi was caught between strong parental expectations and the fact that his parents could not be his sole source of guidance. Research by OiYan Poon and Ajani Byrd suggests that first-generation Asian American students tend to rely more on teachers and counselors to make decisions about and navigate college.[12] Although being a first-generation student drove Shinichi to seek information from his advisor, he was met with dismissive behavior from her. This experience was further complicated by conflicting parental expectations and support of his aspirations. Nonetheless, Shinichi continued to push through in his own ways by engaging his peers and persisting in his own interests.

Shinichi's journey is no doubt uniquely situated within his own familial, racial, social, and cultural contexts. But it also offers a window into several common elements underlying the experiences of many of our students of color. Most important, even though not all of them mentioned encountering specific racial biases, chances are that they did experience those without necessarily knowing or naming it, due to their implicit nature. This assumption is highly tenable given the troublesome finding from our survey analysis I referenced earlier, and the irony is that, because of the strong emotional support these students of color often received from family and friends, they were initially more "out there" in pursuing the transfer potential. Thus they were more exposed to a system not purposefully designed to encourage their success, and accordingly, they experienced more hurdles.

This system is characterized by a frequently implicit, multifaceted burden that students of color often unknowingly endure, as in Shinichi's case, and an explicit wall blocking their educational path forward in the form of huge financial concerns. Quoting Tom, a Latino male student: "I've been thinking about transfer, but my concern and biggest problem is financial aid." (I2) Or Clyde, a Black man: "But money is the only thing, I would say, that stops me from transferring right now." (I2) While financial burdens can be viewed as a universal issue facing the majority of college-going students and families, for students of color, it often intersects with many other hardships, which not only complicates but also jeopardizes their capacity to live a "normal" life. Valerie, a Latina who graduated from Metroshore College without transfer, listed financial burden as the number one issue of concern during her college time, alongside family and cultural issues:

> I would say my economic standing, starting out as a student—I felt that it was really difficult to navigate financially starting out. . . . Or, you know, that is a barrier to continuing your education. Or going to a school of your choice. So, for me, like I told you my mother had

passed away; when I was in sixth grade all the way through high school, that's when she had gotten cancer. She's a single parent, she can't work. Double mastectomy, radiation, chemotherapy. So growing up in a food-insecure environment and a household-insecure environment, with the water getting turned off or our heat getting turned off—that is a detriment to being functional at school. Hence, me taking easy classes just to get through high school. Not being able to go away to school and being immersed in that environment, where, if you're in a dorm you don't have the family pressures. Not having to work. I worked two jobs when I was at Metroshore College. That takes away from your study time—your time that's dedicated to your education. That also was a deterrent to me being able to take internships at City University. I was like, when am I supposed to do that? So I think being economically disadvantaged played a part in me not succeeding in certain aspects of school. And then also I'm Mexican as well. I mean, I know I look pretty white. I haven't faced the same things as my brother has, who looks Mexican. But kind of feeling also torn, where I have this cultural background, but I don't look it. So, you know, not really feeling like I could go to the Latino club. That's what I'm thinking about. Not feeling like I can go there, you know? (I3)

Thus, many of our students of color did not lack the emotional support for school or transfer from their family; in fact, the level of supportiveness from family was statistically the same across all racial groups.[13] But while that support offered a path into transfer exploration, in many cases it was not enough to combat barriers they experienced along the way. Other than finances, students of color are often pulled in multiple directions due to competing responsibilities and values, including a strong sense of family obligation and community.[14] Yet, despite students' desire to have a familial or cultural connection, racial or colorism issues remain not only across groups, but also within ethnic/racial groups.[15] Add to that the fact that community college students of color tend to face food or housing insecurities at higher rates than white students, as in Valerie's case.[16] These intersections can result in the perfect storm, making the road longer and more challenging for these students than it should be.

Although our students invariably shared struggles in juggling multiple demands, whether chosen or imposed upon them, resilience and the quest for community were what kept them going, even if they did not achieve their transfer goals in the end. We already learned that, for Kanda, her resilience and drive to give back to family and community led her to take up a career sooner than transfer would have allowed. If students of color were not able to find the sense of community and belonging they desired at their community colleges, they found a better fit at the type of four-year institution they chose. Case in point: Bubbles, a Latino male student who transferred from Great Lakes College to City University, found his new transfer institution a lot better and "a lot more diverse":

> I feel like here people are—they're more willing to help you out and stuff like—lot of people helped you out at Great Lakes College, I'm not trying to say that. It seems like the mentality is a lot different. Here people are settled in and like willing to embrace the community that's around them. Over at, you know, Great Lakes it seemed like everyone was just there to get their degree and get out. That was kind of like the main thing, you know, I just want to get my general eds so I could get going. I feel like those students, when they transfer off or get where they go, like they kind of settle down and take the people around them for granted. (I2)

Even though many of these students did not transfer, they landed in a place where their contributions extended and transcended the face value carried by a credential. They felt that they made something meaningful out of their experiences at their two-year colleges, and they attached a great deal of value to that education. For example, when reflecting on his experiences across community colleges and four-year institutions,

Chad expressed that, at Metroshore, he learned the need to focus and be "strategic about things." He also shared that, if he could have a do-over, he would have started his college career at Metroshore College, rather than spending so much money at Springbrook University: "I probably would've just taken classes at Metroshore College to begin with." (I3)

Kanda also credited Metroshore, or community colleges writ large, for the diversity, practicality, and the second chances it provides:

> What was great about community college is we met people from all different backgrounds. They were pursuing one degree and their degree ended up not being really something that was practical, or something that could help them get a job. And so they were struggling financially, and they were struggling professionally trying to get somewhere, get experience, and be successful. So they would come back here to Metroshore College and they would get their associate's degree and be like, "We're gonna try this now because my first plan didn't work." And I think that was really motivating 'cause it's like, maybe something the first time you try, it won't really pan out. But it's like, it's not really about how you start, it's kind of how you finish. And really getting to know a bunch of different classmates was super helpful and motivating. (I3)

These stories help reconstruct the perfectly imperfect ways in which community colleges are hosting students of color who pursue transfer in STEM and beyond. Often, the institutions' long tradition as well as current practice of enrolling a diverse population allowed students of color to feel a sense of ease, inclusion, and belonging. The open access, combined with pragmatic training offered through courses or exposure to people's real-world needs and struggles, served as a versatile platform for students of color to acquire something of value that stayed with them beyond their community college education. However, their paths into transfer exploration, even when backed with a strong support system from family and friends, was infiltrated by overt and hidden barriers. Not only did students of color experience the same structural and informational obstructions described in chapter 2, they negotiated these obstructions in conjunction with explicit and implicit racial biases and racism, and all too often, adversities in life that deeply intersected with social class and race.

These were the types of issues our students of color unvaryingly faced one way or another; they endured to overcome these issues with remarkable grace and resilience. Their strengths allowed them to make the most meaning and value of their community college experience. On the other hand, even as we acknowledge, honor, and celebrate these students for all these reasons, we simply cannot accept the fact that institutional action is largely, glaringly absent in these students' stories, which explains the disproportionately lower transfer rates among students of color. These disparities implore us to shift the responsibility away from students and on institutions to create a more equitable STEM transfer pathway that supports the complex identities and situations of these students.[17] This shift (discussed in full in chapters 8 and 9) requires a self-examination as to whether institutional goals explicitly address race and ethnicity as part of their focus on improving participation, persistence, and success in STEM.[18] Do institutional leadership, faculty, advisors, and other college staff support such goals? In what ways are these different individuals carrying or not carrying out those goals?

I want to conclude this chapter with Kooks's journey, a journey that is too rare but one that illustrates how to complete that institutional side of responsibility. Kooks is a Latino student who started at Great Lakes College and successfully transferred into engineering at Fieldcrest University. Like many students of color, he started at his two-year college for its low cost. Kooks transferred early, within the first year of attending Great Lakes College. His entire transfer and post-transfer experience exemplifies how, institutionally, both community colleges and four-year universities can ease the transfer process through building genuine, close personal relationships, something especially important for but not often experienced by students of color in higher education in general.[19]

Speaking about the support for his early transfer, Kooks described how his advisors at the community college not only helped him transfer, but also placed a laser focus on setting up his initial course schedule right when he started at the four-year school:

> I actually had a lot of counselors. They helped me look for classes over at Fieldcrest University to set up my schedule so when I got there—I mean besides the counselors over there helping me choose classes—the counselors here helped me line up my first year so that I could have a very easy path to go onto when I did transfer to Fieldcrest. So besides, you know, just getting me over to the school and saying, dumping me off and saying, you know, "Oh, here's a new environment. Go have fun." They made sure that I had a schedule set so when I went there I could talk to their counselors and see what they advised and then I could have a better understanding of what I should take my sophomore year. So besides the transfer process of just getting over there, they did help me with an educational path as well. (I1)

Kooks transitioned well into Fieldcrest University, elaborating on his pre- and post-transfer experience when we met at Fieldcrest: "The transition was very easy. The counselors here made it very easy for me to set up my classes while I was at Great Lakes College and kind of get me on track with what's going on, what I should be doing on campus, what I'll have to do when I get here. I've had a lot of help with the transfer. It's been very easy. It was pretty much flawless. I actually want to say there was really nothing—there's no troubles in transfer whatsoever so it was good." (I2) Beyond a rather seamless academic transition, Kooks continued to thrive at his four-year school, identifying the personal connections the school helped cultivate as key to his success:

> I guess people in my classes and my professors, they really help me stay on track. My professors, if I ever have any troubles, they're willing to answer and work with me on them. And you know if you start doing

bad in classes, some of the professors will ... although I haven't really had this problem yet, they will sometimes confront the students and say, you know, "Is something wrong? What's going on?" They'll talk to you about what might be going on in your life. It's just—there's a lot of support here for doing—keeping you on track with your education. (I2)

Kooks also saw the value of this type of connection beyond the classroom setting. "There's always been a connection with the teacher while you're in the class. But there's also teachers that'll talk to you outside of class, even about their personal lives, which I think is just fantastic because it helps you connect with the teacher who helps you. I think it makes you—it's made me more comfortable in classes when I'm just sitting there." (I2)

Taken together, Kooks's experiences illuminate the transformative power of the proactive and collective support two-year and four-year institutions can create for including, welcoming, and assisting transfer students of color. Like other students of color, Kooks was also deeply connected to his family and community. However, in his case, they represented more of a safety net only if and when Kooks needed it. They provided a warm background to Kooks's journey as a transfer student of color, buttressed by a strong and inclusive institutional environment traversing both schools that fully embraced, supported, and helped clarify his aspirations. I wish I could say Kooks's story was not an isolated example, but I can't. Nonetheless, I am compelled to end with his story as it illustrates what the STEM transfer picture could and should be for students of color.

5

Waiting to Be Seen

More Student Faces

IN THIS CHAPTER, I focus on students' distinct experiences based on several other identities: as adult learners, as students with mental health issues, and as students with learning disabilities. When reviewing what we found as a whole, the themes around these identities were not always concentrated around transfer, which was especially true for older adults. Also, the breadth and depth of our findings were not as saturated as what we found about gender and race, and this was particularly the case for students dealing with mental health issues and learning disabilities. Their experiences are nonetheless pivotal to learn, as they unravel the ways in which the current system fails to address the many types of diversity in the two-year college science, technology, engineering, and mathematics (STEM) student population and thus underserve and further disadvantage many of these students.

OLDER ADULTS IN STEM: FINDING SPACE AND PACE

" *I know that ageism is kind of prevalent in a lot these technology degrees."*
—Jim (I2)

About 30 percent of our students could be classified as "nontraditional" in age when they started at the two-year colleges in 2014. These students—generally defined as those above the traditional college-going age range of eighteen to around twenty-five—represent a fair share of enrollment at community colleges.[1] Nationally, the average age of community students hovers around twenty-eight, with 38 percent falling in the range of twenty-two to thirty-nine and 9 percent over the age of forty.[2] A larger proportion of community college students in STEM tend to be older than their counterparts at four-year institutions. Over a quarter of older adult community college students start in STEM compared with 4 percent of four-year students.[3] Older adults represent a vital group of our college-educated workforce, yet the STEM and transfer literature has limited insight into how they experience, explore, and find fit or lack thereof in the community college STEM path.

Norman, a white older adult pursuing an information technology (IT) program at Centerville College, described his first-year experience there:

> It's been a real struggle. I mean, it's been a real challenge, returning to school. There's a lot of roadblocks. I don't learn and retain things quite as fast as I did when I was younger. It probably would have been helpful had I connected with somebody that was kind of paired with me, and going through this journey. The other counselors here at Centerville College and other people I talk to about it, but you know, I was kind of, I didn't fit in a lot of the patterns or whatever. I was sort of an odd duck, coming in later in life, looking for a career change, trying to find somewhere where I could blend my previous experiences with something new out there, and I think we could use more support in that area. You hear the term "lifelong learning," and they're trying to

do that, but I think much of the way we're set up is still, "You're born. You go to school. You get a job. You retire. You die." It still seems like it's that linear progression. (I2)

Norman's insights and frustrations poignantly illustrate the larger theme we found throughout our older students' experiences and struggles: they feel like they are navigating and left out of an educational space that is fundamentally designed with more traditional-age students in mind. This is worrisome, especially when considering the fact that two-year colleges are primarily commuter institutions, lauded for accommodating students who are older, working full-time, and have competing responsibilities.[4] While older community college students might have high levels of motivation and achievement, they are also less likely to persist.[5] Community colleges can clearly do better to help this promising group of students realize their education and career goals in STEM.

This lack of intentional accommodation for older adult learners manifested itself in several ways within and beyond the classroom. Inside the classroom, older adults often found activities and group work to be more suited to younger "kids," and their own lives and/or professional experiences were not sufficiently acknowledged and appreciated. Consequently, many older adults' self-perceptions as learners in STEM fields were detrimentally impacted, and they often described themselves as slow or poor learners. For example, Norman viewed his young fellow students as superior academically:

> There are a couple other classmates that were kind of like my son, you know, it's like, the knowledge sponge. We'd get done with a test, and I'd get beads of sweat, walk out, and say, "Oh yeah, I thought the test went pretty good." So, there were definitely a lot of people in there who are much better academically than [me]—they learned things faster, and they seemed to be able to retain it and apply it too, without even doing the projects and stuff. They were just light years ahead of me. (I1)

The age difference also translated into other classroom dynamics that inhibited older adults' ways of learning. Callan, enrolled in agriculture at Metroshore College, was highly sensitive to this age difference, resulting in his initial reluctance to interact with his much younger classmates: "I'm so much older than all of the students in the class, you know? I had a couple people there were my age. At first, like I said, I went back to school I didn't know what to wear, I didn't know what to put on, I didn't know what to—I don't know how to talk to them." (I1)

Similarly, Katy was also having a difficult time wanting to interact with her younger peers, but for a different reason: "And I find maybe it's because I'm a little older, but like I get really frustrated when other students spend their class time on their phones, like with Pinterest or Google or texting each other and giggling about what's in the news, and having side conversations, and so as a learner with ADD, I'm easily distracted anyway. But then to have classmates who are obviously not engaged is very frustrating. And to have an instructor who just sort of ignores all of it, it's like hard." (I2)

Temperance, another older adult, had to struggle and then ignore peer dynamics based on age intersecting with gender: "Well, sometimes with younger guys or whatever, especially when I first started the program, I was coming back after a very large gap in schooling. I'm looking around and going, 'Oh my word, I'm in a room full of babies. Oh my goodness. What am I getting into?' And so sometimes it's just an age factor. They haven't figured out life yet, so I'm not going to take it personally." (I2)

Across all these different instances and contexts, older adults struggled to find an immediate connection with their younger fellow learners, or with an educational space that was not only shared but also dominated, perhaps symbolically, by young people. As a result, they assigned a direct connection between age and the capacity to learn, and they considered their younger student peers as more competent, faster learners who would likely enjoy an advantage when it came to their educational and career attainment. For example, Jim, an older white male student who works for the city, has a family, and is pursuing IT, was concerned about his employment prospects because of his age: "I know that ageism is kind of prevalent in a lot of these technology degrees and stuff. I think a lot of people like tend to pick on the—pick the younger kids because they got more time, more free time and stuff." (I2)

While older adults were self-conscious about their age, affecting their initial academic engagement and outlook on reentering the workforce in potentially new fields, they also viewed their age, often associated with maturity and resilience, as a strength. For instance, although describing himself as a "slower" learner, Norman was confident that his perseverance would be what mattered eventually: "So yeah, I can say, I'm not the smartest person on the planet, I struggle, but I can learn it if I put enough time and effort into it." (I1)

Temperance described her perseverance as the most helpful factor to keep her in her program, despite the challenges she encountered being an older adult student, employed full-time, and studying full-time:

> In my sheer stubbornness, I decided if I was going to go back to school, I was going to do it full-time, get it done as quickly as possible, so a lot of my struggles were all self-inflicted. The "normal," I say that in quotations, the normal going back and getting the degree as an adult or as a full-time employee somewhere, most of these people are taking two, maybe three classes tops a semester. . . . So yes, I sacrificed having a big social life, and I sacrificed being able to go out or to do certain things. But in the long run, I'm glad I did it, even though it was difficult. Had I not been this far in the program, I might not have been as eligible a candidate for the job that I now have, so but yeah, just deciding this is what I wanted and sticking with it, and doing it no matter what, even if I wanted to kick myself for it, was really what got me through. (I2)

From what our students shared in the surveys, there were vast differences between the types of resources and knowledge that older adults and younger students tapped into as they navigated the STEM path.

Important to note is that close to 30 percent of adult students over thirty never talked to their academic advisors for academic purposes, whereas this percentage was around 15 percent among their younger counterparts.[6] From our individual conversations with older adults, we learned that they barely utilized supports and services offered by their institutions due to scheduling reasons. For these students, support for their schoolwork came primarily from their significant others, and interactions related to academic matters largely occurred within the classroom setting, which was more accessible. Talking with advisors, which involved time outside of the classroom, was often out of the question. Overall, unlike their younger peers, older adults were much less likely to seek help from advisors and student peers for transfer and schoolwork. Instead, they turned to family and friends as they navigated and progressed through college.[7]

We already know from the large body of community college research that adult learners' lives do not revolve around courses, peers, or other college activities; instead, these students tend to prioritize their work, family, and other obligations.[8] Therefore, it may not be a surprise that family and friends served as their major source of capital as they worked their way through college. At the same time, if older adults take little advantage of, or have limited access to, institutional resources or knowledge offered by institutional agents, they may not obtain critical information and networks, such as referrals to academic resources or transfer guidelines that could facilitate their success in STEM. This is a delicate equilibrium that must be struck carefully. As some of our older students already voiced, they often felt immense pressure to make expedited returns on their education since many had to care for their kids, along with other external responsibilities that prevented them from being in school for prolonged periods.

How to strike that balance, then? A simple appeal or requirement for academic advising and networking done the traditional way would not suffice. Recognizing the age differences that drive community college

STEM students' experiences and educational outcomes is an initial step. What needs to follow, urgently, is the tailoring of advising services for students from different age groups, as well as the development of creative ways to leverage and combine academic and social venues through which knowledge and resources are built among different groups of adult learners, such as socioacademic integrative moments advanced by Regina Deil-Amen.[9] Older learners face many complicated dynamics in their education and life to begin with, which can be exacerbated if we ignore the unique ways they navigate higher education, learn, and use and consume information and supports.

FIGHTING MENTAL HEALTH ISSUES AND LEARNING DISABILITIES

❝ *I don't have to be alone and feel like a failure."*
—JASMINE (I1)

Although we did not set out to center our work on mental health conditions and learning disabilities, the number of our students who voluntarily revealed their struggles with these often interlaced issues was astounding. While we do not yet have reliable estimates nationally, based on data from several community colleges across seven states (California, Louisiana, New Jersey, New York, Pennsylvania, Wisconsin, and Wyoming), almost half of the students reported at least one mental health issue, a higher rate than their four-year counterparts. The picture is not much better when we look at community college students with learning disabilities.[10] In 2018, the American Association of Community Colleges released a report indicating that about 20 percent of the 7.2 million community college students identified as having disabilities. Among students with disabilities, 26.5 percent disclosed attention deficit disorder (ADD) or attention deficit hyperactivity disorder (ADHD) as their disability, and 4.6 percent identified specific learning disability or dyslexia as their disability.[11] The increasing recognition of the prevalence of mental health and learning disabilities among community college students, however, does not yet translate into a deep understanding of these often intersecting issues, and these students' experiences continue to be sorely overlooked.[12]

Based on what we have learned, many students dealing with mental health issues and learning disabilities find community colleges appealing for the greater access, flexibility, and accommodations that they represent.[13] Overall, a small (or feel-small) learning environment underlies their choice to attend and persist in community colleges. For some of our students, community colleges represent a place they find to be safe or a way out of their struggles. Kelly, a white female student who suffers from anxiety and agoraphobia, described her biotechnology program at Centerville College as "safe." When asked what exactly made her feel safe, Kelly said, "Teachers make me feel safe because I feel like they're trying to teach us to become good, working members in biotech as opposed to trying to test our skills. And the students are great; small class. That helps me feel safe, and it's a small college and I like that too. I just like it here. It's, it's a peaceful place for me." (I1)

Jasmine, an aspiring transfer student in IT enrolled at Centerville College, suffers from chronic depression. She previously went to a four-year school, stayed for a year, and then pulled herself out of it: "I didn't do well there, and I had the same problem, where I was depressed and I missed class and I didn't really interact socially and make friends. I suppose there was probably resources there that I could have reached out, but there wasn't anyone who really came to me and said, 'Hey, you seem like such a promising student. Why have you missed class?'" (I2) Contrasting that experience with her two-year college, Jasmine felt that Centerville College was where she should be: "Yeah. Now when I get stuck, I have people I can go to for help. I don't have to be alone and feel like a failure." (I1)

Depression and anxiety are among the top mental health issues facing our students, which aligns with other estimates.[14] However, in many instances, these concerns of our students intersected with several others, such as financial concerns, being a single parent, and working multiple shifts, that further complicated the prospects of their STEM education and careers. When describing what would stand in the way of her academic success, Jasmine revealed how her mental health issues intertwined with financial issues and how her son was the reason she could not give up: "Money has been really tight. So I'm really looking forward to getting financial aid in the fall. It's hard to do well at school when you have to remember to go to the food pantry. It's hard when money's tight. More so than I think some people realize. Everything gets more difficult. And then I have my depression. My depression and anxiety, and sometimes my brain will tell me that I can't do it, that I should give up. And then I think about my son and I know that I can't." (I1)

Callan, introduced earlier in this chapter, also shared his multiple identities and situations:

> I'm not going to kid you, I have a learning disability, I have dysgraphia. ... Quite a few people in my family have mental issues, and when you've got mental issues or people classify you as something, you have no say-so; when they talk to you, they treat you in the way that they treat anyone else. They don't think that you're a person; they just put you along with that category. I needed some help with, in the process of doing this I was also trying to fix up my—I have child support because I have kids—and I was trying to get that stuff straightened out. And I went downtown, and going to school makes you a little bit happier, so you get a little more confidence, so you can talk to some more people. (I1)

As Jasmine's and Callan's stories show, these students faced an abundance of adversity as they attempted to juggle their identities, lives, work, finances, and school, making them not only vulnerable to their mental health issues and learning disabilities in the first place, but in some cases, exacerbating their mental health and well-being. Add the fact that these students often do not actively seek help or accommodations from the institution for fear of stigma or because they believe that they should manage on their own.[15] Our students who disclosed their mental health issues clearly identified these problems as major barriers to realizing their transfer aspirations, but those same students, although holding a positive view of their experience, did not highlight any institutionalized professional support as an effective solution.

Although these students discussed the obstacles posed by their mental health issues, they were also determined to overcome them to succeed in STEM. When asked what she saw as a major barrier for her future, Kelly said:

> My anxiety, this anxiety ... I'm just always going to have it. I always have and I need to learn how to deal with it and it's going to be a huge barrier to my success ... I'm not, you know I'm just going to fight it and see how far I get and kind of throw it in my anxiety's face, like, "Hey anxiety, look at this. I made it through two semesters." But yeah, that would be a big barrier. Another thing is my dad going to the mental hospital. That really was awful, but again, I got through it. So yeah, I guess just outside familial obligations and my inside anxiety would be a barrier, but I'm going to fight. (I1)

What is revealing about Kelly's words is how much she placed the burden to fight her anxiety on herself. When probed about who or what else helped support her in dealing with her anxiety, she named her proactive approach in sharing her condition and the support from her teachers and peers:

> Oh and—if you can't tell, I talk about it. I let people know about it, so they're not wondering, like, "Hey, what's going on?" My friends and teachers are super supportive. Sometimes I'll have—this is getting really personal—I'll get an anxiety attack in class where I'm gonna pass out, like—that happens to me sometimes. Fun. The teachers got to know me, and my classmates got to know me, and kind of joke about it with

me, which really helps. Like kind of making fun of myself for it, and they kind of josh with me, you know. And I keep—I talk to them about my fears of coworkers and bosses and expectations and they're—they laugh—this is all people in the program—they laugh and say, "Look, your coworkers are going to be like us. Your teachers are going to be like your boss. It'll be fine." So that helps a lot. Camaraderie, I guess. (I2)

While Kelly's approach may be a smart mechanism for coping with both the anxiety and the potential embarrassment she perceived as associated with panic attacks, it is vexing to realize that Kelly, like the majority of her peers suffering from mental health issues, was left to her own devices. This resonates with the overall theme described in detail in chapter 2, but the difference is that the mental health and learning disabilities these students endure can be such a detriment that they amplify the numerous other barriers that students encounter, serving as the final straw that completely breaks their transfer path.

When help is indeed available, it makes a big difference. Jasmine was able to pursue her STEM program through a Trade Adjustment Assistance Community College and Career Training (TAACCCT) grant.[16] This allowed her to enroll in the community college without having to take on a significant financial burden. At the same time, she was a single mom coping with her depression and caring for her son. This resulted in some rough times during her studies, including missing a significant amount of class, which put her behind. Her STEM prospects were looking dim. However, the support of her parents gave her the encouragement needed to push on. She recalled a conversation with her dad:

> I remember toward the end of my first semester, I was on the phone crying with my dad, and I'm like, "I'm not gonna be able to do this. I can't do this." And he was like, "You have to do this. You're not gonna be able to support yourself and your son with just like a minimum-wage job. You need to go back to school. You need to call your TAACCCT coordinator, whoever, and make this right." And I wiped away my tears

and brushed my hair and went to school, and I made an appointment and got back on track. (I2)

As Jasmine tried to get back on the STEM transfer path, she had to wade through a number of resources for help with her mental health issues and the other challenges she was facing. She was doing it mostly on her own. During this process, she realized that her grant coordinator was not as helpful as she had hoped, and didn't even believe in her ability to succeed: "I didn't know that the TAACCCT grant coordinator first was kind of telling people like, you know, 'Don't waste too much time with her. She's not coming to class.' And then I think I impressed some people after I had been around for three semesters or so." (I2) Indeed, she held on and eventually was able to stumble on a counselor to help her reconcile her classes and mental health issues: "Having him [the counselor] know what resources were available at school that I could reach out to and helping me reach out to them, and helping aid in knowing what kind of communication to have with my professors when I did miss class, because of being depressed, helped. And just feeling like there was someone here who was trying to help me succeed helped." (I2)

The positive interactions with the academic advisor gave Jasmine the information, resources, and assistance to carry on. Most important, they gave her the sense that someone at school was there for her, and her success meant that she no longer had to do it on her own. Jasmine's story gives hope to what community college supports and services can look like for these students. The current reality, though, is that even though mental health issues are more prominent among community college students, there are simply not enough resources or services to match their needs. According to a survey by the American College Counseling Association's Community College Task Force, 73 percent of community colleges provide mental health counseling services, but 86 percent do not have a psychiatry resource on campus.[17] Community college student usage of mental health services is even lower, hovering around 30 percent.[18] How can these students possibly use something they are not aware of or do not have information about?

In many ways, the realities facing students with mental health issues also ring true among students with learning disabilities. Most distressingly, in a similar way, despite the appearance of available services, there is an equal lack of substantively helpful support on the part of the institution. Katy provides a prominent example; she attempted to return to college several years back and figured out a few resources at that time. So when she enrolled in 2014, she was already aware of the publicized services she would need to help with her ADD. However, there was a disconnect with her instructors in understanding her needs. Speaking of her first chemistry lab:

> I think by the time I realized I was super overwhelmed, I had talked to my professor and he's like, "I feel like you're doing fine. Like I don't feel concerned about your progress. I think you're doing okay." I mean, you know? So I was like, "Well, I must not appear to be struggling." . . . I don't think I had the awareness to say anything like, "I don't get the lab. I don't understand how to work with other people when there's noise, and movement, and fire, and chemicals ." I just don't know what I'm doing. (I1)

In a well-intended but unhelpful way, the instructor dismissed Katy's ADD and anxiety as having overly high expectations for herself, and thus missed a pivotal opportunity to fully integrate the available services into Katy's learning experience.

In other cases, some students did not find out about assistance or services until well after the fact. Mathias, a Native American male in engineering at Metroshore College, recalled his struggles with an online course that failed to accommodate his Asperger's: "I just finished science and technology. And it was an online course. So, online it's kind of hard. But I got through it. Even though my outcome was a D. Having Asperger's kind of did that a little bit. I didn't get the special accommodations

I should have had gotten, because I didn't know about them right away." (I1) Eventually, Mathias independently found the resources he needed to help him through his courses. Yet, when asked why he felt he had to figure things out himself, he responded, "Well, to me, with a community college sometimes I feel that they will help you. And they'll have like the things out there. It would just be your responsibility to actually take advantage of them." (I1) Mathias fully believed that community colleges do help their students. However, he still placed the responsibility of obtaining the assistance on himself.

A few of our students shared insight into what community colleges could do to better help students with mental health and learning disabilities, so they could access what they needed when they needed it. Katy talked about a more streamlined process:

> It's just at college, I feel like Centerville College has a little ways to go to streamline their process, to make sure everybody's getting funneled through the right supports. A lot of people come in with, you know, economic disadvantages, learning disadvantages, and they aren't well supported, because it's not a streamlined process to get in. So I think Centerville College has been really effective at pulling in a lot of students. I think they're great at casting that wide net, but as far as processing people, I think their structures could be a little more effective. (I2)

Jasmine called for a more heightened focus on mental health issues:

> Okay, well, if you want to go really big picture, I would like to see more support for people with mental health problems. Like I said, my coworker and friend who used to be my student instructor here had similar struggles that I did as far as self-confidence, so I'd guess I'd just like to see like a little more assistance, a little more acceptance of those kinds of struggles, like a little more recognition that it's a real struggle and it's not just someone being lazy or something like that. (I2)

But what hits me even harder than the voices of Katy and Jasmine is the invisible heavy weight carried by these words from a first-generation student (taking a break trajectory) on our final survey:

> While much of what Metroshore has to offer is great on paper, it actually does very little in practice. I currently go through the Veterans Affairs at Metroshore (along with many other Metroshore programs) for help with my ADHD and mental issues and how it greatly interferes with my schoolwork. While there are a lot of people to talk to, honestly it ends up being just talk. Information is great, but I am already able to find such information or try and self-motivate myself. It boils down to grades and GPA. In my situation, I can learn the material and know it well enough to tutor my peers, but my own grade will barely be passing (or even failing). I view mental health treatment as a valued service, but ultimately a game of guesswork and wishful thinking, until it finally stumbles upon a mild success. I'm realistic about the time restraints of an academic environment, and how colleges will probably not accept me. Basically, while I would love to take classes, pass, and move off to a four-year college, I'm aware this may not work out. *Not because I'm unable to learn, but because I'm unable to fully participate in the whole process* [emphasis added]. My GPA will always need heavy explaining. I'm a risk in a competitive field that no college admissions staff is likely to take. Also my VA college money will run out, and with my low GPA, will limit any future financial assistance I can receive. I cannot think of anything anyone can do to help me, any more than what I already get. (S3)

The issues raised here deserve serious reflection on what counts as truly meaningful and transformative supports for these students. Not only do we need to consider new approaches to address their unmet needs; we must rethink what the practices and services already in place are really doing with and for these students. Are the extant support channels designed, coordinated, and communicated to fully recognize and address students' unique situations and issues related to mental health and learning? Do they include creative, nonconforming, and self-authoring ways to recognize and celebrate these students' talents and accomplishments?[19] If institutions are not genuinely committed to seeking answers to these questions, these students remain unsupported, misunderstood, and left to figure out their STEM path alone.

What we learned from the groups of students in this chapter, as with women in chapter 3 and students of color in chapter 4, urges us to interrogate how existing and emerging mechanisms intended to support transfer students in STEM and beyond influence historically underserved students across the wide range of their identities, especially those minoritized students. Only by taking a critical look inward can we truly support these students as an invaluable talent pool and make impactful change toward more equitable STEM pathways.

6

Tempered Aspirations

IN 1960, SOCIOLOGIST Burton Clark published his to be widely cited, highly contested, and often misunderstood landmark piece, "The 'Cooling-Out' Function in Higher Education," where he engaged in a vivid, realist ethnography of how community colleges' institutional agents participated in a systematic process of weeding out students who were not "qualified" or malleable enough to become "qualified" for baccalaureate education.[1] According to the cooling-out notion, institutions, such as community colleges, that serve students deemed underprepared for collegiate education track these students into subbaccalaureate options leading to a job that does not require a bachelor's degree. Intentionally or unintentionally, institutions thus maintain the social status quo, and keep the poor where they are by managing, redirecting, and eventually diminishing their baccalaureate aspirations.

But should community college students' transfer aspirations be managed and redirected to serve their best interest? A more contemporary argument may suggest a "yes." That is, the "college-for-all" ethos, touting that all students could and should participate in postsecondary education, inflates college aspirations, regardless of how realistic those aspirations may be.[2] Some argue that central to the college-for-all ethos is a problem: students arrive at college with little understanding of what they need to do to get from point A to point B, as well as limited awareness of potential barriers that they may encounter along the way.[3] Pertaining to community college students in particular, add to that argument the fact that many of them come in undeclared because they are not yet sure what they want to study or pursue as a future career. As a result, some contend that although the vast majority of community college students may hold baccalaureate aspirations, influenced by the college-for-all mind-set, they may still wander aimlessly because they do not know what they want to do.[4]

If this second argument holds true, it is inherently expected that community college students lower their transfer aspirations because of the volatility and uncertainty of such aspirations in the first place. Indeed, there was a downward course in our students' transfer aspirations: although the majority of our students arrived at college indicating an intent to transfer, four years later, only around 40 percent of these students actually transferred, and close to 30 percent of the initial transfer-aspiring students no longer held such a desire.[5] But how exactly did these two propositions play out in the journeys of our transfer-aspiring students? In this chapter, I describe whether and how upward transfer, as a key measure of two-year college student success, fit into the larger scheme of students' lives and their own definitions of success. I begin by telling the stories of Bethany and Clyde, briefly introduced earlier in chapter 1 (Bethany) and chapter 4 (Clyde). Both indicated an intent to transfer in the fall of 2014, which they ended up letting go.

❝ *I'm going straight into full-time work in my field.*"
—BETHANY (I2)

Bethany attended Centerville College initially reporting transfer as her intent. Although she had started in a science transfer program and was close to reaching transfer, she ran out of money and had to put school on hold. When she returned to Centerville in fall 2014, she switched into the biotechnology program. When we saw her during the second interview in 2016, she was about to complete her program. While she did mention transfer, she talked about it in an idealist sense: "I'll hit graduation and I'm probably just going to go straight into like, full-time work in the field. I would be interested in doing a four-year degree in molecular biology if I can afford to take a break from being in work." (I2) Thinking about her envisioned major if she were to attend a four-year school, Bethany clearly knew that there was no way to pursue a baccalaureate degree without disrupting her job. She would need to take classes on campus and during normal work hours: "There's no way to do these kinds of classes online. Like, you have to have the time to go in, and like I said, it's so hard to get part-time work in my field that I'm like, I don't even know if I even could. I can't do another science degree, because you do have to be in class for that—you can't do labs at home." (I2)

The pull of a job in her field was the major incentive, though. It was enough. Bethany felt that if she got a four-year degree, she might not be able to find work in her field. Moreover, like many of our students, regardless of where their transfer aspirations took them, the financial security of having a job offer was what she sought: "I feel like if I go into a four-year degree, there's a strong chance that I won't be able to work in my career field. I feel like once I have a degree, I'll probably want to be using it. So, I'll be wanting to work. And I'll also have student loans that I want to pay off. I mean, I know it's harder to like, go back to school once you've been working and making money." (I2)

For Bethany, another key motivation shifting her interest away from transfer was simply the idea of immediately starting to make small, incremental contributions to society by finding a solid job in her field of interest, and that was sufficiently exciting and satisfying: "You have to really just think, well, I'm gonna get this awesome job that I enjoy doing. I mean, we don't make that much, but I feel like it contributes to society and the betterment of people when we develop new products. Especially with my interest in the medical applications. I'm like, that is why I joined. I want to make a difference, even if it's just by being a part of a little team in one little company. But, you know, I want to be making a difference." (I2)

> *But now it's like fifty-fifty."*
> —Clyde (I3)

Hailing from Haiti, Clyde moved to the state in 2013. His interest was really in Centerville's civil engineering program, but due to a capacity issue by the time he applied, Clyde had to change direction and went for the architectural engineering program, which, according to the college's website, is an applied science program aimed at developing the skills to enter the architectural field or transfer into a bachelor's degree program in architecture. Clyde's goal was to achieve exactly everything the program promised to offer: to finish his associate's degree and then transfer into a bachelor's program. Preoccupied with the potential to transfer, during his first year at Centerville alone, Clyde went on three trips to visit the four-year school to which he was hoping to transfer and planned on doing more in the future. However, under the impression that the requirements for earning the associate's degree and those for transfer fell under two distinct categories, Clyde felt that he made the mistake of avoiding transfer classes during his first year:

> But the mistake I made—I should have started taking classes to be transferred. So now I'm not taking any transferring classes. That's the mistake that I made from the beginning. I didn't really know because I did not talk to my advisor about that, because I thought if I take transferring classes, I may not have my associate degree. That's what I thought. So this is why I was only taking classes to get my associate

degree. I did not know if I take transferring classes I'll be able to get my associate degree anyhow. (I1)

Initially, this bump in the road did not alter Clyde's aspirations to transfer. A huge motivating factor was his hope to use his education to help out communities in Haiti: "My education, my degree from here... It can be really, really useful for the people out there [in Haiti]. If I can get the bachelor's degree, that will be wonderful. There's much more I could do with it." (I1) As Clyde was completing his architectural engineering program, he realized that he did not have enough money left to transfer and pay four-year tuition right away: "Honestly, I could not afford it, since I'm currently on my own—like, when it comes to paying my tuition. So, a two-year college education is more affordable to me—for someone in my situation." Having wandered around this much, Clyde was not as sure as before when speaking of his transfer prospects: "But now it's like fifty-fifty. If I have the opportunity, I can afford it; I would transfer to get a bachelor's degree." (I3)

ASPIRATIONS REVISITED FOR IMMEDIATE FULFILLMENT

Bethany and Clyde illustrate the two major groups of students who initially aspired to transfer but later gave up this goal. The first group of students, such as Bethany, can be described as those who initially said they would transfer because they viewed transfer—and eventually earning a bachelor's degree—as something that would signify a life accomplishment in idealistic ways. But as they progressed through college, they did not necessarily see the value of transfer and found it hard to factor transfer into their life right away or within the foreseeable future. Thus, they readily revisited and relinquished their transfer aspirations, because something else in life fulfilled them in a more immediate and tangible sense.

For instance, Bethany graduated from her two-year institution set on getting a job. Although she still talked about earning a bachelor's degree, it was more as something distant that would be nice to have, the way anyone might talk about life dreams, instead of an immediate goal. What was of utmost importance to Bethany was financial independence so she could start making a difference in society, even on a modest income. In the end, not having a bachelor's degree as part of her near future plans was fine with Bethany. The ultimate reason that she was able to find peace with this reality was that, with or without transfer, her intrinsic motivation was satisfied, as long as she worked in a professional field about which she truly felt passionate. That allowed her to matter and to make a contribution. Among this group of our students who lowered their initial transfer aspirations, we found their desire to give back to the larger community and society to be particularly powerful in sustaining and fulfilling them. It was what propelled them toward completing their associate's degree, certificate, or coursework, and working in a STEM field without transfer.

Like Bethany, many of our students originally intending to attain a bachelor's degree viewed transfer in a more symbolic sense: great to have it but fine if not. Unlike Clyde, they were never really torn between work and school, because work was always winning out. Temperance, in a mechanical design technology program at Metroshore College, indicated intent to transfer during her first semester. However, when I spoke with her after her first full academic year, she expressed that she now mainly viewed her program as a path to a better-paying job than to transfer: "I like this degree. I like the program. I think I want to work in it a little bit before I decide to go back to school for a third time." (I1)

Having been in college before, and keen on getting back into the workforce, Temperance wanted to work in her field and gain experience before she made any decision to transfer. Similarly, Nelkowicz, enrolled in the industrial maintenance technician program at Centerville College, vaguely described the prospect of completing a four-year degree: "I'd like to get a bachelor's degree in industrial maintenance or some sort of design engineering. I have no idea what." (I1) Yet, work was definitely taking precedence. Before completing his program, Nelkowicz landed a job as a safety and compliance officer at a company providing solar energy, electric, plumbing, and energy services. Speaking about his job, he was way more excited than how he sounded when describing the transfer potential: "It seems like a really smart move to try to get into a field I'm interested in at a time when it's like just starting to become a big thing in a company that's rapidly growing. I've never been in a good position like this. It feels exciting." (I2)

Although they were not oblivious to the value of a bachelor's degree, for this group of students, that value was more abstract and easily gave way to a more pressing and present desire to work in their field of interest. For them, transfer represented one of life's many open, figurative options, one that they were more than willing to forgo, as long as something else was right within reach that supported them and their family's needs and fulfilled them as an individual. Because of this, delaying or letting go of transfer was not a forced choice.

A Cautionary Note on Jobbing Out

While not transferring is far from a failure for this group of students, we must exercise caution with regard to the phenomenon called "jobbing out."[6] To job out means that students take a job before finishing their credential or degree. In most cases, those job-outs are unlikely to come back to finish their program. Nelkowicz's insights help further unpack this issue. Nelkowicz's program is in the trades—industrial maintenance. Many students enroll in this program specifically to get jobs, with some jobbing out almost before finishing a credential. Thus, retaining students until they finish a credential has become a serious issue for the program leaders: "That's a big problem with our industrial maintenance program. I was helping them [program leaders] to write surveys and stuff to find out what they needed to keep retaining students. And I don't think it's so much a lacking in the program and what they're learning." (I2)

Some other students were also tempted by the prospect of getting a job before finishing school. When a highly appealing employment opportunity to work in the city came along during her final semester, Temperance was nearly on the verge of becoming one of those job-outs who never returned to finish a degree. However, with her extraordinary grit, Temperance fought through it all:

> Opportunity presented itself when I had to act when I did, when the job came available for the city at probably the worst time possible for me. So starting a brand-new job, trying to finish up the last of the semester, and I was pulling out my hair. I didn't know if I was actually going to make it. It was the first time I sat down and I was like, "I bit off more than I can chew." It was a real low point for me, because I'm like, "I might not make it. I don't know if I can do this." So just being so busy with the difficult load of classwork and starting something so brand new, it really was rough. I was struggling so much to keep my head above water, and to keep deadlines straight, and coursework along with, you know, those little checkmarks at work for, you know, "We'd like you to be able to accomplish this by this checkpoint, and this by this checkpoint," and just keeping it all around. (I3)

Temperance's experience is telling. Taking on a new job while nearing completion of a program is an enormous challenge that would lead most students, including Temperance, to seriously consider deferring to the job, as it can immediately earn them what they ultimately signed up for: a potentially exciting employment opportunity that pays. The temptations for jobbing out are high—students are able to spend less money on and time in school, enter the workforce quickly, and start earning a living. However, we are finding that, although jobbing out may be appealing in the short term since students have an immediate job and some financial security, it is not necessarily the best choice in the long run.[7] Actually, education researchers Mina Dadgar and Madeline Joy Trimble found that students are better off if they complete their program and earn at least a certificate or associate's degree.[8] Therefore, sticking with it, as Temperance did, can provide greater long-term benefits that can make the difficult times well worth it. While it may feel like "work won't wait" for students whose real intent eventually becomes employment-oriented, finishing out their program will reap greater rewards and keep their options open later on if they wish to revisit them.

This cautionary note aside, for Bethany, Nelkowicz, Temperance, and other students in similar situations, their experiences at school and work have been rewarding. Being able to attend their community colleges has been a confidence boost. In many such cases, these students described how their experiences at two-year colleges allowed them to express their individualities and to thrive, and they were thus no longer interested in transferring to prove their self-worth. It is often the success stories of these students that do not get celebrated, as conventional measures of student and institutional success do not capture the incremental value the two-year college experience adds to one's educational and career advancement, which is so difficult to quantify and measure. However, this remains juxtaposed with the lack of concrete information about transfer and the constant pull of the practicalities of needing to make a living plus wanting that degree. It seems that guidance that helps fit all the pieces together would really help students like Bethany, Nelkowicz, and Temperance even more.

ASPIRATIONS DISCOURAGED BY A MUDDLED TRANSFER PROCESS

Clyde and the second group of students whose initial transfer goals diminished came in with a much more determined mind-set to transfer, and their stories behind the dwindling of their transfer aspirations paint a more troublesome picture. We already learned from Clyde that financial burdens placed an indefinite pause on his transfer outlook. We also saw that his change in transfer plans was not due to his lack of initiative and motivation. Despite actively seeking out services and information on transfer, Clyde found his efforts fruitless, yielding confusing and conflicting pieces of advice. The information that he did gather to figure out transfer led him to take less transferable courses, creating a longer and more ambiguous road to transfer. This aligns with what we found from surveying all of our students, revealing that acquiring transfer information bore no positive relationship to sustaining students' momentum toward transfer.[9]

Paul's experience sheds a different light on the second group's vanishing transfer aspirations. A Black man with an international background, Paul was pursuing the Information Technology Systems Administration Specialist program at Centerville College. He came from a difficult situation in his home country of Sierra Leone, including but not limited to the Ebola crisis in 2014. Determined to transfer, Paul managed to survive his first year where "everything was somewhat different." (I1) With limited resources, he believed that he could still make transfer happen while working by implementing his "plan." He spoke of how he liked the training at the two-year institution because it kept up with technology and was practical. However, to transfer, he needed guidance: "I actually need guidance on how the program goes. What are some of the procedures? What are some of the things to do to qualify you for transfer? Yeah. I need to know those things. I need to have an education on those things. What can actually qualify you to transfer, or what are you supposed to do, in order for you to transfer?" (I1) While all these appear to be the right kinds of questions to ask about transfer, it was hard for Paul to put into words how this would all come together—finishing a two-year degree, and then going on to complete a bachelor's degree.

The most recent time I caught up with Paul, he was completing his associate's degree, but was no longer interested in transfer. Paul's journey up to this point was plagued by so many challenges it's hard to say which was his biggest hurdle—that his cultural experiences and expectations were so different, that he had limited resources anywhere nearby, or that he had to acclimate to a completely new environment, among other challenges. Any one of them would be enough to derail someone's ambitions entirely. However, although he clearly articulated precisely the right questions on which he needed guidance, nowhere across our conversations did I hear distinct evidence that such questions were addressed by college staff. Other than describing his transfer vision, Paul did not elaborate on whether and how that goal would be operationalized or, at minimum, on how to get help from someone adept at translating that vision into action.

Stella's experience adds yet another intricate layer to this group's waning transfer aspirations. Stella is a white female student pursuing the biotechnology program at Centerville College. She initially voiced a strong desire to transfer: "I'll probably end up kicking myself for it [if I do not transfer] later." (I1) However, Stella experienced a hitch in her transfer aspirations. The sheer idea of plunging into the transfer process and facing many unknowns overwhelmed her. Other than her trepidation about the actual path to transfer and the complexities that transfer might entail, Stella had other concerns that further muddled her ability to visualize transfer, such as the perceived competitive nature of the four-year institutional environment and lack of financial assistance. Although she viewed Centerville College as a highly encouraging environment for transfer, she remained hesitant. Without ever having engaged in the transfer process—she admitted that she had never really talked to anyone—all the pressure and uncertainties she anticipated to be surrounding the process scared her and left her with a fuzzy outlook.

For Stella and many students in this second group, "not right now" was a common phrase related to pursuing a bachelor's degree. Life circumstances certainly contributed, but there was a distinct reason that separated them from the first group of students who lowered their transfer aspirations. This second group gave up on transfer mainly because they saw that transfer into a four-year program was far from a smooth route. Instead, transfer was viewed as a convoluted process. As we already saw from Clyde, Paul, and Stella, with or without their own initiative in seeking out information or resources, the end result was the same: they could not visualize transfer with clarity, confidence, and a sense of ease. Further, quite a few of them, such as Tom, realized much later the tough reality that they could not transfer credits within their major, and would need to retake the major courses that they had just completed. Tom, a Latino in the IT Network Security Specialist program at Centerville College, was already on the verge of graduating and had landed a full-time job. After some time working in his field, he had a nagging feeling he would have to go back and get his bachelor's degree to advance in his career. However, Tom became aware that his program courses would not transfer. When asked how he found this out, he said, "One of my instructors is actually the advisor of the IT department. So, I had an appointment with him and I asked him, 'Will one of these classes transfer in the future, if I'm going to go to a different school for a bachelor's?' And he was like, 'Well, general eds, like English and psychology—those classes might transfer, if they are transfer classes. But the IT classes, they won't transfer.'" (I3)

The tempered transfer aspirations of these students in the second group reiterate that students should not be left to their own initiative to figure out transfer. Corresponding with the main argument of chapter 2, community colleges should ensure that accurate information on transfer be formalized as part of transfer advising services, which must act as the main source of transfer information for students. That way, they can resolve any ambiguities or confusion and keep students on a clear, informed path toward transfer. With better articulation, counseling, and preparation well ahead of transfer, students would be able to make informed choices and make the necessary adjustments sooner so that, even if transfer is not something they can choose at the moment, they can come back to it without having to start over. In addition, this may mean providing more options for students who have already completed a full complement of courses that could transfer. This might include certain courses or blocks of courses that can transfer if students perform at a certain level. In doing so, more students would be able to realize their dream of a four-year degree regardless of their timeline and program of study.

The stories from these two groups of initial transfer-intending students depict, in various ways, whether and how upward transfer fit into the larger scheme of students' lives and their own definitions of success. These students' experiences and journeys told us that such a downward trajectory in their aspirations was neither just a random change of heart (as many would say, "Students don't know what they want"), nor an intentional, systematic process of weeding out by the institution (what Burton Clark would call "cooling out"). Rather, it represents the complex interplay between how students make sense of their educational goals within the larger context of their motivations and lives, and how opportunities are constructed, communicated, and provided within and beyond the institution.[10] For some of these students, transfer represented one of life's grand accomplishments, but the value and fit of transfer within their individual contexts remained questionable. In figuring out what they needed and wanted, some of these students arrived at a place where they no longer desired transfer, but were achieving success by their own definitions, which often no longer involved transfer and a bachelor's degree. Other students' vanishing transfer aspirations presented a more trying and puzzling journey that illuminates a need for intentional supports and optimized information delivery to help them fully develop or revisit the prospect of transfer. Rather than navigating (and potentially abandoning) transfer alone, these students need a help line within reach to forge on toward transfer.

I close this chapter with some additional contexts and insights from Temperance. When she and I met for the third and final interview in the summer of 2018, Temperance had been working with the city as a technician for two years. She received a promotion over those two years and generally liked where she was. During her time at Metroshore and even after she took the job at the city, Temperance did look into transfer options and was particularly drawn to a program at a local private four-year school that offers engineering programs geared toward full-time employees: "And I'm like, 'Oh, look. They have the program planned for a working adult coming back.' So it was only a couple of classes each semester. And they already have the program planned there, and I was looking at it, and going, 'Oh man, they're really making this easy.' So yes, I have actually seriously kind of looked to see what was out there." (I2) So, as we wrapped up our conversation, I asked her if she would still consider transfer in the longer term and she said, "Check back with me in a decade. It'll come back to bite me if I say it'll never happen. 'Cause that's just how the world works. So . . . it will depend on where life takes me. If I'm still with this job. If I move someplace else. It'll all depend on that, so I'm not naïve enough to say I'm never getting another degree. Right now, I'm enjoying where I'm at. I'm just gonna wade in this pond for a while and see what it yields." (I3) Temperance, who described herself as someone who "fought tooth-and-nail against myself" to get where she was, teaches us that, even if transfer turns into a "not right now" thing, we should never say never.

7

Momentum Trajectories and Embedded Inequities

AS PREVIEWED IN THE INTRODUCTION, our transfer-aspiring students eventually landed on four momentum trajectories, each briefly illustrated by the profiles of Jordan, Seamus, Kanda, and Katy. These trajectories serve as sort of interim outcomes that provide some answers to the questions that I set out to study. However, despite the directions they appeared to be taking at any given point, I view them as momentum trajectories to reflect a central message to be learned from the students in the study and the two-year colleges that serve them. Regardless of whether their success, as defined by the student or the institution, is yet to be determined, these students have made something of their time at the two-year institutions they attended, gaining momentum toward something of value in the grand scheme of their lives. While some of the students may have lost that momentum at times, I have reason to believe that community colleges hold remarkable promise for their open access and their genuine will to serve historically marginalized students who would not otherwise have attended college. But they are due for a reform that positions them to do even better in cultivating an enriching experience for their students. Through that process, future students going or coming back to these institutions will gain and build momentum toward great success.

MOMENTUM TRAJECTORIES: WHO WENT ON WHICH PATH?

I now delve deeper into each of the four trajectories our transfer-intending students landed on four years later and reveal their undergirding factors and contexts. The first trajectory is *linear upward*. Students on this path transferred to a four-year institution without much delay. Jordan is a prime example of this trajectory. We already learned that, straight out of high school, Jordan arrived at his two-year college with a sure sense of his future success. His journey was not without hurdles, especially in regard to transfer into a specific major. But it is fair to say that Jordan's path to transfer was and has proven to be a sure bet.

The second trajectory is *detoured*. Along this winding path, students maneuvered among multiple institutional or program routes to transfer to a four-year institution, after recognizing that their original institutional or program selection was not a good fit to set them up for success. Seamus's path to pursue a bachelor's degree or more was detoured after flunking out of Capital. She enrolled in Centerville's biotechnology program and loved it. However, missing a key transferable course, plus apprehensions about an unfriendly four-year environment due to her initial negative advising relationship, cast doubt around transfer. Her concern not to "waste" any more time, ironically, continued to keep her transfer prospect on an indefinite pause.

The third trajectory is *deferred*, where students initially determined to transfer had to forgo this possibility to pursue a more terminal credential and make immediate financial returns on their education. Kanda's story matches this profile. The lack of articulation from public institutions regarding her areas of interest left her with no affordable transfer options. Although her family provided unwavering support, she was acutely mindful of the fact that her parents took care of her two brothers, who are disabled, one her twin who had started college as well. For Kanda and students like her, transfer was a dream delayed.

The fourth trajectory is *taking a break*, which characterizes those students who left their two-year institution without receiving any credentials during the study period. The impossibility of getting through the chemistry lab steered Katy away from STEM fields, but she still believed that education was key to achieving financial and professional success: "I presume that who I am and what I have and what I've done are not adequate for my success financially or professionally, so my assumption is that if I'd like to get ahead and get out of the sort of low end loop of jobs that I always am in, my assumption is that I have to have a way to get out of those, and education seems like the thing." (I2) Katy tried to push through despite the multitude of barriers she was facing, but her experience at Centerville did not provide the kinds of accommodation she needed. Eventually, she had to take a break. Katy and her peers on this trajectory faced the most uncertain future.

Inequities Embedded Within Momentum Trajectories

Early in chapter 2, I argued that, though all our students appeared to be largely on their own to negotiate transfer, with or without a choice, their access to information and resources was uneven, resulting in inherent differences in the utility of the insights they gleaned through their own initiatives. Here, four years later, these differences played out in a more pronounced way to shape our students' momentum trajectories. If we circle back to the preface and take a further, more intentional look, we see that there were fundamental differences in our students' backgrounds that set them apart from the onset. Not in terms of their individual capacity, motivation, and effort; rather, these differences translated into the four trajectories through the uneven and unequal access, processes, and experiences that lay ahead of them from the moment they enrolled in college.[1]

Here's a quick refresher of these initial differences in the four students' backgrounds. Jordan identifies as a white male. He comes from a single-parent, lower-middle-class family. His mom went to college and completed a bachelor's degree. In high school, he took a wide range of math and science courses, and finished calculus. His immediate and extended family was extremely supportive of his education. Although not from an affluent family background, his mom has ensured that he has the needed financial support for transfer.

Seamus, who identifies as a multiracial Black woman, has a background similar to Jordan's in many ways. She also comes from a single-parent household with a college-educated mom. She, too, had rich exposure to math and science during high school, and finished calculus. She had strong support from her family, especially her mom, for any and all of her educational pursuits.

Kanda identifies as a Native American woman. She had three years of math and science courses and completed algebra II before college. Although she had a great deal of support from her parents to transfer, there were limited financial means to do so. Compared with Jordan, Seamus, and Kanda, Katy had substantially less math and science during high school, with only two years of math, including algebra I. A first-generation student from a low-income background, Katy indicated that she had only a little support for transfer from family and in terms of finances.

These differences underlying the four students' momentum trajectories were not isolated, incidental variations. They were indicative of the larger patterns of disparities in our students' backgrounds and contexts that were associated with the specific trajectory on which they eventually ended up. Figure 7.1 illustrates a few notable examples, showing that students of color disproportionately were found in the taking a break trajectory.

FIGURE 7.1 Percentage of students on the taking a break trajectory, by race

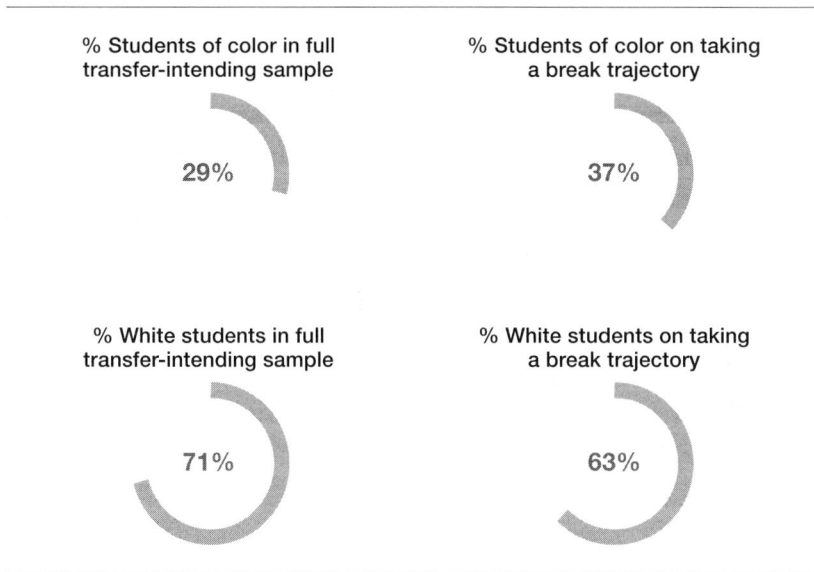

% Students of color in full transfer-intending sample	% Students of color on taking a break trajectory
29%	37%

% White students in full transfer-intending sample	% White students on taking a break trajectory
71%	63%

Further, family income was a notable, almost linear function that appeared to drive students onto distinct trajectories, with the linear upward trajectory more likely to be followed by students from more financially resourced families, and taking a break with a concentration of students from low-income families (see figure 7.2).

Closely related, proportionately fewer first-generation college students followed the linear upward trajectory compared with other trajectories (figure 7.3).

Table 7.1 offers a more complete picture that lays out the four distinct momentum trajectories our students fell under four years later and the kinds of backgrounds and contexts associated with each trajectory.

Looking across these patterns, it becomes clear that the students on the linear upward trajectory were from the most advantaged backgrounds from the get-go in most if not all aspects of the educational and financial resources they brought with them. Individuals on the linear upward trajectory had the most material resources at their disposal, and those

FIGURE 7.2 Percentage of students on the four trajectories, by family income

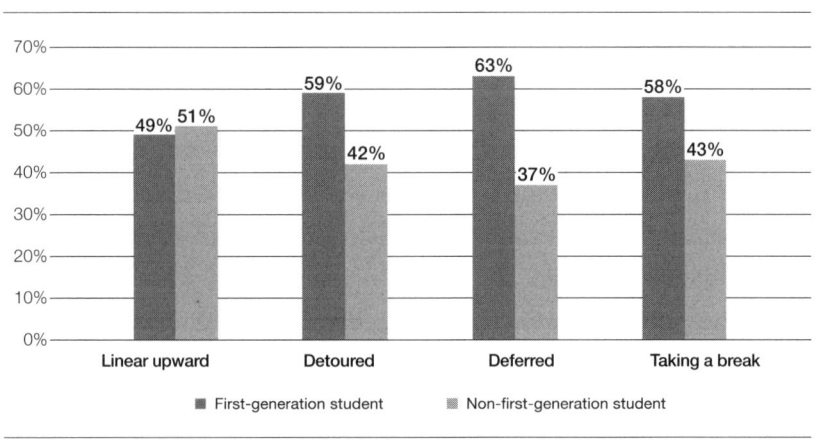

	Linear upward	Detoured	Deferred	Taking a break
Less than $30,000	23%	32%	33%	41%
$30,000 to $59,999	22%	28%	29%	26%
$60,000 to $89,999	28%	23%	16%	19%
$90,000 to $119,999	19%	10%	13%	10%
$120,000 to $149,999	4%	5%	5%	3%
$150,000 and above	4%	3%	4%	2%

FIGURE 7.3 Percentage of students on the four trajectories, by first-generation status

	Linear upward	Detoured	Deferred	Taking a break
First-generation student	49%	59%	63%	58%
Non-first-generation student	51%	42%	37%	43%

taking a break the minimum. Further underneath these trajectories were the pronounced ways in which these students' backgrounds were transmitted into their college experiences, often in unchecked, indiscernible

TABLE 7.1 Momentum trajectories and associated background characteristics

BACKGROUND CHARACTERISTICS		LINEAR UPWARD	DETOURED	DEFERRED	TAKING A BREAK	TOTAL
Sex	Female	46%	51%	46%	37%	43%
	Male	54%	49%	54%	63%	57%
Race/ ethnicity	Students of color	23%	25%	31%	37%	29%
	White	77%	75%	69%	63%	71%
Age	18 to 19	71%	60%	57%	59%	64%
	20 to 23	14%	21%	14%	18%	17%
	24 to 29	8%	10%	17%	10%	10%
	30 and older	7%	10%	11%	14%	10%
Working hours	Less than 20	33%	30%	18%	20%	26%
	20 to less than 40	38%	38%	45%	38%	39%
	40 plus	29%	32%	37%	41%	35%
Income	Less than $30,000	23%	32%	33%	41%	32%
	$30,000 to $59,999	22%	28%	29%	26%	25%
	$60,000 to $89,999	28%	23%	16%	19%	23%
	$90,000 to $119,999	19%	10%	13%	10%	14%
	$120,000 to $149,999	4%	5%	5%	3%	4%
	$150,000 and above	4%	3%	4%	2%	3%
First-generation student	Yes	49%	59%	63%	58%	55%
	No	51%	42%	37%	43%	45%
Single parent	Yes	1%	6%	4%	8%	5%
	No	99%	94%	96%	92%	95%

Note: Column percentages may not sum to totals due to rounding. Reported percentages are weighted using adjusted longitudinal weight. Analysis based on transfer-intending students only.

ways by both the students themselves and the instructors or advisors they ended up working with during college.

On the linear upward trajectory, Jordan attributed his success to his own hard work, laser-like focus, and resilience:

> I care about what I'm doing. I guess motivation and passion for what I want to do is the thing that's gotten me from where I was to where I am now. Yeah. I don't really know what else, because I feel as though it's all been on me. College itself is, people want you to succeed, sure, but

they're not going to do everything they can to help you succeed. You got to do it on your own. It's all about you. I don't say I'm this bright individual. I say I'm an incredibly hard worker. That's what I want to be remembered as. Somebody that said he was going to do something and went at it with everything he had. (I3)

Jordan's reflection mirrors a strong individualistic, meritocratic point of view. While Jordan is everything he describes himself to be—resilient, focused, independent, and so on—what he could not realize (and this is by no means Jordan's fault as that's the way he has been socialized) is that, as a white male, his proactivity and autonomy are rewarded matter-of-factly by his instructors and advisors. The opportunities he was provided were earned but with easy access. He got handpicked by one of his math instructors to work on campus as a tutor, which further honed his study and communication skills that paved his transfer. Earlier in chapter 2, I described how Jordan experienced challenges in figuring out transfer into his desired major. Other than that, Jordan's experience with transfer advising was positive: "I walked in there, they [advisors] helped me figure out classes. They figured out, like, which colleges would be the best. And that's where I decided for sure Capital, was in the walk-in advising." (I1) Although his later meetings with transfer advisors were not described as helpful, each provided him with information that led to the next piece. Jordan viewed education as "an individual, independent, isolated kind of activity," (I2) yet he may not have realized that his "on my own" path worked out for him due to the privilege he had over his peers that came with his white, male, and middle-class background, which also positioned him to be socially and therefore academically "advantaged" from the get-go.

My point is not that the resources at the disposal of Jordan and his family were not hard earned; they were. And it is not that Jordan did not fight to get where he was. He did, and his transfer to Capital was a true testament to his persistence and resilience. My point is not centered at the individual level, on Jordan or his family. Rather, my focus is at the societal and systemic level—where resources, advantages, and privilege are unequally distributed and thus inequitably accessed based on race and class and their intersection. This mechanism, powerful as it is, manifests itself invisibly at the systemic level, but is demonstrated at the individual level, misperceived as solely individual merit and hard work.

This all starts way before college, far back in our history, and is deeply rooted in the complexity of educational disparities as a culmination of historical, economic, sociopolitical, and moral issues, as pedagogical theorist and teacher educator Gloria Ladson-Billings points out.[2] The educational debt for minoritized groups, especially racially minoritized students, is not only still overdue; it continues to manifest itself in the inequitable access and opportunities at the postsecondary level among students.[3] As John Diamond and colleagues argue, societal forces of race and socioeconomic status are still at work creating and perpetuating inequities.[4] In particular, disparities among Black and white students' family income, parental education, residence location, and achievement set these students on two very different tracks.[5] One track offers students access to higher-level coursework and achievement, likely leading to smooth sailing ahead toward college. The second track places students into one disadvantageous course placement after another, never getting them where they need to be when it comes to attending college. As a result, talking about achievement gaps understates the issue when in reality there are much larger structures at work that shape the schools, access to opportunities, educational experiences, and so on, compounding the effects as students move through each educational level. These inequities end up paving roads for some students, like Jordan, and blockading those for others from minoritized backgrounds.

Jordan also fits the ideal image of someone instructors and advisors perceive to be college material, especially the image of an aspiring engineer. Spanning all education levels and public domains, there has been a widely held (mis)perception—by instructors, counselors, advisors, and students themselves—of scientists and engineers as white males.[6] White male dominance in STEM fields is not only embedded in the realities and perceptions of student faces, but it is deeply seated within instructional and institutional practices. Although there has been an influx of diversity initiatives to recruit more women and students of color into STEM, they often stop at the surface level of structural diversity. Consequently, such initiatives are incapable of challenging the status quo in STEM fields, which continue to reflect the white male ways of knowing and learning, and ultimately do not remove the barriers and challenges for women, especially women of color, as indicated by Heidi Carlone and Angela Johnson, as well as Sarah Rodriguez and colleagues.[7]

Therefore, Jordan's being a white man on an engineering path in and of itself did not raise the same kinds of extra barriers faced by Seamus, Kanda, Katy, and others who do not share his racial and gender identities. Although Seamus was heavily recruited by Capital University as part of a "diversity" recruitment effort in engineering, once she was on campus, there were no purposeful curriculum and advising efforts to engage and support her as a woman of color in a male, white-dominant field. By every standard, Seamus and Jordan are similar in their precollege backgrounds except for their racial and gender identities. And that difference was magnified once they set foot in a predominantly white institutional, programmatic, and classroom environment. Four years later, Jordan was on his way to completing his baccalaureate engineering degree, and Seamus had long left the same four-year campus from which Jordan was graduating.

Also a woman of color, Kanda's first semester in college, particularly her programming course, seriously jeopardized her sense of belonging in the information technology (IT) field that she fell in love with during high school:

> To be completely honest, I am probably not going to stay in a STEM field. I've entered Metroshore College in hopes of becoming a computer

programmer because I had so much fun in high school programming. Sadly, the same experiences didn't carry over in college. I feel like I'm not up to speed with my classmates in my programming courses, and I feel so lost that I don't feel I'll succeed in the field in the future. I've exhausted all resources I could think of to help me try to be successful in this program, but it's clear that I don't belong in this field. Going from being a 3.9 GPA student to barely treading water in a subject I enjoyed is something that really disturbs me. I've been told by my current instructor that programming is a field where talented people succeed, and I guess I don't have that talent. (S1)

Kanda's programming course was full of white male students, many of whom perhaps were like Jordan, whom the instructor readily categorized as "talented." Now having learned the rest of the story, we know that Kanda *has* the talent plus everything else to eventually earn her near-perfect GPA. But had it not been for her own tenacity and drive to serve those around her, a widely shared tendency among Native students and women of color, she would have dropped out of IT or Metroshore altogether due to that seemingly innocent but truly harmful remark made by her instructor.[8]

Katy, from a low-income and first-generation background, did not have sufficient exposure to rigorous high school math and science. This left her with a fear of learning math, which was viewed as foundational across STEM subjects. Her learning disability, mental health issues, lack of financial resources, and role as a single parent converged with everything else to complicate her STEM path from her very first chemistry course, and none of those vital facets of who she is had been intentionally supported or even fully acknowledged. As we wrapped up our final conversation, Katy reflected on the many dimensions of her identity: "I recognize sometimes the most impactful parts of our identity, we don't have an awareness of. Like, I'm a privileged, white woman in the Midwest. And I don't know that I would've spent a lot of time thinking about any of those aspects during the course of my education. I would've said, 'I'm in pretty difficult emotional and economic circumstances.'" (13)

Katy's words reveal both the struggles acutely present that interfered with her educational journey and her introspective awareness of her white privilege. Here it is important to look beyond Katy and reflect on the multiplicity of our students' experiences based on their identity, which brings up a key consideration of intersectionality. This term was coined by Kimberlé Crenshaw in her original analysis of the failure of antidiscrimination law to address Black women's distinctive, intertwined experiences of racism and sexism.[9] The notion of intersectionality has since been popularized to elucidate the fact that, since an individual's identity is constructed through the intersection of multiple dimensions of social life, we must avoid oversimplification and instead embrace complexity to fully understand and analyze how various forms of underrepresentation cause compounded forms of marginalization, which cannot be addressed through a unidimensional solution. Given that intersectional analysis is difficult to achieve in its entirety as it is nearly impossible to fully harness its complexity, here it makes sense for me to focus closely on the dimensions that illuminate marginalization and disadvantage at a systemic level in the STEM context. In that light, across these four students alone, we see gender, racial, and class (low-income and first-generation background) differences, and implicitly, the disparities in their experiences underlying these explicit differences.

The first such intersectionality is between gender and race. Unlike Jordan and Katy, the unique, heightened challenges endured by Kanda and Seamus as women of color had to do with their questioned belonging and fit in a predominantly white setting. However, in another light, the intersectionality between gender and class, in Katy's case compounded by her first-generation status and many other struggles, such as her learning disability, was also protrusive. In this sense, we can say that women and students of color in STEM fields are subject to a systemic disadvantage, and in addition, when gender and race converge with other marginalized identities, the system becomes one that jeopardizes the educational prospects of our most vulnerable transfer-aspiring students.

To further illustrate, students on the taking a break trajectory, in contrast to those on the linear upward path, did not have the same level of educational resources at their fingertips. With a high concentration of students of color and low-income and first-generation students, many students on this trajectory did not have access to rigorous math and science preparation during high school. Also, many did not have college preparatory courses and many were the first in their family to attend college. They may not have felt that they "fit in" at college. A lot of them didn't know anyone with jobs in the fields that they wanted to pursue. This left the students at a disadvantage and put them off the college track without a credential. Intersecting with and further exacerbating the lack of access to educational resources was the fact that many students on this trajectory did not have the financial resources to complete a college degree. Thus, their college experiences were often fundamentally different from Jordan's because of these prior differences.

One of the survey participants, a first-generation Asian female coming from a family with an annual income of less than $30,000, was on the taking a break trajectory and put all this into a stark and sobering context:

> In the last three years I have tried and failed and tried again to enroll in a program that makes sense for me. I have not been able to talk to a human being about any of it, and have spent hours at a time crying over the shitty, terrible website, wishing "academic advisor" was a real thing and not a sarcastic and unreachable illusion presented by the outdated college advertisements. My first year of college I was working two jobs to pay for it, and was enrolled in a liberal arts transfer program, which makes no sense. I dropped out, because it was too many hours (forty-five working hours, fourteen credits). No one helped me then and no one helps me now. I have frankly no idea how to even

enroll in programs of my desired field. Work and poverty combine to make it nearly impossible for me to get through school, and it feels as though the entire system was designed to encourage me to drop out. It makes me angry to think about all the people who did their precalc or chem in high school, are now buying their way into four-year degrees, having no other responsibilities, and will graduate into engineering degrees. The point of this awful rant is that if I had the money, and more importantly, if Centerville College offered even the most cursory counseling and human assistance with enrolling, I would be getting a useful and fulfilling degree, instead of voicing my frustration now. (S3)

Students on the detoured trajectory seemed to possess some of the educational and financial resources that they needed to successfully transfer, but were missing other pieces to make the leap. Many of them are students of color who heavily relied on family, peers, and themselves to help guide them through. Shinichi, profiled in chapter 4, found the transfer information unclear and his transfer advisors unhelpful. He has a close relationship with his parents and an extended larger community from similar backgrounds. But in this community, his and most of his peers' parents did not graduate from high school or college, and some did not attend school at all. Given this reality, Shinichi did not feel that parents could lend the best insight into college: "I didn't know if that was a barrier, so I had to either do it for myself, ask friends, ask others. Kind of like, I'm on my own. So like, rather than getting help from parents . . . you know, [I relied on] students, friends." (I2)

Because of the inadequate information he could formally obtain in relation to transfer, he resorted to peers who had successfully transferred, and this hadn't changed when I saw him during our final interview: "Other people I've asked, who've already graduated from college . . . they did the whole Centerville College–Capital University transfer." (I3) The result of that strategy, however, was that Shinichi did not transfer in a "timely" fashion. He does, however, get a lot of support from his parents in terms of living arrangements: "They're still giving me a roof and we both pay for food and stuff. I'm not paying any rent to my family right now, but they're still, you know, my loving parents." (I3) With these necessary but insufficient supports, Shinichi is waiting to take the leap of transfer.

Students on the deferred trajectory consistently described transfer as their firm educational goal over the years we followed their journeys. However, these students did not make it to four-year colleges and ended up taking a two-year college credential due to financial constraints. For Kanda, continuing to a four-year college came at the cost of financial independence and security, so she deferred transfer for a job to relieve her family's burden. Kanda's financial concerns, at strong odds with her sturdy desire to transfer, were shared by other women of color on the deferred trajectory. A first-generation, Hmong female student from a low-income background expressed her disappointment at not being eligible for the only seemingly fitting shot at financial assistance:

> I am saddened to know that the National Science Foundation does not consider Hmong students as underrepresented in the STEM majors; therefore I am unable to participate in the [program name redacted] Program here at Centerville College. Even though that was a major disappointment, I will still continue to strive for the best academically and professionally. Being a minority, low-income student, it will be financially difficult to fund my education, as I proceed to transferring to Capital under the Guaranteed Transfer contract, with intentions of majoring in computer science. (S3)

Much as this student has the passion, clarity, and knowledge about that transfer path, she did not end up transferring, but instead took a job due to tightly constrained financial circumstances.

As shown by our students' journeys, the preexisting and lasting disparities in their access to education resources, their experiences with teaching and advising, the conundrum between their support from and for family, among others, converged and diverged to propel them onto different momentum trajectories in their quest for transfer. At the onset of this project, I was determined to reveal, through following these students' college careers, a clear path to transfer in STEM. But as those journeys unfolded, I realized the numerous types of tension that caused abundant friction and acted against student momentum. The types of tension, which I describe in detail in the final two chapters, are by no means an individual student's problem to resolve. Instead, they are deeply reflective of, at the systemic level, the promising and yet still inequitable transfer pathway that community colleges represent. Those instructors and advisors who appear in this book through students' voices were by and large well-intended and committed practitioners invested in their students' success, but as shown, collectively they fell short at constructing and coconstructing truly engaging, effective, and empowering experiences for students. The unintended and unrecognized consequence is that these practitioners often default to the "on my own" mentality or may even espouse the individualist value of that mentality, which this book has shown to be insufficient for students to achieve their success in meaningful ways. Yet practitioners, like students, are also subject to the tensions of institutional structures and resources, making it all the more challenging for them to fill in the gaps so students have a shot at successful transfer. In what follows, I discuss the educational, social, and political dynamics that situate this book's findings and how to resolve inequities and build student momentum toward transfer in and beyond STEM. I also offer some tangible approaches practitioners can adopt as community colleges continue to wrestle and work with numerous internal and external forces to resolve those tensions.

8

Reducing Friction to Level the Playing Field

I have very much this sort of mentality, like I'm going to do it on my own. I'm going to bootstrap, do it the American way, all of that bologna, which has really been something that I've believed very pervasively throughout my life. And now, as I'm reaching these precipices and making decisions about my future, I'm thinking, "I can't make this decision on my own. I need more information."

—Katy (I2)

KATY SHARED THESE THOUGHTS with me during our second conversation in the summer of 2016, at which time she was trying hard to get back on track after failing her introductory chemistry course. By now, we had already learned that, despite these insights and the efforts that ensued, Katy ended up on the taking a break trajectory. Her words and her story epitomize this book's title, *On My Own*, from both within and without. From within, it embodies what I call agentic and aspirational momentum in the motivational sense, which our students were trying to maintain for themselves; and from without, it mirrors the raw reality of how our students interacted with a vaguely envisioned path to transfer—that is, on their own.[1] This central storyline was not restricted to the Katys who were taking a break; to a varying extent, it was underlying virtually all trajectories, as illustrated in the stories of a number of our students profiled throughout the book so far.

Having followed these students for four years, and especially having spent the past two years making sense of what I learned from them, I keep thinking what "on my own" means for the notion of *momentum* for two-year college student success—in STEM or not. In 2017, I published a monograph in which I advanced a model of momentum for community college student success.[2] In conceptualizing momentum, I highlighted key domains and forms of momentum concerning curricula, teaching, and learning, as well as motivation. I called for a comprehensive and holistic institutional approach to building momentum among community college students, through engaging students in meaningful and impactful educational experiences. I further advocate for a shift in our narrative around community colleges and their students away from cooling-out and student deficits, and toward a cumulative process of building momentum to guide and empower students in their agentic pursuit of a promising educational journey toward their own success.

So exactly what does "on my own" mean and how does it impact the momentum of our transfer-aspiring students? I have learned that the internal side of "on my own" means that our students started strong with, and often held on to, abundant momentum in the motivational domain, in the form of what I call aspirational momentum and agentic momentum, as well as their perseverance. Although for some students, "on my own" appears to be a manifestation of their preexisting tendencies of self-reliance and hesitance in seeking help, it soon was reduced to the only source of momentum as students started to experience friction in other domains—when the external side of "on my own" comes into play. Essentially, the system as it is now serves to create multiple forces of counter-momentum friction. Instead of building momentum, the process has become one by which students are pushing through friction points, fueled for the most part by their own motivational momentum.

And what does "on my own" then do to the momentum of transfer-aspiring students? Regardless of which path students are currently on, linear upward or taking a break, "on my own" means that all of our students experience friction in various spaces that counteracts their momentum. Our students are still left much in the dark to figure out transfer by themselves, with or without an intentional choice. The even bigger and more vexing consequence of the external "on my own," however, is that it essentially serves to further advantage only those students with more preexisting privilege and capital in the social, cultural, financial, and academic domains, such as Jordan, and leave out those with fewer prior resources in these regards, such as Kanda, Seamus, and Katy. In this sense, the current state of transfer in STEM fields and beyond has not evolved into an inclusive and seamless process, and more problematically, it acts as a mechanism that perpetuates and worsens inequities in the transfer access, experiences, and outcomes that I laid out in chapter 7. I summarize these takeaways in figure 8.1, which captures the spaces where friction resides and the larger societal structure and forces that come into play.

To build momentum for all our students, but especially for students like Kanda, Seamus, and Katy, means that the external "on my own" must be disrupted, so that the internal "on my own" acts as an asset if needed instead of the sole helpline. To set the stage for this discussion, I need to share my biggest, somewhat unexpected takeaway from this work. That is, I have come to realize how much of the process of building momentum, in the STEM transfer context, rests with removing the counter-momentum friction that exists in so many spaces, including where momentum is supposed to be gained, instead of lost. Although in my earlier monograph I discussed in detail the kinds of counter-momentum friction and the need to remove them, in truth, my lens was more focused on generating momentum. While my positionality has not changed and I still strongly believe we need to support students in building momentum,

FIGURE 8.1 Domains where counter-momentum friction resides

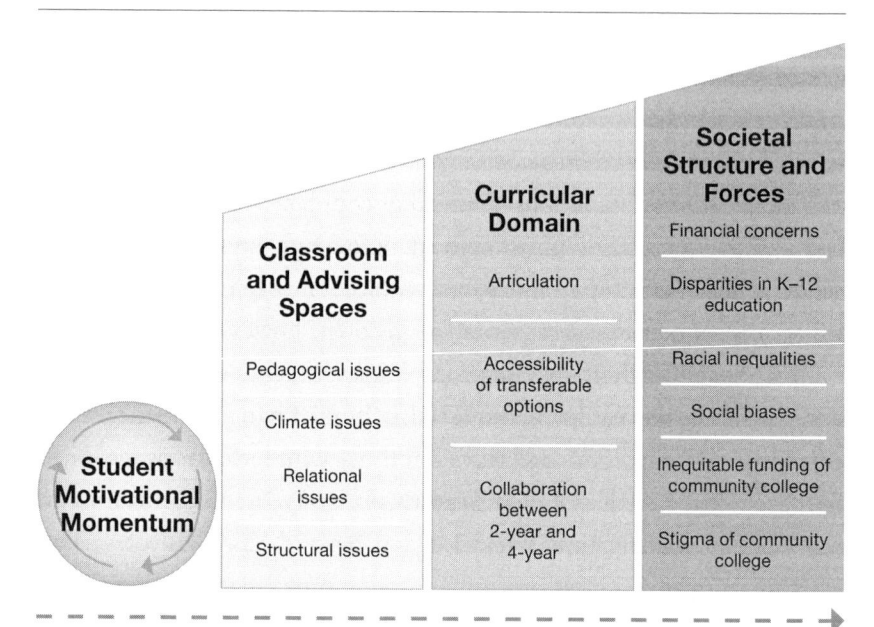

Student Motivational Momentum	Classroom and Advising Spaces	Curricular Domain	Societal Structure and Forces
	Pedagogical issues	Articulation	Financial concerns
	Climate issues	Accessibility of transferable options	Disparities in K–12 education
	Relational issues	Collaboration between 2-year and 4-year	Racial inequalities
	Structural issues		Social biases
			Inequitable funding of community college
			Stigma of community college

the stories and findings from these 1,670-some students have brought me even closer to the acute reality that, for transfer-aspiring students, we must first remove friction that is inherently ingrained in certain spaces, differentially and negatively impacting minoritized students, before we even begin to approach those spaces as ones for building momentum—namely, the motivational, teaching and learning, and curricular domains in my original model.

This focus on leveling the playing field by removing friction that causes inequities is critical given the current policy context that highly prioritizes timely college completion through efficient transitions. A prime example is the guided pathways reform that was articulated around 2012, resulting in a full-fledged book in 2015 by Thomas Bailey, Shanna Jaggars, and Davis Jenkins. From that point, guided pathways has extended its reach and impact, with institutions across the country adopting related reforms. The guided pathways movement is grounded in decades of research on community college completion, primarily by researchers at the Community College Research Center of the Teachers College at Columbia University.[3] Guided pathways is a response to community colleges' traditional approach to offering courses and programs that may not always align. The consequence of this "cafeteria-style" model, Bailey and colleagues contend, is that students are facing too many choices and too little structure, with limited useful help from advisors who can also be under- or misinformed by an overwhelming set of options. Ultimately, under the traditional "cafeteria" model, students tend to make less than optimal decisions, which, the researchers argue, increases their risk of dropping out of college. The guided pathways approach, instead, promotes early planning and program entry; timely monitoring of student progress for assessment and needed intervention; integrated basic skills and college-level courses; and highly structured and coherent programs that match students' educational and career goals.

The central idea undergirding guided pathways is a rigorous one: providing clear educational paths as well as holistic support to students. Both my earlier research and this book's findings support that larger idea in principle. At the same time, what I have laid out in this book complicates guided pathways by unraveling some of the unspoken assumptions in the current model. In particular, while guided pathways is predicated on the idea of removing barriers, the kinds of barriers that are currently being centered in implementation are primarily structural—procedural changes to practices and policies, such as accelerated developmental math, reading, and writing coursework; mandatory orientation, advising, and monitoring; program maps; bridge programs from K–12 to higher education; and so on. Essentially, these efforts involve shifting, restructuring, adding, and in some cases eliminating the educational spaces where students intersect with community colleges. Reconfiguring these operational approaches to fit these educational spaces may serve the notion of efficiency, but it leaves other critical barriers unnamed, and that comes with a highly plausible cost: it does not drive deep into the experiential and relational dynamics within these educational spaces. Nor does it cast a deep and critical view on practitioners' attitudes and mind-sets that have a qualitative impact on students through those dynamics and in those spaces. However, as this book shows, there are numerous friction points *within existing* educational spaces, and they must be removed before students can even begin to benefit from guided pathways or any similar initiatives aimed at charting clear educational routes toward success that are meaningful to students. And more pressing to note are the disparities deeply seated in the types and volume of friction experienced by students based on their backgrounds, identities, and social contexts.

As chapter 7 showed, students on the linear upward trajectory shared background characteristics that placed them in an advantaged position. They benefited from having preexisting educational resources such as college preparatory coursework that allowed them to take more advanced science or math courses early on, family members who had attended college and were supportive of postsecondary education, and family members or acquaintances of high status in fields that students wanted to pursue. Others were able to gain traction toward upward transfer by participating in programs specifically designed to give students a boost. These students had a distinct advantage relative to those who had none of these things. In short, they had a lot of momentum to begin with.

It does not mean that their path was seamless. Like Jordan, whose quibble concerned transfer into specific majors, students on this trajectory largely commented about transfer in relation to their desired areas of study. Regardless of how "linear" and smooth transfer appeared for Jordan and others on this trajectory, this most advantaged group of students still experienced friction, particularly in the curricular domain, which I describe later in this chapter. I don't want to diminish the import and urgency of their struggle, but at the same time, the fact that Jordan and others on the linear upward trajectory were positioned to wrestle with these issues speaks to their relative privilege and the absence of the many friction points encountered by students from less privileged backgrounds who followed other trajectories. Those students, equally aspiring to transfer, were not even close to that point. In this scenario, a focus on structural change in the articulation of majors would touch Jordan positively, for sure, but it would not reach the range of friction other students encountered before even reaching the point of transfer.

Clearly, we cannot really build student momentum through structural reforms alone, especially if we do not tackle the friction inequitably experienced by students in "organic" educational spaces that are typically not touched by structural reforms. Otherwise we run the risk of having our efforts only deepen inequities. And we cannot tackle the friction if we do not explicitly name it. That is, we cannot do equity work "on top of" building a completion or transfer pathway; we have to name and embed such efforts explicitly and inherently within the pathway. Only when such friction and disparities are tackled head on can guided pathways or any college completion initiatives really live up to their promise of building momentum for all students. It is heartening to see an increasingly intentional focus on the issues of equity by leading researchers and organizations of guided pathways. Community College Research Center researchers Davis Jenkins and John Fink recognized the importance of gauging whether and for whom equity is truly emerging from reform efforts.[4] The Bill and Melinda Gates Foundation echoes this issue, pointing out that when making improvements in student success, institutions should recognize challenges around which student groups are actually making the most gains, and which ones get left behind.[5] Acknowledging institutional and systemic barriers is a crucial first step toward scrutinizing reform efforts to determine whether they are truly benefiting all students, particularly those who continue to be underrepresented and underserved.[6] Further, efforts to reduce friction and bring equity front and center need to be situated within multiple levels and contexts of community college STEM education, in consideration of the social and political tensions to be resolved. I turn to this discussion next.

REMOVING FRICTION

Recently, I was invited to speak at a professional development workshop for community college instructors across the country about my momentum model. After I shared the model, an instructor raised a question: "In sports, you see these small, precipitating events causing an instantaneous shift in momentum. How often do you see that in the students you study?" I cannot recall how many examples raced to my head in that very moment. I thought of the time Seamus missed that one transferable chemistry class, which pushed her back another whole year. Or when Kanda learned the dollar amount of the private options for her transfer along with the fact that none of her credits would transfer to public institutions. Or when Katy could no longer handle the noise in her lab due to her attention deficit disorder. Or when Gwyneth sensed that she was not taken seriously by others due to her gender and her small stature. Or when Shinichi's advisor told him he was not confident enough to transfer despite his proactivity. So many faces and stories came to mind—countless friction-causing moments that set off a domino effect, changing students' entire STEM and transfer trajectories. With the limited time that I had, I shared with the instructor Katy's example, given his instructional area. I then invited him to think about how oftentimes well-intended instructional and advising practices assume a neutral approach that does not account for the many identities and contexts of our students, which get washed away in our hasty and seemingly "objective" ways of resolving vital and difficult education issues.

Essentially, this experience captures and crystallizes a lot of what I have been thinking about as I wrap up this book. In this reflective journey, I have gained renewed, firsthand insights into the many spaces in which counter-momentum friction occurs, and how it happens in ways that are disproportionately hurting students from marginalized and minoritized backgrounds. As a necessary but insufficient precondition for building STEM transfer momentum, the following areas that cause friction must be named before they can be fully addressed.

The Money Factor: Financial Barriers Facing STEM Transfer

Financial barriers are one of the top counteracting forces that cause counter-momentum friction. We know that the vast majority of community college students face severe financial burdens.[7] Concerns about financing their education, both current and future after transfer, as well as limited or no financial resources, can often dissuade highly talented community college students from finishing a credential or transferring to a four-year institution.[8] We surveyed our students three times over the course of four years since we initially got in touch with them. During our final survey, we asked the students what the key barriers were in deciding whether to transfer to a four-year school. Financial concerns rose to the top, with 45.1 percent of students saying finances posed "a great deal" of a barrier (S3). Earlier in chapters 4 and 6, I shared the experiences of Kanda, Clyde, and others, and how the money factor both represented the top barrier and exacerbated other concerns facing these already underserved students.

These financial barriers led to recent policy discussions and efforts associated with free tuition at community colleges, a huge step toward reducing the financial friction that hinders the forward momentum of community college students.[9] These policies and efforts include promise programs and scholarships that can be especially helpful to students in STEM, considering time and amount of work required to complete these degrees.[10] However, as appealing as it sounds, free tuition has not touched transfer, a core mission of community colleges and why many students enroll in the first place. It may help students get started, but it does not help see them through the process and beyond. In particular, the cost of transfer into a STEM major is higher than that of a non-STEM major, as STEM bachelor's degrees cost more.[11] Many students attend community colleges due to their already limited financial resources. Then they encounter the prospect of STEM transfer and find their efforts to save precious money to be all for naught. How are these students supposed to follow such a counterintuitive plan? As long as transfer is not given the same value as freshmen recruitment and admissions in the form of generous financial aid packages, the financial concerns experienced by low-income students and students of color, such as Kanda and others, will continue to pose the most severe friction.

Friction in the Curricular Domain

Our transfer-aspiring students soon experienced two key sources of friction in the curricular domain. One had to do with the sheer scarcity of articulated coursework and programs for transfer. This led to extra credits simply to explore their field, only to find out that they didn't transfer, such as in Seamus's and Clyde's cases. Many of our students were deeply affected by this process of wading through articulation and transfer, taking them longer than desirable to reach the point of transfer—that is, if they had not already left college. The counter-momentum friction caused by the lack of broad articulation and transferability of coursework then resulted in additional expenses because of the extended time in school. This concern cannot be decoupled from the affordability of transfer and particularly hurt low-income students and students of color, as shown in Kanda's case. These two intersected concerns manifested their biggest consequence through the limited transfer "menu," which restricted options that were affordable for, truly appealed to, and embraced the diverse range of our students' interests and contexts.

Another major area of friction lay in the much narrowed access to the courses and programs that were indeed articulated and transferable. This access issue especially revolved around timing, as with Seamus, whose required organic chemistry course was offered only once a year. Or in Clyde's case, the transferable program he was initially interested in closed its door too soon for many students like him due to a capacity issue. It appears that, to access the right transferable courses or programs at the right time, many pieces all need to be in the right place: accurate information, money, schedule, work, and in some cases, childcare and transportation. If one piece is missing, the whole transfer prospect has to wait, or in some cases, wane.

The result of these two major sources of curricular friction is that many students are left with limited to no understanding with regard to what and how credits or programs transfer to their desired four-year institution. Roughly 40 percent of our transfer-aspiring students said they well understood which courses at their college were transferable to a four-year school. Interestingly, though, this pattern has not changed with the passing years, as the percentage hovered around the same level all three times we surveyed students.[12] As chapter 2 conclusively showed, this in fact was not because students were not putting forth the effort to learn these things—many of them were. But because everything about accessing a course, a curriculum, or a program has to be so granularly precise, it is very easy to miss the whole train—yet often the blame is placed on the passenger for being late.

Removing friction in the curricular domain is a major feat, a conundrum where systemic change must happen and politics must be navigated. The fact of the matter is that there remain contentious politics around two- to four-year articulation. Much of this has to do with limited or lack of trust between two- and four-year faculty, including the general stigma around community colleges, power issues around who controls the curriculum, student learning expectations and outcomes, and ultimately, which courses are deemed "rigorous" enough to transfer. Four-year faculty are a crucial part of making articulation and transfer work. However, the issue is complicated by their general lack of initiative, understanding, and respect for the quality of two-year courses, deeply rooted in a biased perception of community colleges and faculty hierarchy that unfairly places two-year college faculty at the bottom.[13] Higher education scholar Alicia Dowd cautioned that the power status and dynamic can be even more magnified among four-year and two-year STEM faculty, which can intensify curricular distrust and misalignment.[14] Establishing trust between two-year and four-year institutions cannot be emphasized enough for cultivating a strong, sustainable institutional partnership.[15] Without it, the community college stigma and related biases and power dynamics will persist, preventing both parties from coming together as equal collaborators for their students' transfer and success.

Further, when it comes to determining transferable course and program options within institutions themselves, politics and several inherent challenges muddle the picture. These include how institutional stakeholders see their mission and value. In particular, two-year college faculty in certain technical fields that are more vocationally oriented may struggle to see facilitating transfer as part of their role. In these instances, two-year college faculty are often expected to cultivate industry relationships and help students with job placement instead of transfer. This relates well with the experiences of a number of our students who were interested in transfer, but their program and faculty were not exactly set up for that option. As a result, faculty, particularly those working with STEM transfer aspirants, may view transfer as conflicting with the program mission or their own desired outcome for students.

An equally complicated issue has to do with the accessibility of transferable options. Structure and sequence dominate most STEM curricula, but as we saw in Seamus's and other students' situations, some foundational courses were only offered at a particular time, so if students were unable to access them during certain semesters, or even academic years, they were derailed from the STEM path. Although offering multiple sections across the year is a much desired and needed option, this comes at a cost. The reality is that institutions have their own resource constraints, and faculty workloads tend to be bursting at the seams.

Friction in the Teaching and Learning Domain

We know that the reason so many community college students did not progress rests with what happened—or didn't happen—in the classroom. For the most part, our students had limited exposure to teaching and learning approaches that engaged them in constructing knowledge as active, instead of passive, learners. The lack of these types of classroom experiences only served as friction and impeded student momentum toward STEM transfer.

Compounding and intertwined with this problem was the rarity of a truly inclusive STEM classroom. Consider Gwyneth or Greer, who encountered less than welcoming class environments for women. We have Katy, who struggled to feel completely heard, included, and supported in her courses due to her ADD. She was often distracted and misunderstood. There were Jim and Temperance, feeling old and disconnected in the classroom. More troublesome, the sheer concentration of students of color experiencing classroom difficulties is telling of the racial biases that implicitly and explicitly permeated the STEM classroom. The stereotype threats based on race, gender, ability, age, and other identities tended to be experienced by the students from their peers or even instructors. We saw that instructors didn't really challenge their own assumptions and biases, or go out of their way to fully understand the whole person's context and embrace their unique strengths and qualities. Although by principle, the contemporary community college aspires to be an inclusive institution, it still has a long way to go in creating spaces where all students feel welcome, supported, and valued, and this is a particularly thorny issue in the STEM context.

This is not to question the good intentions of faculty, but good intentions alone are far from demonstrating inclusive teaching and a genuine mind-set to combat the biases, stereotypes, and other negative perceptions or experiences that infiltrate the classroom and cause the most insurmountable friction for students from minoritized backgrounds. This involves a process of building faculty capacity toward cultivating robust and inclusive classroom settings. To begin, such efforts would require professional development ranging from implicit bias training to instructional training and curriculum development, along with other resources to support faculty as they strive to improve their courses and teaching. These efforts can be met with pushback, especially if institutions don't have a strong culture of professional development and growth among faculty in addressing issues of inequity. One way to ensure such efforts truly take effect, at least on behavior at first, is to attach them to accountability measures such as review and promotion. However, this takes strong commitment and willpower from top institutional leadership.

Friction in the Motivational Domain

This book has shown that students possessed abundant motivational momentum, which they brought with them and continued to draw upon. Thus, the friction I describe in this domain exists primarily in the external college contexts students negotiated, particularly with regard to advising. I also need to make clear that any friction that occurred in the curricular and teaching and learning domains acted as a deterrent to motivational momentum, directly or indirectly. But since I discussed those domains earlier, I now turn our attention to the types of friction outside of those domains that directly worked against students' motivational momentum.

Important to note is the friction caused by inadequate, or complete absence of, advising. The first facet of this issue is more technical. It concerns STEM course and program selection.[16] As Jordan's experience showed, even the most "advantaged" students who could hit the ground running with their coursework tended to be faced with confusing choices that may not have contributed to cohesive progress toward their intended outcomes.[17] Inadequate advising in course and program selection is known to negatively affect community college students' outcomes, and poor or no advising in this area may lead students to take "wrong" courses in general or courses that they do not need or will not transfer.[18] We saw this happen to Clyde. He ended up with a bunch of courses that were not transferable and a slew of others he would have to take to get even remotely close to transfer.

The second facet of the advising issue that causes friction is far more complex and profound. It is relational. With few exceptions, we see a general lack of a humanistic, culturally receptive and responsive advising relationship, and its absence is especially glaring among and detrimental to the experiences of students of color, as shown throughout this book. Given these realities, advising that is inadequate or lacking is a major source of counter-momentum friction in the motivational domain. It induces "on my own" as the only way to make it. It acts against aspirational momentum, keeps exhausting perseverance, defaults to agentic momentum, and challenges a growth mind-set as students do not see their own efforts leading to progress.

While I lay out these types of friction to motivational momentum caused by inadequate, inaccurate, and in some cases, utter lack of advising, problematizing "on my own" as the major way in which students navigate transfer does not mean pointing fingers at advisors as individuals. As I briefly touched on in chapter 2, this issue has more to do with pervasive problems in the actual structures of advising. Many community colleges are severely underresourced, with a student-to-advisor ratio as high as in the hundreds or even thousands. At the two-year colleges where our students enrolled, the caseload for advisors has consistently been in the hundreds since fall 2014.[19]

As we can imagine, such an advising load is unsustainable and untenable with advising done the traditional way. Recent efforts to redesign advising to resolve the capacity issue include burgeoning online advising services at community colleges.[20] These online options vary, ranging from students sending inquiries to a designated advising email address, submitting an online form, web conferencing, and live chat, among others. These approaches are intended to fill in the gaps when walk-in or in-person appointments are not available or feasible given the capacity issue and schedule constraints. Nudging, which consists of automated and/or personalized text messages sent to students, is another new approach. These prompts "nudge" students regarding tasks they should complete to help them prepare and progress through college, as well as remind them of other college information and resources available to them.[21] However, this strategy has both benefits and drawbacks, which I discuss further in chapter 9, with suggestions to overcome any potential challenges.

But even with these innovative strategies, the relational aspect of advising remains an essential but missing piece. How do we build a humanistic and empowering advising relationship to especially better serve students of color? Obviously, the same challenges with faculty development I discussed earlier hold for cultivating advising capacity and need to be resolved. But a precursor to fully addressing this question is to tackle the mismatch in the profiles and identities between community college students and their advisors. This same matter also applies to faculty but represents a more urgent though less talked about issue for advisors, as student–advisor interactions are often not situated within a structure that inherently allows them to develop trust. Education researcher Courtney Luedke found that trust represents one of several vital elements of a rich, supportive relationship between students of color and college staff.[22] The current challenge is that community college advisors and other college staff are proportionately more white than the student body they serve.[23] Without an authentic process of building trust, it can be difficult for students of color to fully engage with and benefit from these key individuals.

Also, I would be remiss if I did not underscore the general lack of recognition of both the power held and responsibility to be shouldered by four-year institutions in this process. By default, community colleges have been held responsible for transfer and transfer advising, despite resource challenges. The boundaries of these responsibilities need to shift, as both community colleges and four-year institutions are accountable for transfer students.[24] This requires the removal of some major hurdles in policy and practice, with the most pressing being the lack of a supportive policy environment for student and credit transfer from two-year to four-year institutions. At present, four-year institutions and community colleges are not sufficiently rewarded for receiving and sending transfers. Further, transfer success metrics that incentivize and reward both ends are yet to be developed. Currently, reporting and tracking of transfer and related student outcome information gets rather messy, which can further deter four-year institutions from getting involved in the transfer process. However, these realities bear significant consequences for students, as they are the ones left feeling the biggest loss of all—credits, information, and support—and lacking the much-needed lifeline to move forward on their STEM pathway.

In this chapter, I have outlined the kinds of counter-momentum friction implanted within several key educational spaces that disproportionately disadvantage students from minoritized backgrounds, perpetuating and intensifying inequities already in place. If we rely on reforms that solely revolve around removing structural barriers, we run the risk of lifting a small group of already privileged students at the cost of not addressing, and thus exacerbating, inequities. Therefore, any major reform with equity in mind must operate at both structural and individual, qualitative levels to remove frictions residing in both. This is obviously a tall order and a tough issue for transfer-sending and transfer-receiving institutions. Some may pose questions such as: Which level should institutions prioritize given resource constraints? Does one have to be addressed before the other, or can both be tackled simultaneously? While these questions are completely reasonable, I also don't, and challenge institutions not to, view this as a balancing act. Our students traversed both the structural and individual levels in compounded ways. Both levels shape a student's transfer trajectory, and neither should nor can wait.

9

Toward Equitable Access to Transfer

IN CHAPTER 8, I centered a culminating synthesis of this longitudinal project around the importance of naming and eliminating the friction that thwarts student momentum in several key domains. I highlighted how issues of inequity permeate the access, experiences, and outcomes of students throughout their journeys, further cementing the friction already ingrained in the imperfect transfer system to affect minoritized students in more disparaging ways. These types of friction must be removed, but entrenched politics, resistance to change, and naïve belief in good intentions (or more precisely, lack of reflexivity) pose major challenges. The process of resolving these challenges is a painstakingly long one that involves a real shift in both mind-set and action.

But they are not insurmountable. Overall, colleges, both transfer-sending and transfer-receiving, must rethink the ways in which they support students. What we learned from our students illuminates a number of big-picture directions to guide our collective transformation toward a new way of conceptualizing equitable transfer in STEM fields and beyond.

PUTTING MONEY WHERE THE MOUTH IS

The biggest friction, financial barriers, must be removed. Financial aid must fully include transfer admits. Plain and simple. The current policy narratives stress supporting college students, but transfer access is barely factored into the picture. Case in point: promise programs in states such as New York, Tennessee, and many others tend to focus on two-year or four-year colleges in isolation, leaving out the transfer connection between the two.[1] Transfer students, who make up 36.7 percent of the entire college student population, are *not* intentionally served by the current financial aid system across federal, state, and institutional levels.[2] Without generous financial investment, upward mobility through two-year to four-year transfer is only a hollow slogan.

In conceptualizing how financial support works for transfer-aspiring community college students, we cannot ignore the other salient factors that intersect with financial barriers and feed into the financial friction, such as the need for transportation and childcare, which prevent students from gaining momentum.[3] Add in other college costs, like textbooks, course materials, school supplies, and unforeseen fees, and students may think twice about continuing down their transfer path. Pioneering financial aid programs such as City University of New York's (CUNY) Accelerated Study in Associate Programs (ASAP) thoughtfully cover additional costs such as transportation and textbooks, but there are two unanswered issues.[4] The first one concerns sustainability and scalability, which requires major reallocations of all sorts of resources within and across institutions and the education system as a whole. But these are issues that policy can fix, provided a strong political will.

The second issue, however, reflects a removal from the experiential aspects of college-going among community college students. Students from families with limited means—and this is especially complicated for those from racially minoritized backgrounds—tend to shoulder many life obligations that often include the need to financially support their family members on top of their own education. These students may still need to work despite what appears to be a generous scholarship package. These circumstantial aspects are inherent parts of our students' realities that make stringent scholarship eligibility such as continuous full-time enrollment per term unsustainable, as it is out of touch with these students' lives. Relaxing the full-time enrollment requirement may appear counterintuitive, as taking fewer credit hours per term might slow down student momentum. However, we are still doing addition instead of subtraction since this arrangement means not only do students continue to accrue credits, but the removal of financial friction allows them to build further momentum in all other domains.

To ensure steady progress toward an ultimate outcome desired by students, setting a minimum mandate that is lower than full-time enrollment, say six credit hours per term on a continuous basis, or allowing a mixture of full-time and part-time attendance, would represent a happy medium. By and large, scholarship programs are contingent upon continuous full-time enrollment, and the few that strive to accommodate part-time attendance cover tuition only for a limited number of terms, emphasize credential completion instead of transfer, and thus remain an incomplete solution to a long-standing problem.[5] Making transfer an integral part of the financial aid system and providing full financial support without full-time enrollment strings attached is where we need to be heading if we are to effectively dismantle financial friction. This is a significant point of departure, as financial friction works in tandem with other friction points that we need to break down.

WIDENING AND DEEPENING TRANSFERABLE OPTIONS—ARTICULATION

To resolve friction in the curricular domain means to revamp the current structure of both articulated options and how articulation operates. And engaging in this work in productive ways cannot be decoupled from cultivating a state policy environment that is supportive of and conducive to transfer. Over the years, many states have attempted to develop articulation policies to improve transfer from two-year to four-year institutions. Yet, the effectiveness of articulation policies has been questionable, at best, as found by Josipa Roksa and colleagues.[6] While this may not be directly caused by an intentional lack of state support for community colleges and transfer, the reality is that states have a long history of undervaluing and underfunding community colleges.[7] To make things worse, performance- or outcomes-based funding further deepens the funding inequity with regard to transfer, as transfer often is not part of the formula applied to both community colleges and four-year institutions. When we look at the study's state, transfer is not even reflected in the outcomes-based funding formula of one of the two major two-year college systems that contains some institutions with transfer as one of their core missions. What do the policies like this assume? Whom are they intended for and whom are they *not* benefiting? This is a reflection of the larger policy landscape where the potential of community colleges to facilitate transfer and advance social mobility is not reflected through explicit and concrete equity-oriented goals, targets, and measures in state policies. These policies inherently trickle down to institutions and practitioners to operationalize. This reinforces the need to push back on such measures and develop state policies that not only facilitate transfer, but also support the institutions trying to help students make the two-year to four-year leap.

While state policies are an overarching and crucial support in facilitating transfer, we cannot overlook the vital role institutions play in this process. In reality, state policies only go so far, and it is how they are implemented (or not) that counts. What matters even more is when both two-year and four-year colleges step in and flesh out institution- and major-specific articulation agreements, as they can account for changes in programs, requirements, and other regulations.[8] Challenging as collaborative efforts are in the area of transfer articulation, such endeavors can reap significant benefits. As discussed in chapter 8, articulation efforts do not happen overnight for any institution, system, or state, and we must disrupt norms and power structures to pave the way for smoother transfer paths; but the "how" is the difficult part, especially when it comes to changing cultures and structures. This is where equitable, egalitarian cross-sector faculty collaborative models are crucial. This process has to be designed in such a way that power and authority are equally distributed between community college and four-year faculty. One segue into this effort is to appeal to and engage the commonalities among faculty regardless of their institutional type, including, for a start, the basic desire to be responsive to their students' needs and success.[9] Further, it is critical to build a mind-set that views learning at the undergraduate level as developmental, rather than hierarchical; earlier stages as foundational instead of basic or general; and progression across all milestones as uniformly essential rather than tiered. Once the stage is set where both parties are equally responsible for equally important areas and stages of learning, faculty can engage in cocreating learning objectives, streamlining courses across institutions, and aligning course requirements.

Moreover, within institutions, faculty involvement in articulation and transfer efforts is integral, since they interact so frequently with their students and far more than advisors.[10] To transform faculty mind-sets and campus culture toward greater faculty involvement in transfer articulation, institutions need to redefine faculty roles and responsibilities to explicitly include transfer efforts. To integrate this element as part of accountability structures bears significant symbolic meaning, especially for four-year institutions that historically hold the power but enact little intentional effort to actualize their role as transfer-receiving institutions. This may mean making adjustments to existing faculty workloads, especially in programs that tend to attract a lot of transfer students.

WIDENING AND DEEPENING TRANSFERABLE OPTIONS—ACCESSIBILITY

Several things can be done to solve problems of limited access to transferable courses due to a highly structured and narrowed course pathway. First, institutions must center their course scheduling around students as opposed to what's always been done as well as what and when faculty want to teach. The reality is that courses are typically scheduled based on precedence and faculty preference, with little if any consideration of when students *can actually take* them. Tailoring course schedules toward students' needs and constraints has major implications, as this can relieve financial friction (among other types) when full-time enrollment is not an option. For example, one promising option is block scheduling. This would allow students to attend several classes during a concentrated time window, helping students make more efficient use of their time and reduce transportation barriers and conflicts with external commitments. Adjusting course schedules by broadening their access would enable students to take more courses within their constraints with an informed sense of their own time line toward transfer and completion.

Equally important, we might reconsider the current structures and sequences of STEM programs. I think it is worth asking whether those gateway or gatekeeper courses really have to be foundational—that is, the first courses students must encounter and complete to progress in their programs. While part of this is about improving the ways in which these foundational courses are taught for a much richer student experience, as I described in chapter 1, perhaps existing course sequences do not have to be structured and sequenced the same old way. In fact, I have found that taking STEM subject-matter courses first, followed by math, contributes to a more robust transfer pathway in STEM.[11] Rather than strict course sequences and requirements that move from general to program-specific, students should be able to explore their STEM disciplines so they are able to make connections across various courses and feel less constrained or even blocked from progressing in STEM. Allowing space for this intentional flexibility would help broaden access to transferable courses and embrace the many life contexts of our students.

CULTIVATING AN INCLUSIVE CLASSROOM ENVIRONMENT

Momentum does not exclusively imply going through the motions of taking the "right" sequence of courses; it also taps into the actual learning and teaching that occur inside the classroom—a key venue where friction arises for our minoritized students. A truly effective process of building momentum should allow enriching and meaningful learning experiences for students to engage with and succeed in. And such learning experiences hinge upon an inclusive classroom environment.

A path toward that means institutions and faculty need to make a total mind shift and revisit their current practices. For example, instructors cannot and should not focus solely on who the majority is in the classroom or the overall satisfaction level when it comes to student feedback and course evaluations. Challenging ourselves as instructors and pinpointing problem spots can transform the classroom experience, especially for students who feel marginalized and overlooked, while defaulting to the "majority" would only further marginalize those already unseen. This means checking and addressing implicit bias, stereotype threats, racism, sexism, and so forth head on. This would allow instructors to start removing previously unchecked counter-momentum friction within the classroom, and move toward transforming the STEM classroom as a safe haven for minoritized students to explore and cultivate their interests, and to safeguard them from other friction forces at play around the college and in society. Addressing counter-momentum forces in classroom interactions and climate would better support STEM momentum among these students. Plus, making these changes can have a spillover effect, which students can carry with them throughout and beyond their program. Attending to these issues for underserved groups can lead to larger changes in terms of retaining valuable STEM talent and transforming STEM education and work environments.

Along the same lines, instructors need to honor and encompass more diverse learning styles and cultivate culturally responsive approaches to better support students of color, women, older students, and other underserved students. Active learning and contextualization are a few promising strategies that get students to engage with learning, work in groups, develop multiple ways to solve problems, make relevant connections between content and their lives, and much more. But more important, such approaches and strategies would yield the most value for students when grounded within the principles of culturally responsive and relevant education. According to education researcher Geneva Gay, culturally responsive education means situating the students—their backgrounds, experiences, cultures, perspectives—within the content, knowledge, and skills to create more meaningful and engaging learning experiences.[12]

Equally important, scholarship by Gloria Ladson-Billings on culturally relevant education speaks to confronting and challenging issues and systems, expecting and cultivating high levels of success, and drawing upon students as sources of skills and knowledge.[13] These approaches create a communal, collaborative learning environment, where everyone has value and a contribution to make, all positioned within students' contexts and lives. This includes instilling a community or family environment—a significant cultural component for students of color.[14] The community element can transform STEM classrooms from the all too often individual and isolated effort to one of collaboration, pooling knowledge and talents to challenge and solve problems in creative, innovative ways.

Integrating social and cultural aspects of students' experiences is especially crucial. These include role modeling and providing successful examples of people who look like the students. Fostering community and networking among underrepresented students sharing the same goal is incredibly helpful, as these students would have others like them to confide in and relate to, but also celebrate with throughout their journeys. Mentoring and developing personal relationships create vital, accessible resources that can amplify students' progress and success. Developing strong identities as STEM learners and professionals also plays an important role in keeping underrepresented student groups interested and on track in STEM.[15] This can be particularly powerful for women of color who find recognition as a "science person" to be an important part of developing a science identity.[16] Supporting the whole person also means acknowledging and accommodating students' obligations to their families and jobs, addressing financial concerns, and being responsive to varying cultures and norms. These are just a few of the many ways instructors can validate and assist students' rich contexts and situations. The knowledge that they are seen, heard, understood, and valued can create a pivotal turning point in students' journeys toward achieving their educational goals.

TAPPING INTO AND STRENGTHENING MOTIVATIONAL MOMENTUM

Before discussing motivational momentum, we need to consider the strong aspirational momentum students bring with them and hold on to, as well as the significant and persistent challenge of how to accurately measure and account for the highly diverse and fluid educational goals of community college students. Creating alignment between student goals and clear education options still remains a critical piece of the puzzle. This means bridging students' aspirational momentum with other types of momentum, such as those in the curricular domain, to help remove the misalignment problem and translate aspirations into actionable and viable educational plans.

Given the friction students experience in the motivational domain largely due to advising, an advising redesign is in order. This redesign must be systemwide. These broader efforts toward more effective advising have included early and regular contact, and helping students set clear goals from the onset. Specific advising approaches that have emerged in higher education include proactive or intrusive advising, appreciative advising, strengths-based advising, learning-centered advising, and nudging. These and other related strategies essentially aim to retain students, help them overcome challenges, leverage their existing knowledge, skills, or motivation, and place them in a more active or central role of the advising relationship. As a result, when such strategies are used, students tend to feel that their college cares about them as an individual and about their success, making them more likely to persist and accomplish their educational goals.

However, these efforts, though promising and well-intended, are more complicated in practice. Let's look at nudging, for example. With this approach, advising and related resources can be at students' fingertips, quite literally. At the structural level, it gives advisors the opportunity for more timely reminders and interactions with students at students' convenience, possibly avoiding the time, transportation, and scheduling conflicts that frequently arise when students try to set up an in-person meeting with their advisor. However, technology alone is not the solution to improving advising and cannot replace human interactions between advisors and students.[17] It is pivotal to remember that, at the core of an effective advising redesign, whether technology based or not, is relationship building, and approaches such as nudging may not achieve it if not done right. A recent report examining nudging scaled up at the state and national levels in relation to financial aid found that it actually didn't work.[18] Why would a scaled version fare so poorly, contradictory to earlier evidence from smaller models? It is possible that although more students were reached, it came at the cost of building individual, substantive relationships with students. These messages may not have been as tailored to students' individual contexts and the communities in which they lived. As a result, students may have been left feeling that they were being bothered with impersonal messages, instead of purposeful ones coming from people they truly knew and who were invested in their success. Thus, relationships are essential and nonnegotiable in revamping advising efforts.

Another overhaul has community college educators support students not only through their teaching, but also advising built within teaching. Considering how intimately involved faculty are with courses and programs, they would be invaluable in ensuring that students select the suitable courses for their programs. This does not imply that faculty would have to take on all the responsibilities of an advisor, as this would be daunting. What I suggest is equipping faculty with advising information and techniques within the confines of their teaching. For instance, when registration for future classes is coming up, faculty can take some time to present subsequent course options to students depending on their program. Also, instructors can clarify from the onset the transferability of courses and highlight important content or skills students will need to have post-transfer. In addition, instructors can bring advisors into classroom spaces, which could count toward advising time, maximize time spent per student, build strong relationships, and send a message that instructors and advisors are a team—collective change agents—supporting students in their programs and facilitating transfer and success. Of course, none of this is possible without the necessary professional development, along with building a culture and accountability system that views and celebrates advising as teaching and teaching as advising.

UNFINISHED WORK—A REFLECTIVE PATH FORWARD

What I describe above certainly requires major changes in the higher education system. As the field continues to wrestle with these challenges and potential solutions, what can practitioners do in the near future without waiting for massive changes to occur? Instead of setting forth "best practices," I opt to provide a few main ideas and questions that we must hold on to in our efforts intended to support equitable transfer in STEM and more broadly. I adopt this approach out of two considerations. For one, abundant resources have been developed by researchers and educators committed to equity issues across education sectors. With appropriate contextualization, these are the funds of extant knowledge ready for adoption by reflective practitioners. I reference some of these resources below whenever possible. A more important consideration is that the emphasis on "practices," perhaps unintentionally, obscures the difficult, deep thinking that must happen as part of the transformative reflection leading to change in practices. In my own experience working with practitioner colleagues at both community colleges and four-year institutions, I have increasingly realized that when we use the term "best practices," regardless of how rigorous and impactful they might be, the message we are sending is counterproductive to supporting a sustained, iterative, and truly reflective journey toward a real shift in mind-set that drives action to address inequity.

Before we can even begin this path forward toward change, we must start with deep, honest reflection. This focus on self-checking is driven by the book's key arguments that while there are numerous domains of counter-momentum friction facing all students, they disproportionately affect marginalized and minoritized students. In reality, I found that the most disproportionate impact of counter-momentum forces lay in the classroom and advising experiences for these students. Therefore, the most urgent and targeted approach to cultivating equitable transfer in STEM would involve addressing classroom and advising experiences. This task cannot be seriously and honestly tackled without the foundational initial step of explicit reflection among practitioners.

An imperative condition and first step is to fully understand and act upon the concept of equity-mindedness, developed by the University of Southern California's (USC) Center for Urban Education (CUE), led by Estela Mara Bensimon.[19] When practitioners are equity-minded, they recognize persistent racial and ethnic inequities, holding themselves and their institutions responsible for practices, policies, and structures that address or perpetuate those inequities. USC's CUE also put forth twelve equity-minded indicators that institutions can pose regarding racial and ethnic participation, recruitment, reporting across campuses, programs, courses, and so on.[20] These indicators are excellent material for reflective questions practitioners can ask themselves in the context of STEM education and transfer in community colleges, especially in regard to making changes to advance racial equity. The Office of Community College Research and Leadership (OCCRL) at the University of Illinois at Urbana-Champaign, directed by education professor Eboni Zamani-Gallaher, also offers a rich range of equity-guided resources, including webinars on addressing gender and racial microaggressions and on equity outcomes and assessment, along with relevant consulting, professional development, and assessment and evaluation toward equitable student outcomes.[21] OCCRL's timely resources and support keep institutions and staff engaged and working toward transformative, equity-driven change.

Equity-mindedness leads practitioners to critically reflect on and revisit their practices, including questioning their beliefs, assumptions, and behaviors, as they work toward change and equitable student outcomes. In that spirit and taking stock of what I have learned from our students through this reflective journey, I invite practitioners who work with students similar to ours to pause and think about the following questions. Though I've organized these reflective prompts loosely by the broad domains for which they apply more immediately, the larger idea transcends professional contexts.

General considerations across all spaces:
- Do I have an ideal student in mind? If so, what does that student look like? Where does that ideal come from? Do I compare all students to that ideal student?
- Whom do I praise and when? Who doesn't receive praise?
- When I think about the programs I know of or work with in my institution that focus on recruiting and retaining "diverse" students

in STEM, what assumptions about how to help those students succeed are built into those programs? What types of activities do those programs entail? Is there enough relationship and trust building in these programs?
- Do I have access to students' data on who they are and how they perform academically through my institution? If not, whom do I work with to gain access to the data? If I have access to the data, do I look beyond the general trends and disaggregate the data based on students' backgrounds and identities? When I see areas of struggle for certain groups of students, what assumptions about their struggle do I hold? What do I do to provide stronger support?
- How much do financial concerns and/or lack of acceptance of coursework at public four-year institutions create counter-momentum friction among my transfer or transfer-aspiring students? Which students tend to experience this type of friction? What are some actionable approaches to resolving this?

Classroom and advising spaces:
- When a student appears to be struggling, where do I look for solutions? Do I tend to think that the student may not have worked hard enough? Do I tend to be overly encouraging without hearing the student out more?
- Am I giving my students opportunities to learn and succeed in ways to which they are most connected? Do I include all students in my efforts to help them learn and succeed?
- Do I consistently attempt to develop my students' cultural competence? Am I committed to increasing the sociopolitical and critical consciousness of my students? Do I do the same for myself as an instructor?
- Do I pay purposeful attention to group dynamics among students—especially who gets to talk, participate, and engage more, and who is

left out? When and if I notice that, have I done anything on the spot to change the dynamics?
- What types of course evaluation do I give and how do I use course evaluation results? Do I look beyond the big picture to identify any differences based on student backgrounds? Do I investigate unexpected negative evaluation feedback for possible blind spots in my teaching? Do I reflect and take deliberate action on the evaluation data?

Curricular domain:
- Thinking about foundational courses in my field(s), how might they act as a gateway instead of a gatekeeper? How might they serve as a space to cultivate cognitive, metacognitive, and motivational momentum among transfer-aspiring students?
- How might "guaranteed" or "articulated" transfer programs be a vehicle to cultivate momentum among my transfer-aspiring students?
- What might an aligned, supported curriculum look like?
- Are the programs currently being accessed by all students in equitable ways?

This set of questions represents my experiential takeaways from our students' stories. It is by no means exhaustive or prescriptive, though it serves as a model touching upon both broad and specific contexts for practitioners working with transfer or transfer-aspiring students. Revisit the stories of Jordan, Seamus, Kanda, Katy, and others in this book, and think about how each of their journeys could have been a bit smoother if such reflexivity had been intentionally guiding institutional practices. For instance, Seamus might have continued on her path to a four-year degree in engineering right away had her first-year courses been more engaging and her advisor been more proactive in guiding her toward resources and supports to bolster her success and connection at Capital. Kanda would not have had to give up on transfer had there been articulated transfer programs she was interested in between her school and in-state, public, four-year institutions. Even better—if there had been designated financial support for transfer students in IT like her. Katy might have passed, instead of failed, her chemistry class, had her instructor waited to hear out her full set of struggles and addressed her learning needs by allowing her to indicate what her ideal classroom setting would be; a quiet space with a tutor to walk her through some of the materials might have made all the difference. Jordan's journey might have been even more straightforward had he been given easily accessible and clear information on guaranteed transfer into specific majors. While we cannot rewrite the paths already traveled by these students, the experiences they lived and shared let us imagine that if the same societal support structures that are in Jordan's favor had been in place for all students, and in particular for Seamus, Kanda, and Katy, then all of them might have experienced smoother pathways, or at least, they would not have had to fight against the various friction points feeling that they were on their own.

Authentically engaging in questions like these in our day-to-day teaching, advising, and other interactions with students is an essential first step toward transforming our assumptions and resultant actions. And as we continue our collective quest for more equitable transfer access in STEM areas and beyond, reflective questions like these invite and embolden us to meet the challenges inherent in change. This is a fluid and dynamic process where both our thinking and practice are guided by constant reflection and self-checking, and by asking the *biggest set of self-reflective questions of all: Do our efforts serve students justly by addressing their unique needs? WHO is still NOT supported by our efforts, and how can we CHANGE that?*

APPENDIX A

Methodological Notes

THIS BOOK is the culminating product of a longitudinal, mixed methods research program that I developed with one overarching research question in mind: What are the factors influencing upward transfer among students beginning in science, technology, engineering, and mathematics (STEM) fields at two-year institutions, and how do students describe their experiences pertaining to these influential factors? From fall 2014 to fall 2018, I worked with my research team to follow a cohort of roughly 1,670 students beginning in STEM programs and courses at three large two-year institutions in a Midwestern state. The mixed methods research undergirding this book draws upon survey data, in-person interviews, and administrative records in documenting students' journeys and experiences as they moved toward or away from potential transfer to a four-year college.

MIXED METHODS DESIGN

I anchored the longitudinal research program behind this book in the proposition that transfer in STEM and beyond is the outcome of a deeply contextualized process, involving the interplay of multiple individual, motivational, learning, institutional, and social factors. Accordingly, I chose a mixed methods design to account for the problem's complexity. Aligned with Johnson, Onwuegbuzie, and Turner, I view mixed methods research as "an intellectual and practical synthesis based on qualitative and quantitative research ... that recognizes the importance of traditional quantitative and qualitative research but also offers a powerful third paradigm choice that often will provide the most informative, complete, balanced, and useful research results."[1] Often situating mixed methods research is pragmatism, which reflects my larger paradigmatic stance. Pragmatism acknowledges differences in paradigms but views methods and paradigms as distinct. Thus, it centers around creating "shared meanings and joint action" by combining qualitative and quantitative approaches to tap into their nonoverlapping strengths, and thus minimize their respective limitations.[2]

Pragmatism focuses on identifying practical solutions to social problems and attaches utmost importance to the research question, which captures my long-standing belief that research design should be solely driven by the question.[3] I was always drawn to and find it natural to learn and apply both quantitative and qualitative methods depending on the question at hand. My stance is aligned with pragmatism also in that I believe knowledge can be both contextual and generalizable if analyzed for broader transferability.[4] As a pragmatic researcher, I am open about my subjectivity in my reflections and also strive to maintain a level of "objectivity" in data collection and analysis. In all, a pragmatist paradigm rejects the incompatibility thesis, which maintains that qualitative and quantitative research are incompatible and thus cannot be employed together in conducting social science research. On the contrary, a pragmatic stance maintains that research paradigms can be separate, but research approaches, methods, and techniques from different paradigms can be integrated to best answer a given research question.[5] Especially in the context of the culminating analysis underlying this book, mixed methods allowed me to combine qualitative and quantitative approaches for achieving breadth and depth in our understanding of the question at hand and corroboration of our findings.

Timing, Integration, and Priority of the Mixed Methods Design

Essentially, I adopted *a sequential Quantitative (Quan) → Qualitative (Qual) mixed methods design* that was embedded within each of the three waves of the longitudinal study in a highly iterative and interactive fashion. See the procedural diagram in figure A.1 depicting the overall design. As a constantly evolving field, mixed methods research contends with a multitude of methods considerations that can complicate what appears to be a simple process of naming a specific mixed methods design. Three key dimensions anchor the design and execution of a mixed methods research study or program: *timing or sequence, integration or mixing, and priority or weighting.*[6] Timing or sequence can be either concurrent or sequential, capturing the temporal order by which qualitative and quantitative strands of data collection and analysis occur. Integration or mixing refers to the act of interfacing quantitative and qualitative approaches in a mixed methods study, often through combining and reconciling results for a joint interpretation, or linking the two methods in data collection with findings from one strand to shape the design and data collection of the other. Priority or weighting speaks to the relative importance of qualitative and quantitative methods in addressing the research question.

Situating the issues of timing, integration, and priority within this research, a sequential Quan → Qual design was implemented for each of the three waves of original data collection, where quantitative survey

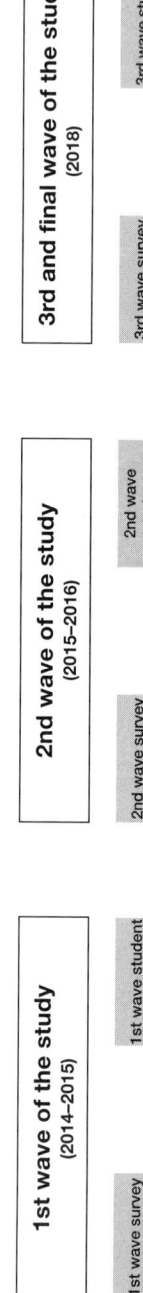

FIGURE A.1 Procedural diagram of the longitudinal sequential mixed methods design

data collection occurred first, followed by the qualitative interviews with students. During each wave, this sequential timing allowed us to utilize quantitative survey data to immediately inform the qualitative data collection. Specifically, we relied on the survey sampling and findings to identify students for the follow-up qualitative interviews, which is one way in which integration occurred as one strand completed and the other commenced. In addition, within each wave of the study, integration also took place when findings from both strands were interpreted together. As a team, we made sense of each study wave's findings together as they became available, with the quantitative results mainly identifying influential factors and salient patterns in the survey and administrative data; we used qualitative interview data primarily to explain or offer context for the identified factors and patterns, and in some cases, reveal new directions for further inquiry.

Assigning priority in a mixed methods study is a challenging task. The mixed methods literature agrees that there is not a unifying way to do this, especially in research where both strands feature rich volumes of quality data. Typically, a sequential Quan → Qual design implies a priority given to the quantitative strand. Although this was indeed in my original conceptualization, the issue of priority played out in complex ways as my research program evolved. Several factors and contexts contributed to this good problem. First, I soon realized that the fullness of our qualitative data was not to be confined solely to an explanatory, elaborative, or confirmative role, left to mostly support the quantitative findings. That is, often our student interviews revealed insights that warranted their own complete treatment independently as an empirical inquiry. In these cases, quantitative data were rightfully consigned to the background, playing a supporting role, if anything at all. For instance, the women we interviewed frequently referenced their life experiences and multiple identities when they talked about studying in a STEM field and transfer to a four-year institution. These facets emerged in such rich and powerful ways that we recognized that our quantitative analysis would not do them justice. As a result, postdoctoral researcher Kelly Wickersham and I resorted to using narrative inquiry to dive into this theme, focusing primarily on the qualitative interview data, drawing on some background survey data elements to complement the narratives we built. This narrative inquiry study is featured as part of chapter 3 on women. Second, and out of a more practical consideration of affordances as well as constraints, the large volume of data we collected over the years allowed my team to publish a number of studies along the way. Most of these studies tended to be substantively and narrowly focused, drawing upon specific quantitative or qualitative approaches. Inevitably then, operating within a larger mixed methods research program, priority shifted from study to study depending on the specific question each sought to answer. Also, in full transparency, mixed methods research can be difficult to publish due to a variety of practical and political reasons such as constraints around time and resources as well as skepticism regarding the value or utility of mixed methods, among other things.[7] This reality was further compounded by the fact that my research team was made up primarily of graduate students, whom I am personally and professionally committed to developing and growing with. Because of this, we developed pieces appropriately aligned with their areas of research and methodological training, all within the larger confines of the project aim and scope.

All these intellectual, substantive, and practical considerations make the issue of assigning priority for this book nearly impossible or perhaps unnecessary, as this issue also mirrors the highly iterative and interactive nature of our evolving mixed methods design. Indeed, the priority or weight assigned to the quantitative or qualitative strands shifted over the course of the project. In some cases, qualitative approaches drove our efforts in analyzing and interpreting the data. In other cases, quantitative approaches guided our survey data analysis and findings. In analyzing data for this book, often both approaches deserved equal weighting and it was hard to decide which one should be given priority. This can be seen throughout the book—in the introduction, chapter 1, chapter 2, and others. In this sense, although there is a chronological sequence of the quantitative and qualitative strands, it doesn't make our study as straightforward or less "messy" as a typical sequential approach. *Interactive or iterative longitudinal sequential mixed methods design* is likely the most appropriate "label" for our research. We approached our analysis within and across three iteratively linked waves, tightly coupling quantitative and qualitative strands to inform each another. Also, data collection through both approaches occurred in an alternating pattern throughout the course of the study to ensure an informative process that allows for continuous revision.

For my book, this mixed methods approach allowed me to make the biggest possible picture of the study in its entirety through triangulation and complementarity; specifically, the use of quantitative and qualitative methods and data sources to combine differing strengths of each method and to address any potential weaknesses associated with an individual approach.[8] By drawing upon quantitative and qualitative data in the form of surveys, transcript records, and interviews, along with various analytical approaches that I explain in detail through each chapter's endnotes, I examined how the results from the different data sources converge, diverge, and/or relate to one another, thus creating a holistic understanding of transfer in STEM within and across data sources.

CONFIDENTIALITY AND PROTECTION OF PARTICIPANT IDENTITIES

Before I begin outlining other methodological elements, I must address the issue of confidentiality of the participants and institutions involved in the study. These students and institutions generously shared their information, experiences, thoughts, and more with us, which is not to be taken lightly. We took several forms of actions across the various facets of data collection and analysis to protect participant privacy and confidentiality. The surveys were available both online and on paper, giving students the opportunity to complete the survey in any private location of their choosing. We created mapping tables for translating between sensitive identifiers and internally created identifiers that were used as study IDs for participants. Institutions released administrative records only for those students who gave consent to do so through the surveys.

As for the interviews, we conducted them on students' campuses at a location of their choosing if possible, which tended to be the place most accessible to the students during our first interviews. Other times, depending on timing and availability, we conducted the interviews in other spaces that were convenient and comfortable for students, including coffee shops and restaurants. Students created a pseudonym for themselves to protect their identity and the information they shared. If any identifying information was revealed during the interviews, such as names, places, and so on, we did not include it in any publications or reports, or for other related project dissemination purposes. Students were also allowed to redact anything they said or withdraw their interview if they so wished. Students were provided with consent forms throughout the survey and interview process so they were aware of the benefits and risks of their participation, along with my contact information and that of the Institutional Review Board (IRB) if they had any further questions or concerns.

As for the actual storage and protection of the study data, paper files and consent forms were stored in a secure campus location (specifically, the locked offices and desks of the appropriate and approved team members). All electronic forms of the data, such as interview recordings, transcripts, survey responses, and administrative records, were stored on secure institutional or institutionally approved servers. Much of the data was also password protected, and only approved research team members had access to it. All research procedures and protocols were approved by the IRB of University of Wisconsin–Madison as well as that of all three participating institutions. My research team and I also make regular self-checks through reminders, meetings, reflections, documenting, and so on to ensure we consistently hold ourselves accountable to the highest standards of research and related participant protection.

For the statistics reported in this book, we rounded study sample and subsample sizes to the nearest five or ten as needed, and in some cases when the focus was on general patterns, we only reported percentages adjusted with the sampling weight (see sampling section later). This approach prevented multiple data tables and sources, including qualitative data, from being used together to identify students. Also, although not required by the IRB, for this book, I decided to mask the institutions' names and the state where the study occurred for two key considerations. First, some of the findings I present in this book are based on the experiences of the students who participated in our interviews. Many of these experiences were not among the best, and some of the students shared sensitive personal information. While we had already asked students to create a study pseudonym, making their institutions identifiable still ran the risk of linking student responses back to their colleges and the individuals they interacted with throughout the course of the study. Because of this, we masked institutions and the state to protect students' identity to the fullest extent possible. We also masked website information without changing content to maintain accuracy of the content yet further ensure anonymity of the students and their institutions. We did this to protect the confidentiality of the students and in many cases the instructors and advisors, especially since students pointed out good and bad practices. Doing this not only protected the students, institutions, and staff, but also provided a level of transferability and broad applicability of the findings.

Second, I hope I made it clear throughout this book that some of the students did encounter supportive instructors and advisors who positively shaped their STEM journeys, and that the central argument and key findings are not to place blame on individual practitioners or even institutions for the students who did not receive the support, structures, services, and more that they needed to thrive and persist. All the same, this book's findings and conclusions may not read most favorably upon or flattering to the institutions where the study occurred. However, I don't believe that the issue of "on my own" as portrayed in this book is an issue unique to the three institutions. Rather, it has broad transferability elsewhere across the country to many community colleges and their students, both the agentic part and the more wanting part. I hope by removing the identities of the study sites, readers can see the same broader relevance and engage in this thought process around the issue as a commonly shared one instead of dismissing it as "not my problem." Otherwise, the issue of "on my own" simply loses the crucial point I made about reflexivity in the final chapter of the book.

RESEARCH SITES AND STUDY SAMPLE

During the fall of 2013, I approached three two-year institutions in a Midwestern state, Centerville College, Metroshore College, and Great Lakes College, about their interest in participating in a project like this. With a shared commitment to transfer and STEM areas of study gaining traction as an institutional priority, all three were on board and eventually became my research sites. One of the distinctive missions of each of these institutions is to support student transfer to four-year institutions. Centerville College and Metroshore College are large comprehensive two-year colleges in the state, whereas Great Lakes College's sole mission is to prepare students for transfer. Subsequently during 2013–2014, I worked with institutional researchers at each institution to flesh out several design details (described below) and piloted the survey instrument, all of which paved the way for officially launching the study in fall 2014.

A note on institutional differences: Across the three institutions, there exist slight variations in the survey and administrative data regarding students' experiences and outcomes. Especially, Great Lakes College serves relatively more privileged "traditional" students compared with the other two institutions, where the student population is more diverse. Higher numbers of students starting at Great Lakes ended up on the linear upward trajectory and fewer students cited finances as a major barrier, compared with students starting at Centerville and Metroshore. Students at Great Lakes also tended to report slightly more positive experiences and more frequent interactions with their instructors, advisors, and peers. However, these differences by and large did not amount to the level of prominent institutional differences in such a way that the central arguments and conclusions would change based on the institution. Therefore, the results and data reported across the chapters reflect the study's findings as a whole that cut across the research sites.

Classification of STEM Fields

In this project, STEM fields include four general groups based on the classifications by the National Science Board:

1. Biological/agricultural/environmental life sciences
2. Computer/mathematical sciences
3. Engineering/engineering technologies
4. Physical sciences[9]

Under this general guideline, a combination of the Classification of Instructional Programs (CIP) codes (specifically 01, 03, 11, 14, 15, 26, 27, 40, 41) and institution-specific contexts in regard to STEM program and course offerings that serve transfer were considered when selecting STEM fields. For Centerville College, programs that matched the indicated codes were defined as STEM programs. In addition, Centerville College's Liberal Arts Transfer programs in science and engineering were also included. For Metroshore College, a combination of three criteria were used. The first drew upon the same CIP codes as adopted by Centerville College. The second pertained to the selection of Metroshore's Associate of Science degree programs as part of STEM. Finally, the third allowed the inclusion of additional programs classified as STEM based on a definition specific to Metroshore College. As for Great Lakes College, the same CIP codes were applied to define STEM programs at that institution. Being a transfer-oriented institution, these programs award an Associate of Arts and Science degree. No other criteria were needed or used to define STEM programs for Great Lakes College.

Identification of STEM Courses Designated for STEM Programs

Since many beginning two-year college students do not declare a program of study right away, we also included STEM-aspiring students who had not declared a major but were enrolled in one or more STEM courses that were program-level courses typically required for a STEM program degree. For Great Lakes College, institutional researchers worked with department chairs in developing this STEM course list as previously defined. For Centerville College and Metroshore College, institutional researchers supplied course and program lists, along with program requirements to the project team, who then built a list of STEM courses for each institution.

Study Sample

Students at these three institutions who were eligible to participate in this study were first-year students who had declared a major in STEM, or those who had not yet declared a major but were enrolled in one or more courses within a STEM field in fall 2014. Operationally, students must have met all of the following criteria:

1. They were first-year degree-seeking students in fall 2014.
2. They were enrolled in one or more credits at the research site.
3. They had either declared a major in a STEM field or, if they had not declared a program, were enrolled in a course typically taken by students majoring in a STEM field.
4. They had not indicated a FERPA restriction.
5. They were at least 18 years old.

Survey Sampling. In fall 2014, we sampled roughly a thousand students from each of the three institutions for a final target sample size of about three thousand students. Our sampling approach balanced the need for sufficient statistical power and resource constraints, and was based on the actual distributions of students in specific racial/ethnic groups and STEM fields. Given the small number of students of color in STEM at each institution and the urgent need to better serve them, students of color were oversampled to ensure that the final analytical sample included a sufficient number of these students. In addition, for institutions where enrollment was small within specific STEM fields, sample members were chosen with different probabilities of being selected depending on that STEM field. As a result, the sample was obtained using a stratified sampling design with two strata: race/ethnicity and STEM fields. This approach helped separate the target population into these two strata and select sample members within each stratum.

When we invited students to participate in the longitudinal study through the first survey, we provided information on access to administrative records as part of the study. The students could choose whether to participate in the survey and to permit access to their administrative records. Only students who consented to both were considered study participants. Approximately 1,670 students completed the survey and granted access to their administrative records, for a study participation rate of 56 percent. This group of students became the study cohort whom we contacted for two additional surveys in late fall 2015/early 2016 and spring 2018. About 1,250 students of the 1,670 completed the second survey and again agreed to give the research team access to their academic records, for a response rate of 75 percent. For the third and final survey, 1,260 students participated, for a response rate of 76 percent.

Table A.1 gives a broader understanding of study-eligible students at each research site during the fall of 2014, when the study sample was drawn. To ensure the confidentiality of all study participants, we rounded sample and subsample sizes to the nearest ten.

184　ON MY OWN

TABLE A.1 Fall 2014 enrollment, target sample, and survey respondents

	FALL 2014 ENROLLMENT N	%	TARGET SAMPLE N	%	SURVEY RESPONDENTS (first wave) N	%	SURVEY RESPONDENTS (second wave) N	%	SURVEY RESPONDENTS (third wave) N	%
Centerville College										
Total	1,320		1,000		560		450		440	
Sex										
Male	820	62%	620	62%	320	58%	260	57%	250	56%
Female	500	38%	370	37%	230	41%	190	42%	200	44%
Other/NA	<10	<1%	<10	<1%	<10	<1%	<10	<1%	<10	<1%
Race/ethnicity										
White	1,000	76%	680	68%	380	67%	300	67%	300	68%
Students of color	330	24%	330	33%	190	34%	150	33%	140	32%
Native American	10	<1%	10	1%	<10	2%	<10	2%	0	0%
Black/African American	60	5%	60	6%	30	5%	20	4%	20	5%
Hispanic/Latinx	90	7%	90	9%	50	9%	40	9%	40	9%
Asian American	80	6%	80	8%	50	9%	40	9%	40	9%
Multiracial/unknown	90	7%	90	9%	50	9%	40	9%	40	9%
Metroshore College										
Total	1,000		1,000		500		360		370	
Sex										
Male	660	66%	660	66%	320	63%	220	61%	220	59%
Female	330	33%	330	33%	190	37%	140	39%	150	41%
Other/NA	<10	1%	<10	<1%	<10	<1%	<10	<1%	0	0%
Race/ethnicity										
White	450	45%	450	45%	240	48%	180	50%	190	51%
Students of color	550	55%	550	55%	270	53%	180	50%	180	49%
Native American	20	2%	20	2%	<10	<1%	<10	<1%	<10	<1%
Black/African American	190	19%	190	19%	90	18%	60	17%	60	16%
Hispanic/Latinx	110	11%	110	11%	60	12%	30	8%	30	8%
Asian American	60	6%	60	6%	30	6%	20	6%	20	5%
Multiracial/unknown	170	17%	170	17%	80	16%	60	17%	70	19%

(continued)

Qualitative Sampling. Following a sequential mixed methods design for data collection, it was important that participants in the qualitative phase also respond to the survey. Upon completion of the first wave of survey administration and preliminary analyses of the survey data, we

TABLE A.1 *(continued)* Fall 2014 enrollment, target sample, and survey respondents

	FALL 2014 ENROLLMENT N	%	TARGET SAMPLE N	%	SURVEY RESPONDENTS (first wave) N	%	SURVEY RESPONDENTS (second wave) N	%	SURVEY RESPONDENTS (third wave) N	%
Great Lakes College										
Total	1,570		1,000		610		440		450	
Sex										
Male	910	58%	580	58%	330	54%	230	52%	220	49%
Female	660	42%	420	42%	280	46%	210	48%	230	51%
Other/NA	0	0%	0	0%	<10	<1%	<10	<1%	<10	<1%
Race/ethnicity										
White	1,340	85%	770	77%	470	77%	350	79%	350	78%
Students of color	240	15%	240	24%	140	23%	100	22%	100	22%
Native American	20	1%	20	2%	10	2%	<10	<1%	10	2%
Black/African American	40	3%	40	4%	10	2%	10	2%	10	2%
Hispanic/Latinx	100	6%	100	10%	70	11%	50	11%	50	11%
Asian American	80	5%	80	8%	50	8%	40	9%	30	7%
Multiracial/unknown	<10	<1%	<10	<1%						
Grand total	3,880		3,000		1,670		1,250		1,260	

Note: Sample and subsample sizes rounded to the nearest ten. Column counts and percentages may not sum to totals due to rounding. Reported percentages are unweighted.

purposefully drew the interview sample from survey participants, primarily relying on maximum variation. Given its emphasis on selecting a wide range of cases to achieve rich variation on important dimensions, maximum variation sampling allowed us to capture the most pronounced patterns and core experiences that influenced STEM transfer and that cut across a wide range of students, disciplines, and institutions.[10] Taking advantage of the large number of survey respondents, we applied random sampling techniques through stratification of the survey respondents by research sites and STEM fields, followed by a random selection of a hundred survey participants from the joint distributions. We then augmented this information by adding students' self-reported background characteristics as well as their composite scores along several key dimensions of the survey such as learning experiences, motivational attributes, and transfer-oriented interactions.

Working with these various data sources, we purposefully looked for students who could help us achieve maximum variation along these noted dimensions. We then used directory, survey, and institutional information to reach out to these students, inviting them to participate in interviews. A total of forty-three responded to our invitation and participated in the first interviews, thus forming our initial longitudinal interview sample. Depending on the depth and richness of the interview data as well as areas that invited more questions, we followed up with thirty-four of these students in the second wave of our interview data collection. For the final wave of our data collection, our primary goal was to further solidify, deepen, or confirm/disconfirm patterns and findings from our analysis of the quantitative and qualitative data already collected, and in that spirit, we purposefully selected fourteen previous participants and three new participants to conduct our third and final round of interviews. Table A.2 lists students who participated in our qualitative data collection and several important characteristics of these students.

RESEARCH INSTRUMENTS AND PROTOCOLS

Survey Instrument

We collected the survey data using an original instrument that I developed in 2014. Informed by prior literature on transfer and the social cognitive career theory, this instrument includes a total of 103 items measuring various factors that are hypothesized to contribute to transfer in general and, specifically, to transfer and attainment in STEM areas of study.[11] In addition to the common survey items, our survey included research site-specific items to offer customized information to our research partners. For the specific survey domains, refer to figure A.2, the conceptual model guiding the survey development. The full base year instrument

TABLE A.2 Interview participants

STUDY NAME	CHAPTER(S) APPEARED	RACIAL IDENTITY	GENDER IDENTITY	AGE RANGE AT START OF STUDY	INITIAL STEM PROGRAM/ COURSE AREA
Centerville College					
Adrian		White	M	24–29	BIO/AG/ENV
Bethany	Ch1, Ch6	White	F	20–23	BIO/AG/ENV
Bill		White	M	18–19	PHYS
Clyde	Ch4, Ch6, Ch8	Black	M	20–23	ENG
Hunter		Unknown	M	18–19	ENG
Jasmine	Intro, Ch3, Ch5	White	F	30 and older	BIO/AG/ENV
Jennifer	Ch2	White	F	24–29	BIO/AG/ENV
Katy	Pre, Intro, Ch1, Ch2, Ch3, Ch5, Ch7, Ch8, Ch9	White	F	30 and older	PHYS
Kelly	Ch5	White	F	30 and older	BIO/AG/ENV
Kwesi		Black	M	30 and older	COMP/MAT
Lotty		White	F	30 and older	ENG
Nelkowicz	Intro, Ch1, Ch6	White	M	30 and older	ENG
Nico		White	M	20–23	PHYS
Norman	Ch5	White	M	30 and older	COMP/MAT
Paul	Ch6	Unknown	M	24–29	COMP/MAT
Rain		Hispanic/Latino	M	24–29	COMP/MAT
Seamus	Pre, Intro, Ch2, Ch7, Ch8	Multiracial Black	F	20–23	BIO/AG/ENV
Shinichi	Intro, Ch4, Ch7, Ch8	Asian	M	18–19	BIO/AG/ENV
Stella	Ch6	White	F	30 and older	BIO/AG/ENV
Taylor		White	M	30 and older	PHYS
Tom	Ch4, Ch6	Hispanic/Latino	M	24–29	COMP/MAT
Vern		White	M	24–29	COMP/MAT
Metroshore College					
Callan	Intro, Ch5	Black	M	30 and older	BIO/AG/ENV
Chad	Ch4	Black	M	20–23	PHYS
Gwyneth	Intro, Ch1, Ch2, Ch3, Ch8	White	F	24–29	PHYS
James	Intro	Black	M	30 and older	COMP/MAT
Jennipher	Ch1, Ch4	White	F	18–19	COMP/MAT
Jim	Ch5, Ch8	White	M	30 and older	PHYS
Kanda	Pre, Intro, Ch2, Ch3, Ch4, Ch7, Ch8, Ch9	Native American	F	18–19	COMP/MAT
Mathais		Native American	M	24–29	ENG
Robert		Hispanic/Latino	M	18–19	COMP/MAT
Sam		White	F	24–29	PHYS
Temperance	Ch1, Ch5, Ch6, Ch8	White	F	30 and older	ENG
Valerie	Ch4	Hispanic/Latina	F	30 and older	BIO/AG/ENV

(continued)

TABLE A.2 *(continued)* Interview participants

STUDY NAME	CHAPTER(S) APPEARED	RACIAL IDENTITY	GENDER IDENTITY	AGE RANGE AT START OF STUDY	INITIAL STEM PROGRAM/ COURSE AREA
Great Lakes College					
Alexander		Hispanic/Latino	M	24–29	COMP/MAT
Bubbles	Ch4	Hispanic/Latino	M	18–19	ENG
Elizabeth	Intro, Ch1, Ch3, Ch4	Asian	F	18–19	PHYS
Gertrude	Intro, Ch1	Native American	M	30 and older	COMP/MAT
Greer	Ch1, Ch3, Ch8	White	F	18–19	ENG
J.J.		White	M	24–29	ENG
John		White	M	18–19	BIO/AG/ENV
Jordan	Pre, Intro, Ch1, Ch2, Ch7, Ch8, Ch9	White	M	18–19	PHYS
Kevin	Intro, Ch1	Native American	M	18–19	ENG
Kirsten	Intro, Ch3	White	F	18–19	ENG
Kooks	Ch1, Ch4	Hispanic/Latino	M	18–19	ENG
Scott	Intro	White	M	18–19	ENG

Note: Students chose their own study names. F = Female, M = Male; ENG = engineering/engineering technology, BIO/AG/ENV = biological/agricultural/environmental life sciences, PHYS = physical sciences, COMP/MAT = computer/mathematical sciences.

is available at https://uwmadison.box.com/s/db8k2u7r78ezfs8l07xpjtq56d1bjad1. As this is a longitudinal survey instrument, most of the measures were repeated in the two follow-up surveys. However, in each of the subsequent surveys, we added questions. In the second wave of the survey, we also asked whether students were still enrolled at their institution; whether they transferred, where, and when; if they transferred, which field of study they transferred into; posttransfer experiences, coursework, and sense of belonging; students' current activities if not attending college and reasons for not attending; reasons for and barriers to transfer; and students' mental health or learning disability, if they chose to answer. In the third wave of the survey, in addition to these items, we also asked students about the influence of their pretransfer

FIGURE A.2 Conceptual model guiding the survey development

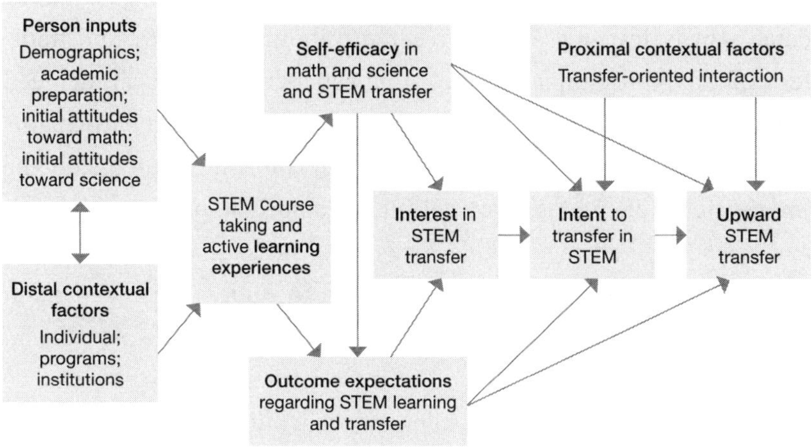

```
Person inputs
Demographics;              Self-efficacy in              Proximal contextual factors
academic                   math and science              Transfer-oriented interaction
preparation;               and STEM transfer
initial attitudes
toward math;
initial attitudes
toward science
                    STEM course
                    taking and          Interest in        Intent to         Upward
                    active learning  →  STEM          →   transfer in   →   STEM
Distal contextual   experiences         transfer          STEM              transfer
factors
Individual;
programs;
institutions                       Outcome expectations
                                   regarding STEM learning
                                   and transfer
```

Source: Xueli Wang, "Upward Transfer in STEM Fields of Study: A New Conceptual Framework and Survey Instrument for Institutional Research," *New Directions for Institutional Research*, January 2017.

experiences on their posttransfer experiences and goals; whether students ever transferred since the fall of 2014; posttransfer experiences and educational and career expectations within students' specific area of study; and internship and research experiences, if applicable.

Qualitative Interviews

We conducted interviews with students following each wave of the survey data collection, as a way to both trace interesting patterns from our emerging survey data analysis and deepen our understanding in ways that survey data cannot. In this sense, the sequential design is meant to be both explanatory and for triangulation. Accordingly, we developed and utilized a core protocol that included general questions on educational experiences and plans as well as factors influencing those plans. On top of this core set of questions, we also crafted three additional sets of questions reflecting key domains of student experiences that were both highlighted in the survey instrument and showed a significant connection to students' transfer intent as evidenced in the first-year survey data (namely, learning experiences, motivational attributes, and transfer capital). For example, the "learning experiences" protocol included specific prompts on learning experiences, focusing on what participants saw as helpful or unhelpful in boosting their confidence in transfer. The "motivational attributes" protocol included specific prompts on math and science self-efficacy beliefs, focusing on what shaped high or low beliefs, and how those beliefs were related to students' transfer intent and plans. The "transfer capital" protocol included specific prompts on transfer-oriented interactions, focusing on what participants saw as boosting their confidence in transfer and what didn't work. All interview protocols are available upon request.

DATA COLLECTION

Survey Data Collection

The UW Survey Center assisted with the administration of the survey. To summarize, each of the three waves of the survey was conducted using a series of mixed mode web and mail surveys. In the first advance letter, a cash preincentive ($5 first wave, $10 second wave, and $10 third and final wave) was given to each sampled student, and a cash incentive ($10 first wave, $20 second wave, and $25 third and final wave) was promised after survey completion. After the initial letter invitation, multiple reminders were sent to the participants. During the first wave in fall 2014, an email invitation was sent out six days after the letter invitation. A reminder letter was sent eight days after the email invitation, and an email reminder sent six days after that. A paper survey packet was sent to students twelve days after the email reminder, with another email reminder sent a week after the paper surveys were mailed. Similar protocols were followed in the two subsequent waves of survey data collection.

Administrative Records

In addition to survey data, each semester we obtained consenting students' administrative records from participating institutions, including transcript records detailing course credits, grades, programs of study, and graduation status. This data was particularly powerful in detailing students' incremental academic building blocks to or away from notable educational milestones such as transfer, graduation, or simply enrollment status during a given time. Administrative records also included student background characteristics that serve as an excellent triangulation and complement to self-reports. Finally, per our data sharing agreement, institutional researchers also requested data from the National Student Clearinghouse (NSC) to allow our team to examine transfer behaviors. NSC gathers enrollment data from more than 3,600 postsecondary institutions in the nation and thus can track student enrollment across multiple institutions and institution types (two-year, four-year, public, private) throughout the country (in-state and out-of-state). Not only were we able to verify and track student enrollment and attendance patterns (even concurrent enrollment at multiple institutions), but we were also able to verify certificates and degrees students received throughout their educational career.

Qualitative Interviews

Following each wave of survey data collection, we conducted in-depth, in-person individual interviews with consenting students. These interviews were semistructured in that they solicited student answers to some predetermined questions described earlier while encouraging participants to explore and follow new themes. Interviews ranged from thirty minutes to well over two hours. The in-person interviews were conducted either at a college campus or public location, such as a restaurant or coffee shop of the student's choosing. Students were given a $10 cash reward upon completion of the first wave interview, $20 for the second wave, and $30 the final wave. Prior to the interviews, researchers underwent multiple rounds of training in which we iteratively reviewed and practiced interview protocols and calibrated among ourselves until we were able to ensure that we consistently addressed all facets of the interview process. In addition, we reviewed survey information and any previous interview recordings and notes (for the second and final interview waves). Upon completion of each interview, we recorded field notes containing any relevant information regarding observations of surroundings, the interview itself, the participants, and other reflections in terms of the interviews and data collection process.

DATA ANALYSIS

We conducted data analysis throughout the entire study to glean and distill insights that allowed us to both examine important interim outcomes (for example, important markers of student motivational momentum, such as their transfer aspirations) and shine a light on new areas to focus on in subsequent data collection and analysis. These carefully timed, incremental analyses resulted in a number of studies and publications (qualitative, quantitative, or mixed methods) focusing on a particular angle of our larger research question along the process and also informed the arguments and conclusions throughout this book.

This book is also in large part based on a culminating analysis of all sources of data collected throughout the study. To harness the rich findings from such a large project, my analysis was not confined to a singular mixed methods design. Rather, the statements, narratives, and findings I present in this book were inferred from an integrated analysis of the vast volume of data from quantitative and qualitative strands of this research program. Below, I provide a general description of the data analysis procedures. For greater details, see each chapter's endnotes for the specific sources of my analysis and applicable technical procedures.

Analysis of Quantitative Data

Throughout our project, we applied a wide array of statistical procedures, ranging from descriptive to inferential, to analyze our survey and administrative data. In preliminary stages, in addition to routine data screening, cleaning, and preparation procedures, we conducted analyses to assess the survey's validity and reliability, detailed later. Due to the complex sampling process involved in selecting sample members, each student's probability of being selected was not equal across race/ethnicity and/or STEM fields. In addition, nonresponse would be another source of bias between the target population and the sample. Therefore, to compensate for the unequal probabilities of selection and to reduce bias caused by nonresponse, we first calculated sampling weights as the inverse of the probability of selecting a student from the target population across the two strata. In addition, response rates across the two strata were computed. By multiplying the sampling weights with the reciprocals of the response rates, we derived the final weights that we applied in all of our quantitative analyses involving survey data.

We examined students' administrative records and NSC data in documenting students' enrollment and degree completion status in a given semester. These data sources, augmented by survey data, allowed us to construct the four momentum trajectories among transfer-intending students from fall 2014 to fall 2018. A student's trajectory was considered to be linear upward if the person's data showed that they had enrolled only in one two-year institution, and their latest enrollment record showed that they had either graduated from or enrolled at a four-year institution. Indicators of a detoured trajectory were that a student was still enrolled in a two-year institution based on the latest records, which almost always meant that they switched across multiple programs, or they had enrolled in multiple institutions before upward transfer happened. A student was classified to be in a deferred trajectory if their last record from the NSC data showed that their highest postsecondary credential was from a two-year institution and they had not transferred to any four-year institution during the study window. Taking a break indicated that as of fall 2018, a student was not enrolled in any postsecondary institution and did not complete any postsecondary credential based on their NSC or survey data.

Analysis of Qualitative Data

Interview data were recorded, transcribed verbatim, and initially coded using an open coding scheme to capture a multitude of concepts and patterns. We undertook this analytical process individually and then as a team to reach an agreement on codes and themes to ensure credibility and trustworthiness of the process. We listened to the recordings and read individual transcripts a number of times, followed by a writing process where meaningful codes were identified, grouped together, and organized into categories, subthemes, and themes. We also developed study- and method-specific codes (narrative and emotion coding for narrative inquiry studying two-year college women's life experiences and identities shaping transfer intent; open, in vivo, and coding significant statements for descriptive phenomenology exploring two-year college students' self-perceptions as STEM learners, as two examples), which we reviewed against each study member's emergent codes and the research questions. In a similar fashion to our overarching data analysis process, we then revisited and revised the codes accordingly as we approached and converged on categories and themes, engaging in an iterative process of reflection and revision toward findings reflective of the research questions and the data.

For the students profiled in the book, I drew upon a variety of narrative inquiry techniques—namely, broadening, burrowing, and storying and restorying.[12] With broadening, I situated students' experiences within both the larger contexts that shaped their personal stories and the study questions themselves. Guided by interview data and supplementary information provided through the surveys and field notes, I was able to create a general profile of each of the students. To further achieve broadening, I grounded students' experiences within the larger literature in search of both bigger contexts and interpretations.

Turning next to burrowing, I scrutinized the interview data by both reviewing transcripts and listening to recorded interviews multiple times with a particular focus on the significant emotions, events, people, and moments of struggle or accomplishment shared by students. During this process, I continued to examine, from the students' perspectives, how their educational experiences in relation to transfer in particular were influenced by these significant occurrences. Last, storying and restorying followed, in which case I used multiple years of data to develop a sequence of events and present each student's experience through a clear story line. Although there are many ways in which a student's story can be interpreted and told, I strove to maintain fidelity to their lived experiences by keeping the story centered on what the student shared with us and treating that as bearing the most significance.

Mixed Methods Analysis

For the most part, the data were analyzed separately as they became available. Results emerging from both quantitative and qualitative analyses were integrated into the interpretation stage, especially when writing this book. In this evolving process, the quantitative analyses and findings motivate the qualitative stage; conversely, the qualitative results provide more depth and insight into the factors influencing STEM transfer as identified by quantitative findings, and in some cases, inspired new interrogation of the survey and administrative data. Essentially, upon the completion of all data collection, from fall 2018 to summer 2019, I analyzed quantitative and qualitative data from the entire project, and combined, compared, contrasted, or corroborated results from all data sources. In many cases, I also included in this iterative analysis empirical studies we published along the process. In this sense, this book is more a product of the meta-inferences I drew from the entire project—"an overall conclusion, explanation, or understanding developed through an integration of the inferences obtained from the qualitative and quantitative strands of a mixed methods study."[13] It is also a meta-level synthesis across many smaller mixed or singular method studies resulting from the same data sources of the research program. These all came together in the culminating stories, findings, and reflections that emerged from this process, encompassing the broader results and takeaways as well as the individual narratives of Jordan, Kanda, Seamus, and Katy. When constructing the narratives for the four key students profiled in the book, I heavily focused on crystalizing the gist of each participant's experiences and journey as reflected across the various sources of data collected, including several years of interviews, multiple waves of surveys, students' transcripts, field notes, and verification of background details and important quotes via follow-up emails and/or phone calls.

QUALITY OF DATA AND INTERPRETATIONS

The quality of the meta-influences drawn from the overall mixed methods study depends on the quality of findings from each of the two strands, as well as the quality of mixed methods design itself. In this section, I first describe the separate procedures we used to assess the quality of data and interpretations of quantitative and qualitative strands, followed by a discussion of my approaches to ensuring the credibility of the meta-inferences I drew from an integrated analysis of quantitative and qualitative findings, especially within an interactive, iterative sequential design.

Reliability and Validity of Quantitative Data and Findings
To assess content and face validity, in spring 2014, the survey instrument was reviewed by a total of thirteen researchers and practitioners with scholarly and/or practical expertise in areas ranging from transfer and higher education research to STEM education and curriculum issues and

leadership around two-year colleges. This panel provided detailed feedback in writing or at a virtual or in-person meeting. We made revisions based on all individual and collective feedback, with the occasional need to reconcile conflicting feedback. I sent the revised version to the panel for additional review and made minor adjustments in light of further suggestions.

Following this process, with the facilitation by institutional researchers at the participating colleges, in summer 2014 we conducted a pilot study with nearly a hundred two-year college students who were similar to but not included in the study population. Based on the data collected from this pilot sample, we performed an exploratory factor analysis (EFA) to identify the factor structure based on the draft items that were assumed to measure latent constructs.[14] Results indicated that the general theoretical structure held, but some items may have caused redundancy or lacked clarity, which led to additional edits to the survey.

In early fall 2014, we conducted cognitive interviews with twelve two-year college students to check the readability of the survey items as well as response process validity—the extent to which survey participants' thought processes indicated that they interpreted the items in the same way as the researcher.[15] Each team member provided participating students with a short excerpt of the survey for them to read through and answer question by question, with the team member following up with one or more questions to gain clarity and insight into students' interpretations of the survey items. Students were also asked if certain language in the questions made sense. If students found language unclear or confusing, we took note of this and also asked for potential suggestions to make the items easier to read and respond to. We also asked students to tell us why they answered the way they did to determine whether students were interpreting the survey questions and response options the way we intended. We took detailed notes back to the team for discussion and resolution to improve the survey. Taking stock of everything we learned in the process described above, we reviewed the close-to-final survey numerous times and made final edits and adjustments before fielding the first wave officially in the fall of 2014.

Upon completion of the first full survey administration, we conducted additional construct validity and reliability analyses. A measure of reliability, Cronbach's alpha, was calculated for each latent construct and ranged from .824 to .956, indicating that the items in each latent construct were highly related to one another. The results from the confirmatory factor analysis showed that the six latent constructs were well represented by the items and the items measured their intended latent constructs well, with good model fit indices (N = 1,668, χ^2 = 5610.564, df = 725, p < .001; RMSEA = .064, CFI = .969, TLI = .967), and factor loadings ranged from .517 to .964. The analysis of each item for each of the six latent traits using item response theory showed that the items represented the attributes observed at certain levels of the latent trait and the item responses were greatly influenced by the latent trait. These analyses were replicated on data from subsequent waves of survey administration and the results retained similar patterns.

The administrative records are part of the routine data collection performed by institutional researchers at the participating colleges. Institutions followed standard protocols established by the Department of Education and NSC. Institutional research staff at the participating colleges partner with NSC to streamline and centralize their student cohort and course data on enrollment, progression, performance, and completion. This provides institutional researchers with tools and metrics for reporting on their individual institutions, as well as opportunities to work on and share this information through grant projects with the necessary contracts and permissions. This granted us access to comprehensive administrative and transcript records for data collection through the project.

For all quantitative analysis, we performed and checked each procedure multiple times. Each individual researcher who took the lead on a given analysis always had at least one other equally qualified researcher to double-check the analyses to identify any inadvertent technical errors. Original analyses reported in the book were performed at least two rounds, one by Yen Lee, the team's quantitative researcher, and one by me to ensure accurate reporting. Finally, we also triangulated administrative and survey data on students' demographic characteristics and found high consistency between the administrative records and students' self-reports, such as sex (99.5% consistency) and age (99.6% consistency).

Trustworthiness and Credibility of Qualitative Data and Findings

We resorted to several approaches to ensure trustworthiness of our qualitative findings. First, because multiple researchers were involved in collecting qualitative interviews, especially during the first wave, we initially individually coded about the same quarter of the interview transcripts of the total collected as a way to compare notes on our coding processes. For example, we independently coded one or two interviews and then met to compare the emerging codes, identify inconsistences, and resolve these discrepancies. For consistent codes and discrepant ones alike, but especially for discrepant codes, we unpacked our individual thinking process that led to its identification in hopes of arriving at a more consistent code or definition to achieve reliability. This often meant additional time for reflection as an individual and a team. To illustrate, one researcher would begin coding a grouping of transcripts independently, followed by a second, and then a third researcher. We compiled a document of the codes, along with explanations and interpretations of the codes. We then went back to those transcripts, reviewed all three researchers' codes, met to discuss and agree upon a common set of codes, and proceeded to code additional transcripts using the common codes (and new ones if applicable). We engaged in this process again to clarify, adjust, and develop codes and coding schemes as needed. This iterative process allowed us to establish interrater reliability in both the codes and the coding schemes used between multiple researchers.

Furthermore, multiple data sources enhanced the trustworthiness of interview data. For instance, since all of the interviewees completed one or more rounds of the survey, we were able to refer back to participants' survey responses to cross-check what participants told us during the interviews. This included common elements or themes around students' perceptions or experiences in both the surveys and interviews. To illustrate, if a student talked about themselves as not being good at math or science, we went back to the relevant survey items, specifically those measuring math or science self-efficacy, to determine whether the individual reported a low score on those items. We noted any alignments or lack thereof. These steps were performed in a similar fashion in other areas that intersected across the surveys and interviews, including learning experiences, attitudes toward math and science, and other college/transfer experiences and services. I recognize that it is nearly impossible to gauge the alignment between the interviews and surveys with complete accuracy, given that both are reasonably subjective and self-reported in nature. However, as a whole, there was a clear alignment between the two data sources. As such, this triangulation approach added to the trustworthiness of the interview data.

Also, as a research team, we constantly reflected to keep our presuppositions and potential biases in check. For example, throughout the research process, we wrote memos to detail and record our engagement with the data, allowing us to disclose and negotiate previously held assumptions and biases. This helped us to withdraw from making potential conclusions about the data based on those assumptions and biases. To take note of our positionality and ensure accuracy within our interview data, we engaged in multiple rounds of coding and triangulation, using the previously mentioned coding techniques to enhance our interrater reliability and address preconceived or biased impressions of these students that might not be accurate. We also participated in reflexive debriefing sessions as an additional venue to discuss our memos, consult with one another regarding our potential assumptions and biases, and develop a shared process to document these observations and perceptions. As a whole, by conducting these procedures, we made a constant and robust effort to reflect on the analysis and emergent findings, as well as minimize bias.

Finally, during each of the interviews, without disrupting the flow, we tried to confirm what participants shared with us, especially significant events or thoughts, with our brief interpretations to ensure the accuracy of the meanings we were making in capturing their experiences or words. In some cases, participants corrected our interpretation or clarified what they meant.

Quality of Mixed Methods Meta-Inference

As the project is situated within the family of sequential mixed designs with a highly interactive and iterative feature, the quality of the meta-inferences was secured through the following procedures. To begin, I utilized Ivankova's three strategies to specifically assess a sequential Quan → Qual mixed methods design: "applying a systematic procedure for selecting participants for qualitative follow-up, elaborating on unexpected quantitative results, and observing interaction between qualitative and quantitative study strands."[16]

With regard to selecting participants for qualitative interviews, we identified students across a wide range of backgrounds, fully utilizing what was available in the quantitative data sources, including survey data and administrative records. Using these quantitative sources, we examined students' STEM disciplines, their institutions, their learning experiences, motivational attributes, and transfer-oriented interactions in order to achieve a robust, diverse sample. Through this systematic approach, we ensured that participants in both surveys and interviews originated from the same sample pool, avoiding divergence and inconsistencies in the inferences due to unsystematic sampling approaches that would contaminate a mixed methods design.

As for seeking explanation for unexpected or surprising quantitative findings, we constantly examined our survey and administrative data to identify any inconsistencies or extreme data. We also interrogated the emerging quantitative results by contextualizing them within our presumptions, existing theory, and state of knowledge in the field to identify unexpected patterns. When such surprising patterns were present, we looked into our qualitative data to seek further understanding, and in some cases, these unexpected quantitative findings led to new interview questions in subsequent interviews. For example, our survey analysis indicated that students' transfer self-efficacy was positively correlated with their active learning experiences. However, active learning experiences had an inverse relationship with students' transfer intent. This contradictory set of patterns prompted us to look further into student learning experiences shared during the interviews. Through these interviews, we found that active learning experiences were often concentrated within nontransferable courses, thus revealing why there continues to be a constant exodus of students from the transfer path. The interview findings supported the urgent need to expand active learning approaches to STEM transferable courses to keep students interested in and progressing in STEM areas of study toward and beyond transfer.

Finally, as I discussed earlier, although there was an assumed linearity or sequence in our mixed methods design, especially in terms of data collection, our research was interactive and iterative, which inherently aided our efforts to ensure meta-inference quality through closely observing the interaction between the two strands. For example, the interview data revealed that, during their first year of study at the two-year colleges, a number of students had interacted with faculty and advisors from a four-year campus, and this experience appeared to build their confidence to transfer. This qualitative finding was highly policy relevant albeit not statistically generalizable. It revealed the need for us to tap into our large sample size survey data to execute additional quantitative analyses to confirm or disconfirm this emergent qualitative finding. As a result, we conducted a quantitative study on the influence of early exposure to four-year faculty and advisors on upward transfer among two-year college students. Using propensity score matching and logistic regression on the matched sample, the results reinforced the positive impact of this early exposure on transfer students' longer-term transfer outcomes. Also, the alarming number of students who revealed their learning disabilities during our interviews prompted several new survey items in our subsequent quantitative data collection during the second and final waves, and led us to examine our interview data to glean additional insight into this issue.

Conversely, observations from our quantitative analysis often served to generate additional and future qualitative data collection and analyses. For example, our survey findings revealed that students of color with more support were less likely to transfer or have intent to transfer, and women with more transfer service usage were less likely to transfer or have intent to transfer. Although these students may have more support or use certain services more, the end result was surprising and worrying, as one would hope and assume these would have a positive impact on transfer and transfer intent. These troubling findings only led to more questions. In our follow-up interviews, we added specific questions about racial, gender, and other significant identities and their influences on students' experiences in STEM at their institutions to help enhance further understanding of the quantitative findings. Through these procedures, for the research program as a whole and the findings reported in this book, we were able to provide various validity checks to arrive at quality meta-inferences.

RESEARCHER REFLEXIVITY

Reflection is not a static hallmark of conducting research responsibly and ethically. Rather it is a prominent ongoing process that threads throughout the journey of inquiry. It was with this spirit and through this process of reflexivity that I came to an increasingly fuller understanding of my positionality as a researcher who had initiated and grown with this longitudinal project. In the preface, I shared how I became involved in transfer research and my assumptions about transfer. In my time as a doctoral student at Ohio State, an institution that accepts and serves many community college transfer students, I was deeply involved with research and assessment projects focusing on or involving transfer students. This led me to cultivate a longtime passion for conducting research on community college transfer with hopes to illuminate and eventually remove barriers to transfer. In conducting this longitudinal study, not only was I responsible for all facets of the project design and execution, I also personally interacted with and collected interview data from my research participants. For these interactions, I constantly reminded myself of where I was situated socially in terms of power and positionality relative to the student I was interviewing. Building rapport with my participants was vital to us, and it took a varying amount of time depending on the students I interviewed. This process reflected the outcome of the complex interplay at work between my own and my interviewees' identities, including but not limited to race, gender, age, and social status. For some students, such as Jordan, the initial interview was shorter, likely attributed to the vast differences in our backgrounds, especially as perceived by Jordan, as he was obviously reserved and a little guarded. In other cases, such as Katy's, we connected much more quickly, likely due to our shared gender identity and smaller age difference. Across all interviews, though, the dynamic I was most acutely mindful of was the power associated with my being a university professor and my interviewees being students who often revered the name of my institution. I tried to minimize the influence of this power dynamic by fully explaining why I was doing this work and all their rights and matters of confidentiality, along with being an open and intent listener, letting their voices and insights direct the conversation to the extent they were comfortable. Looking back, when appropriate, I briefly shared bits and pieces of myself and my reactions to infuse humanity into the conversation. However, this was never done in a planned or practiced way, but rather in situations where such a reciprocal exchange was an inevitable ingredient to an authentic conversation between two human beings. For example, I voiced my genuine congratulations when my participants shared highlights or milestones of their education or career since the last interview. I briefly revealed similar personal struggles when a participant broke down in tears when talking about her mental health issues and couldn't carry on. Yet, I constantly reminded myself that it was always about them and gave my best efforts to make the interview an open, safe space. At the end of the day, I strove to be the authentic and empathetic person and listener that I wish to be every day.

The students I followed throughout the study were appreciably more at ease during our later interviews and the rapport that I had with them grew over the course of the study, evidenced by basic measures such as the increasing length of the interviews with the same person over time, and more complex indicators such as greater richness and depth of the conversations. Many students asked questions about the inner workings of this research program and some have requested and commented on the research articles we published over the course of the project. Some students stayed in touch via email with occasional questions. A particular occurrence to highlight, as it pertains to the heart of this work, is that in almost all interviews, students asked me about how to transfer, likely due to the research topic and my position as a professor at a four-year institution, occasionally during the interview process but most often afterwards. When this happened, I stayed as long as possible and discussed with the students their options based on what I knew, and invited them to follow up anytime via my email or phone contact. But despite my best attempts to address questions or be of help, I left these off-record, transfer-centered conversations with mixed feelings. As in the past, present, and perpetually into the future, I was, am, and will always be in awe of community college students' drive and resilience. At the same time, I left with a somewhat haunted feeling that my answers and offer to help were nowhere even close to getting them through the numerous systemic barriers imposed on their hopes and dreams. This became especially true in follow-up interviews when I was increasingly making sense of the cumulative body of our research.

During this process, in addition to field notes for each interview, I also kept a reflection journal especially about how I may have developed or changed in my understanding as the study unfolded. This reflective process also occurred formally and informally among my team members, especially those engaging with qualitative data collection and analysis, but also including quantitative researchers. Reflecting together with my team members, who hold different lenses and identities, helped us all raise our awareness of elements and dynamics in students' stories that may have escaped our own sense making. Thus, the quality of our interpretations are not dictated by a specific design's "rigor," but rather by how they are richly informed by and connected back to data.

Carrying out this research has been a deeply personal, introspective, and yet collective journey, a journey that has empowered me to embrace my identity as a mixed methods researcher who is committed to research that informs policy making across all levels and practice on the ground.

APPENDIX

B

Annotation for Data Sources

QUOTES AND COMMENTS from study participants are followed by a code denoting the data source from which the statements were taken. These codes are used throughout the chapters:

INTERVIEW	SURVEY
I1 = First Wave Interview	S1 = First Wave Survey
I2 = Second Wave Interview	S2 = Second Wave Survey
I3 = Third Wave Interview	S3 = Third Wave Survey

NOTES

PREFACE

1. Throughout the book I use several different terms to describe postsecondary institutions, particularly those of my focus, community colleges or two-year institutions. It is important to acknowledge that these terms are at best imperfect ways to capture how these institutions strive to meet multiple missions and serve diverse students. On a similar note, the "two-year" or "four-year" designation itself is a misnomer, as students enrolled for associate's and baccalaureate degrees within postsecondary institutions may complete these degrees in more or less time depending on their personal needs, experiences, and contexts. While these descriptors do not fully represent the institutions or, by extension, the students they serve, given the lack of precisely appropriate alternatives, I have to settle for less than perfect terms and simply note these shortcomings in order to move forward.
2. Estimates based on the author's analysis of self-reported degree goals among first-time beginning community college students, using data from the Beginning Postsecondary Students Longitudinal Study (BPS). Degree goals were estimated for the BPS: 96/01, BPS: 04/09, and BPS: 12/17 studies. Six-year baccalaureate attainment and transfer rates were estimated for the BPS: 96/01 and BPS: 04/09 studies, as six-year attainment and transfer data are not yet available for the BPS: 12/17 study.
3. Tatiana Melguizo, Gregory Kienzl, and Mariana Alfonso, "Comparing the Educational Attainment of Community College Transfer Students and Four-Year College Rising Juniors Using Propensity Score Matching Methods," *Journal of Higher Education* 82, no. 3 (2011): 265–91; Di Xu et al., "Are Community College Transfer Students 'A Good Bet' for 4-Year Admissions? Comparing Academic and Labor-Market Outcomes Between Transfer and Native 4-Year College Students," *Journal of Higher Education* 89, no. 4 (2018): 478–502.
4. To maintain the confidentiality promised to study participants, study sample and subsample sizes were rounded to the nearest five or ten as appropriate. This approach prevents the use of multiple data tables and sources, including qualitative data, to identify students. See the methodological appendix for more details about measures to protect participants' identity and information.

INTRODUCTION

1. All institutions' and students' names are pseudonyms. See the methodological appendix for details on measures taken to ensure confidentiality of study participants.
2. The average family income reported by Jordan across three waves of the longitudinal survey was within the $30,000–$59,999 range.
3. Arthur Cohen, Florence Brawer, and Carrie Kisker, *The American Community College*, 6th ed. (San Francisco: Jossey-Bass, 2014). In Jordan's school, this guaranteed transfer program allows students to begin as a freshman at the two-year campus and be guaranteed admission with junior status to any of the public four-year institutions in the state. Digging into the fine print, students need to submit a "Declaration of Intent" form before earning thirty credits at the two-year college. Also, students must keep up a 2.0 grade point average (with the exception of Capital University, which requires a minimum of 2.8) and obtain the number of credits required by the four-year college of their choice.
4. As noted in Appendix B, data source annotations are provided for all study participant quotes or comments: I1, I2, and I3 for the first, second, and third wave interviews; S1, S2, and S3 for the first, second, and third wave surveys.
5. Terrence E. Murphy et al., "College Graduation Rates for Minority Students in a Selective Technical University," *Educational Evaluation and Policy Analysis* 32, no. 1 (2010): 70–83. Summer programs are intended to serve as a bridge between high school and college and equip students with the knowledge and skills in the social, academic, and professional domains. Typically lasting a few weeks, summer programs often entail an introduction to college skills, mentoring, and intensive academic activities such as short courses, field trips, and sometimes research projects.
6. Doug Shapiro et al., *Transfer and Mobility: A National View of Student Movement in Postsecondary Institutions, Fall 2011 Cohort* (Herndon: National Student Clearinghouse Research Center, 2018).
7. Lyle McKinney and Andrea Burridge, "Helping or Hindering? The Effects of Loans on Community College Student Persistence," *Research in Higher Education* 56, no. 4 (2015): 299–324.
8. Lorelle Espinosa, "Pipelines and Pathways: Women of Color in Undergraduate STEM Majors and the College Experiences That Contribute to Persistence," *Harvard Educational Review* 81, no. 2 (2011): 209–41; Frankie Santos Laanan, Soko S. Starobin, and Latrice E. Eggleston, "Adjustment of Community College Students at a Four-Year University: Role and Relevance of Transfer Student Capital for Student Retention," *Journal of College Student Retention: Research, Theory & Practice* 12, no. 2 (2010): 175–209.
9. Dimpal Jain et al., "Critical Race Theory and the Transfer Function: Introducing a Transfer Receptive Culture," *Community College Journal of Research and Practice* 35, no. 3 (2011): 252–66.

10. Linda Serra Hagedorn and Daniel DuBray, "Math and Science Success and Nonsuccess: Journeys Within the Community College," *Journal of Women and Minorities in Science and Engineering* 16, no. 1 (2010): 31–50.
11. National Academy of Sciences, National Academy of Engineering, and Institute of Medicine, *Rising Above the Gathering Storm: Energizing and Employing America for a Brighter Economic Future* (Washington, DC: National Academies Press, 2007), 3.
12. National Academy of Sciences, National Academy of Engineering, and Institute of Medicine, *Rising Above the Gathering Storm, Revisited: Rapidly Approaching Category 5* (Washington, DC: National Academies Press, 2010).
13. National Academy of Sciences, National Academy of Engineering, and Institute of Medicine, *Rising Above the Gathering Storm*, 163.
14. American Association of Community Colleges, *Fast Facts* (Washington, DC: American Association of Community Colleges, 2018).
15. Xueli Wang, "Community Colleges and Underrepresented Racial and Ethnic Minorities in STEM Education: A National Picture," in *Community Colleges and STEM: Examining Underrepresented Racial and Ethnic Minorities*, ed. Robert T. Palmer and J. Luke Wood (New York: Routledge, 2013), 23–36.
16. Tatiana Melguizo, Gregory Kienzl, and Mariana Alfonso, "Comparing the Educational Attainment of Community College Transfer Students and Four-Year College Rising Juniors Using Propensity Score Matching Methods," *Journal of Higher Education* 82, no. 3 (2011): 265–91; Di Xu et al., "Are Community College Transfer Students 'A Good Bet' for 4-Year Admissions? Comparing Academic and Labor-Market Outcomes Between Transfer and Native 4-Year College Students," *Journal of Higher Education* 89, no. 4 (2018): 478–502.
17. Wang, "Community Colleges and Underrepresented Racial and Ethnic Minorities in STEM Education."
18. President's Council of Advisors on Science and Technology, *Engage to Excel: Producing One Million Additional College Graduates with Degrees in Science, Technology, Engineering, and Mathematics* (Washington, DC: President's Council of Advisors on Science and Technology, 2012), 34.
19. The Center for Women in Technology, "T-SITE Scholars," https://cwit.umbc.edu/tsite/. The Transfer Scholars in Information Technology and Engineering (T-SITE) program at University of Maryland Baltimore County, supported by the National Science Foundation, provides transfer students in information technology and engineering fields with scholarships that can be awarded over multiple years. National Science Foundation, "NSF Scholarships in Science, Technology, Engineering, and Mathematics (S-STEM)," https://www.nsf.gov/funding/pgm_summ.jsp?pims_id=5257. Also, the Scholarships in Science, Technology, Engineering, and Mathematics Program (S-STEM) is an example of a national initiative by the National Science Foundation that encourages partnerships among institutions (including two- and four-year) and offers

scholarships to low-income academically talented students with demonstrated financial need studying STEM.
20. Becky Wai-Ling Packard, "Effective Outreach, Recruitment, and Mentoring into STEM Pathways: Strengthening Partnerships with Community Colleges," in *Community Colleges in the Evolving STEM Education Landscape: Summary of a Summit*, ed. Steve Olson and Jay B. Labov (Washington, DC: National Academies Press, 2012), 57–80; Becky Wai-Ling Packard et al., "Women's Experiences in the STEM Community College Transfer Pathway," *Journal of Women and Minorities in Science and Engineering* 17, no. 2 (2011): 57–61.
21. To account for the various ways in which educational intent is referenced in everyday language, we included the following items to gauge students' transfer intent: "At this point, do you intend to transfer from your current college to a four-year college or university?" ("Yes" as the response option to indicate intent); "What is your primary goal in attending this college?" ("Transfer to a four-year college or university" as the response option indicating transfer intent); "What is the highest credential you plan to obtain?" ("Bachelor's" and response options above "Bachelor's" as indicating transfer intent). Ultimately, we conducted quantitative analyses restricted to the transfer-intending students using the first two definitions, and the findings and patterns were essentially the same. For reporting consistency, in this book I present results pertaining to transfer-intending students based on those who reported "yes" to the question, "At this point, do you intend to transfer from your current college to a four-year college or university?" given this question's greater specificity.
22. National Science Board, *Revisiting the STEM Workforce: A Companion to the Science and Engineering Indicators 2014* (Alexandria: National Science Foundation, 2015).
23. ACT, *The Condition of STEM 2014*, http://www.act.org/content/dam/act/unsecured/documents/National-STEM-Report-2014.pdf.
24. National Science Board, *Revisiting the STEM Workforce*.
25. Definitional details of STEM are offered in the methodological appendix.
26. The inclusion of these three different institutions allowed us to examine our quantitative and qualitative findings across institutional settings both analytically and substantively. Refer to the methodological appendix for a more detailed discussion on this.
27. Estimates are based on the first wave of the longitudinal survey using the survey item, "At this point, do you intend to transfer from your current college to a four-year college or university?" Weighted percentage is roughly the same.
28. Michelle Van Noy and Matthew Zeidenberg, "Community College Pathways to the STEM Workforce: What Are They, Who Follows Them, and How?" *New Directions for Community Colleges 2017*, no. 178 (2017): 9–21.
29. Daniel Kuehn and Diane Auer Jones, *Sub-Baccalaureate STEM Education and Apprenticeship* (Washington, DC: Urban Institute, 2018).

30. Table A1 in Appendix A offers additional details of the study sample by participating institutions.

CHAPTER 1

1. Elaine Seymour and Nancy M. Hewitt, *Talking About Leaving: Why Undergraduates Leave the Sciences* (Boulder, CO: Westview Press, 2000), 394.
2. National Academy of Sciences, National Academy of Engineering, and Institute of Medicine, *Rising Above the Gathering Storm: Energizing and Employing America for a Brighter Economic Future* (Washington, DC: National Academies Press, 2007); United States Department of Education, *STEM 2026: A Vision for Innovation in STEM Education* (Washington, DC: United States Department of Education, 2016.)
3. Anne-Barrie Hunter et al., "*Talking About Leaving* Revisited—A Multi-component Research Study Exploring Factors Influencing Undergraduate Switching from STEM Majors: Preliminary Findings from the Persistence Study," https://www.aplu.org/projects-and-initiatives/stem-education/science-and-mathematics-teaching-imperative/smti-conferences-meetings/SMTI%202016%20National%20Conference/Hunter-Poster.pdf.
4. Michelle Van Noy and Matthew Zeidenberg, "Community College Pathways to the STEM Workforce: What Are They, Who Follows Them, and How?" *New Directions for Community Colleges 2017*, no. 178 (2017): 9-21.
5. Xueli Wang, Ning Sun, and Kelly Wickersham, "Turning Math Remediation into 'Homeroom': Contextualization as a Motivational Environment for Community College Students in Remedial Math," *Review of Higher Education* 40, no. 3 (2017): 427–64.
6. Debra D. Bragg, "Two-Year College Mathematics and Student Progression in STEM Programs of Study," in *Community Colleges in the Evolving STEM Education Landscape: Summary of a Summit*, ed. Steve Olson and Jay B. Labov (Washington, DC: National Academies Press, 2012), 81–105.
7. Elvira Abrica, "'Thank God I'm Mexican': Cognitive Racial Reappraisal Strategies of Latino Engineering Students" (PhD diss., University of California, Los Angeles, 2015); Erin E. Doran and Anupma Singh, "'It's All About the Ganas': Incorporating a Multicultural Curriculum in Developmental Education," *Community College Journal of Research and Practice* 42, no. 7-8 (2018): 476–88.
8. Anthony S. Bryk and Uri Treisman, "Make Math a Gateway, Not a Gatekeeper," *Chronicle of Higher Education*, April 18, 2010.
9. Debra D. Bragg, "Examining Pathways to and Through the Community College for Youth and Adults," in *Higher Education: Handbook of Theory and Research*, vol. 26, ed. John C. Smart and Michael B. Paulsen (Dordrecht: Springer, 2011), 355–93.
10. Xianglei Chen, *Remedial Coursetaking at US Public 2- and 4-Year Institutions: Scope, Experiences, and Outcomes* (Washington, DC: National Center for Education Statistics, 2016).

11. Our base year descriptive survey data indicated that 75.2 percent of students thought that it was "very" or "extremely" important to know math to succeed at college, and 87.7 percent thought that they would at least "somewhat" need math for their future career.
12. Valerie Lundy-Wagner, "Developmental Mathematics and the Community College STEM Pipeline" (paper presented at the American Society for Engineering Education Conference, Indianapolis, IN, June 2014).
13. Clifford Adelman, *The Toolbox Revisited: Paths to Degree Completion from High School Through College* (Washington, DC: United States Department of Education, 2006); Gloria Crisp, Amaury Nora, and Amanda Taggart, "Student Characteristics, Pre-College, College, and Environmental Factors as Predictors of Majoring in and Earning a STEM Degree: An Analysis of Students Attending a Hispanic Serving Institution," *American Educational Research Journal* 46, no. 4 (2009): 924–42; Will Tyson et al., "Science, Technology, Engineering, and Mathematics (STEM) Pathways: High School Science and Math Coursework and Postsecondary Degree Attainment," *Journal of Education for Students Placed at Risk* 12, no. 3 (2007): 243–70; Xueli Wang, "Why Students Choose STEM Majors: Motivation, High School Learning, and Postsecondary Context of Support," *American Educational Research Journal* 50, no. 5 (2013): 1081–1121. Higher college admissions test math scores, high school grade point average, and the level of math and science courses taken in high school would be expected to enhance expectations of success and lessen the chances of having academic difficulties in college STEM courses.
14. Charles C. Bonwell and James A. Eison, *Active Learning: Creating Excitement in the Classroom* (Washington, DC: George Washington University, 1991); Noel Capon and Deanna Kuhn, "What's So Good About Problem-Based Learning?" *Cognition and Instruction* 22, no. 1 (2004): 61–79; Katelyn M. Cooper, Virginia R. Downing, and Sara E. Brownell, "The Influence of Active Learning Practices on Student Anxiety in Large-Enrollment College Science Classrooms," *International Journal of STEM Education* 5, no. 23 (2018): 1–18; Christopher Justice et al., "Inquiry-Based Learning in Higher Education: Administrators' Perspectives on Integrating Inquiry Pedagogy into the Curriculum," *Higher Education* 58, no. 6 (2009): 841–55. To truly engage students intellectually, active learning involves higher-order thinking activities, such as analysis, synthesis, evaluation, and problem solving. A variety of techniques can be used to carry out active learning in classrooms, such as group discussion and peer instruction, problem-based learning, inquiry-based learning, and cooperative learning. Although there are unquestionable differences in these practices, they all center on the idea of actively involving students and placing them at the center of their learning process.
15. President's Council of Advisors on Science and Technology, *Engage to Excel: Producing One Million Additional College Graduates with Degrees in Science,*

Technology, Engineering, and Mathematics (Washington, DC: President's Council of Advisors on Science and Technology, 2012).
16. Scott Freeman et al., "Active Learning Increases Student Performance in Science, Engineering, and Mathematics," *Proceedings of the National Academy of Sciences* 111, no. 23 (2014): 8410–15.
17. Dolores Perin, "Facilitating Student Learning Through Contextualization: A Review of Evidence," *Community College Review* 39, no. 3 (2011): 268–95.
18. Wang, Sun, and Wickersham, "Turning Math Remediation into 'Homeroom.'"
19. Xueli Wang et al., "Does Active Learning Contribute to Transfer Intent Among 2-Year College Students Beginning in STEM?" *Journal of Higher Education* 88, no. 4 (2017): 593–618. To answer this question, we conducted a path analysis using the first wave of survey data to explore the relationship between active learning, transfer self-efficacy, and intent to transfer. We measured active learning using a mean scale of fifteen observed survey items that gauged the extent to which students engaged in various active learning activities in their STEM courses. Transfer self-efficacy was the mediating variable based on a single survey item measuring students' confidence about their ability to handle the process and requirements for transfer. Transfer intent was the dependent, multicategory variable with three outcome scenarios: intent to transfer in STEM, intent to transfer in non-STEM, and no transfer intent. We adjusted for a set of student characteristics and postsecondary contextual factors. The full list of variables includes students' gender, race/ethnicity, and age; their initial goal of attending the current two-year college; the financial and emotional support they received from family and peers; their childcare obligations and employment situation; the type of institution they were currently attending; whether they enrolled as a part-time student; and the number of courses completed during their first semester of study.
20. Hsun-yu Chan and Xueli Wang, "Interact for What? The Relationship Between Interpersonal Interaction Based on Motivation and Educational Outcomes Among Students in Manufacturing Programs at Two-Year Technical Colleges," *Community College Review* 44, no. 1 (2016): 26–48.

CHAPTER 2

1. Elizabeth M. Cox and Larry H. Ebbers, "Exploring the Persistence of Adult Women at a Midwest Community College," *Community College Journal of Research and Practice* 34, no. 4 (2010): 337–59; Virginia Montero-Hernandez and Christine Cerven, "Adult Student Development: The Socio-Agentic Approach and Its Relationship to the Community College Context," in *Understanding Community Colleges*, ed. John Levin and Susan Kater (New York: Routledge, 2018), 109–34; John Levin, *Nontraditional Students and Community Colleges* (New York: Palgrave Macmillan, 2014).

2. Rebecca D. Cox, "'I Would Have Rather Paid for a Class I Wanted to Take': Utilitarian Approaches at a Community College," *Review of Higher Education* 32, no. 3 (2009): 353–82.
3. Descriptive estimates based on first and final waves of the survey.
4. The Campaign for College Opportunity, *The Transfer Maze: The High Cost to Students and the State of California* (Los Angeles: Campaign for College Opportunity, 2017).
5. Stephen J. Handel and Ronald A. Williams, *The Promise of the Transfer Pathway: Opportunity and Challenge for Community College Students Seeking the Baccalaureate Degree* (New York: College Board, 2012).
6. Xueli Wang, "Course-Taking Patterns of Community College Students Beginning in STEM: Using Data Mining Techniques to Reveal Viable STEM Transfer Pathways," *Research in Higher Education* 57, no. 5 (2016): 544–69.
7. Arthur Cohen, Florence Brawer, and Carrie Kisker, *The American Community College*, 6th ed. (San Francisco: Jossey-Bass, 2014); Peter Riley Bahr et al., "Unrealized Potential: Community College Pathways to STEM Baccalaureate Degrees," *Journal of Higher Education* 88, no. 3 (2017): 430–78.
8. Valerie J. Morganson et al., "Using Embeddedness Theory to Understand and Promote Persistence in STEM Majors," *Career Development Quarterly* 63, no. 4 (2015): 348–62.
9. Anthony P. Carnevale, Ban Cheah, and Andrew R. Hanson, *The Economic Value of College Majors* (Washington, DC: Center on Education and the Workforce, Georgetown University, 2016); Alyssa N. Bryant, "ERIC Review: Community College Students Recent Findings and Trends," *Community College Review* 29, no. 3 (2001): 77–93.
10. Linda Banks-Santilli, "Guilt Is One of the Biggest Struggles First-Generation College Students Face," *Washington Post*, June 3, 2015.
11. Thomas R. Bailey, Shanna Smith Jaggars, and Davis Jenkins, *Redesigning America's Community Colleges* (Cambridge: Harvard University Press, 2015).
12. Center for Community College Student Engagement, *Show Me the Way: The Power of Advising in Community Colleges* (Austin, TX: University of Texas at Austin, College of Education, 2018); Thomas J. Kerr, Margaret C. King, and Thomas Joseph Grites, eds., *Advising Transfer Students: Issues and Strategies* (New York: National Academic Advising Association, 2004).
13. Judith Scott-Clayton, "The Shapeless River: Does a Lack of Structure Inhibit Students' Progress at Community Colleges?" (CCRC Working Paper No. 25, Community College Research Center, New York, NY, 2011), https://ccrc.tc.columbia.edu/media/k2/attachments/shapeless-river.pdf.
14. The Campaign for College Opportunity, *The Transfer Maze*.
15. Richard Kahlenberg et al., *Policy Strategies for Pursuing Adequate Funding of Community Colleges* (Washington, DC: Century Foundation, 2018).
16. Analysis was based on student responses to the following item on the first

wave of the longitudinal survey: How often do you contact each of the following individuals to discuss matters related to transfer to a four-year college or university? The item was repeated for four groups of individuals: instructors, student peers, academic advisors or counselors, and family members or friends. Response options included never, rarely, sometimes, often, and very often. Student response percentages were cross tabulated by groups of individuals and by the four momentum trajectories.

CHAPTER 3

1. Christianne Corbett and Catherine Hill, *Solving the Equation: The Variables for Women's Success in Engineering and Computing* (Washington, DC: American Association of University Women, 2015); Catherine Hill, Christianne Corbett, and Andresse St. Rose, *Why So Few? Women in Science, Technology, Engineering, and Mathematics* (Washington DC: American Association of University Women, 2010); National Girls Collaborative Project, *The State of Girls and Women in STEM* (Seattle, WA: National Girls Collaborative Project, 2018).
2. Hill, Corbett, and Rose, *Why So Few?*
3. Xianglei Chen, *STEM Attrition: College Students' Paths into and out of STEM Fields* (Washington, DC: National Center for Education Statistics, 2013).
4. Hill, Corbett, and Rose, *Why So Few?*
5. National Science Board, *Science and Engineering Indicators 2018* (Alexandria, VA: National Science Foundation, 2018).
6. Jackson, Dimitra Lynette Jackson and Frankie Santos Laanan, "The Role of Community Colleges in Educating Women in Science and Engineering," *New Directions for Institutional Research* 2011, no. 152 (2011): 39–49; Becky Wai-Ling Packard et al., "Women's Experiences in the STEM Community College Transfer Pathway," *Journal of Women and Minorities in Science and Engineering* 17, no. 2 (2011): 57–61; Soko S. Starobin and Frankie Santos Laanan, "Broadening Female Participation in Science, Technology, Engineering, and Mathematics: Experiences at Community Colleges," *New Directions for Community Colleges* 2008, no. 142 (2008): 37–46.
7. We analyzed integrated survey and administrative data among students who completed the first and second wave of the survey. Students who indicated intent to transfer in STEM from the first wave of the survey and maintained this intent as indicated in the follow-up survey, or who had already transferred upward into STEM areas of study, were defined as maintaining their aspirational momentum. Information on students' transfer service usage, transfer-oriented interactions, support received for transfer, and transfer information acquisition was collected in the first wave, each factor measured using multiple survey items. We used a logistic regression model to explore the relationship between these factors and aspirational momentum for transfer in STEM. Then, we added interaction terms between each key independent variable and

gender as well as with race/ethnicity to explore any variation based on gender and race/ethnicity. We found gender differences in the relationship between transfer service usage and aspirational momentum. Male students were more likely to have aspirational momentum as they used transfer services more frequently. In contrast, the likelihood that female students would have aspirational momentum was negatively associated with their transfer service usage. We also discovered racial differences, discussed in chapter 4.

8. Xueli Wang et al., "How Do 2-Year College Students Beginning in STEM View Themselves as Learners?" *Teachers College Record* 121, no. 4 (2019): 1–44.

9. Lynn Farrell and Louise McHugh, "Examining Gender-STEM Bias Among STEM and Non-STEM Students Using the Implicit Relational Assessment Procedure (IRAP)," *Journal of Contextual Behavioral Science* 6, no. 1 (2017): 80–90; Corinne A. Moss-Racusin et al., "Science Faculty's Subtle Gender Biases Favor Male Students," *Proceedings of the National Academy of Sciences* 109, no. 41 (2012): 16474–79.

10. Linda L. Carli et al., "Stereotypes About Gender and Science: Women ≠ Scientists," *Psychology of Women Quarterly* 40, no. 2 (2016): 244–60; Jane Margolis and Allan Fisher, *Unlocking the Clubhouse: Women in Computing* (Cambridge: Massachusetts Institute of Technology, 2003).

11. Jennifer LaCosse, Denise Sekaquaptewa, and Jill Bennett, "STEM Stereotypic Attribution Bias Among Women in an Unwelcoming Science Setting," *Psychology of Women Quarterly* 40, no. 3 (2016): 378–97.

12. Sapna Cheryan et al., "Ambient Belonging: How Stereotypical Cues Impact Gender Participation in Computer Science," *Journal of Personality and Social Psychology* 97, no. 6 (2009): 1045; Sapna Cheryan et al., "Do Female and Male Role Models Who Embody STEM Stereotypes Hinder Women's Anticipated Success in STEM?" *Social Psychological and Personality Science* 2, no. 6 (2011): 656–64.

13. Estimates based on the first and final waves of the survey combined with NSC data to account for credential completion and transfer not captured in the survey data.

14. Xiaodan Hu and Justin C. Ortagus, "A National Study of the Influence of the Community College Pathway on Female Students' STEM Baccalaureate Success," *Community College Review* 47, no. 3 (2019): 242–73.

15. Sarah M. Jackson, Amy L. Hillard, and Tamera R. Schneider, "Using Implicit Bias Training to Improve Attitudes Toward Women in STEM," *Social Psychology of Education* 17, no. 3 (2014): 419–38.

16. Packard et al., "Women's Experiences in STEM."

17. Kristie R. Rankin, Stephen G. Katsinas, and David E. Hardy, "Community College Retention and Access Issues: A View from the Field," *Journal of College Student Retention: Research, Theory & Practice* 12, no. 2 (2010): 211–23.

CHAPTER 4

1. Sylvia Hurtado et al., "Enacting Diverse Learning Environments: Educational Policy and Practice," *Review of Higher Education* 21, no. 3 (1998): 279–302; Matthew J. Mayhew, Heidi E. Grunwald, and Eric L. Dey, "Breaking the Silence: Achieving a Positive Campus Climate for Diversity from the Staff Perspective," *Research in Higher Education* 47, no. 1 (2006): 63–88; Gary R. Pike and George D. Kuh, "Relationships Among Structural Diversity, Informal Peer Interactions and Perceptions of the Campus Environment," *Review of Higher Education* 29, no. 4 (2006): 425–50.
2. Eduardo Casillas Arellano, Mónica F. Torres, and Kathryn Valentine, "Interactional Diversity in Border Colleges: Perceptions of Undergraduate Students," *Journal of Hispanic Higher Education* 8, no. 3 (2009): 282–97; Pike and Kuh, "Relationships Among Structural Diversity."
3. Nicholas Bowman, "Structural Diversity and Close Interracial Relationships in College," *Educational Researcher* 41, no. 4 (2012): 133–35.
4. Marie-Elena Reyes, "Unique Challenges for Women of Color in STEM Transferring from Community Colleges to Universities," *Harvard Educational Review* 81, no. 2 (2011): 241–63; Isis H. Settles, "Women in STEM: Challenges and Determinants of Success and Well-Being," *Psychological Science Agenda*, October 2014, 28.
5. Analysis based on the following item repeated across all three waves of the survey, using adjusted weight: "What is the highest credential you plan to obtain from any postsecondary institution?" The percentage of students of color indicating bachelor's degree or higher was similar to or slightly higher than that of white students—81 percent for both students of color and white students based on the first wave survey, 70 percent for students of color and 68 percent for white students based on the second wave survey, and 65 percent for both students of color and white students based on the third wave survey. This pattern held after desegregating by racial and ethnic groups (for example, analyzing Asian students as a separate group).
6. Analysis based on first and third wave of the survey data.
7. We analyzed integrated survey and administrative data among students who completed the first and second wave of the survey. Students who indicated intent to transfer in STEM from the first wave of the survey and maintained this intent as indicated in the follow-up survey, or having already transferred upward into STEM areas of study, were defined as maintaining their aspirational momentum. Information on students' transfer service usage, transfer-oriented interactions, support received for transfer, and transfer information acquisition was collected in the first wave, each factor measured using multiple survey items. We used a logistic regression model to explore the relationship between these factors and aspirational momentum for transfer in STEM.

Then, we added interaction terms between each key independent variable and gender as well as race and ethnicity to explore any variation based on gender and race and ethnicity. We found with more support for transfer, white students were more likely to maintain aspirational momentum, while students of color were less likely to do so.

8. Varaxy Yi and Samuel Museus, "Model Minority Myth," in *The Wiley Blackwell Encyclopedia of Race, Ethnicity, and Nationalism*, ed. John Stone et al. (Hoboken, NJ: John Wiley & Sons, 2016), 1–2. The model minority myth can be traced back to nineteenth-century Chinese immigration to America, followed by Japanese and other Asian groups, and the pressures to conform to American society and perform well at work to counter racist perceptions and sentiments.

9. Samuel Museus and Peter Kiang, "Deconstructing the Model Minority Myth and How It Contributes to the Invisible Minority Reality in Higher Education Research," *New Directions for Institutional Research* 2009, no. 142 (2009): 5–15; OiYan Poon et al., "A Critical Review of the Model Minority Myth in Selected Literature on Asian Americans and Pacific Islanders in Higher Education," *Review of Educational Research* 86, no. 2 (2016): 469–502.

10. Museus and Kiang, "Deconstructing the Model Minority Myth."

11. Samuel Museus and Varaxy Yi, "Asian American College Students," in *Today's College Students*, ed. Pietro Sasso and Joseph DeVitis, (New York: Peter Lang Press, 2014), 45–55.

12. OiYan Poon and Ajani Byrd, "Beyond Tiger Mom Anxiety: Ethnic, Gender and Generational Differences in Asian American College Access and Choices," *Journal of College Admission*, 2013, 23–31.

13. This conclusion was based on our analysis of the emotional support scale across racial groups using one-way ANOVA. We used multiple post-hoc tests such as Tukey's honestly significant difference (HSD) test to determine which racial groups differed significantly from one another. Pairwise comparisons showed no statistical differences.

14. Andrew J. Fuligni, "Family Obligation and the Academic Motivation of Adolescents from Asian, Latin American, and European Backgrounds," *New Directions for Child and Adolescent Development* 2001, no. 94 (2001): 61–76; Andrew J. Fuligni, "Family Obligation, College Enrollment, and Emerging Adulthood in Asian and Latin American Families," *Child Development Perspectives* 1, no. 2 (2007): 96–100.

15. Ekeoma E. Uzogara and James S. Jackson, "Perceived Skin Tone Discrimination Across Contexts: African American Women's Reports," *Race and Social Problems* 8, no. 2 (2016): 147–59.

16. Sara Goldrick-Rab et al., *Still Hungry and Homeless in College* (Madison: Wisconsin HOPE Lab, 2018); J. Luke Wood, Frank Harris, and Nexi R. Delgado, *Struggling to Survive, Striving to Succeed: Food and Housing Insecurities in the Community College* (San Diego: Community College Equity Assessment Lab, 2016).

17. Lindsey Malcom-Piqueux and Estela Mara Bensimon, "Taking Equity-Minded Action to Close Equity Gaps," *Peer Review* 19, no. 2 (2017).
18. University of Southern California, Center for Urban Education, *Developing a Practice of Equity Minded Indicators*, https://cue.usc.edu/files/2016/02/Developing-a-Practice-of-Equity-Mindedness.pdf.
19. Becky Wai-Ling Packard and Kimberly C. Jeffers, "Advising and Progress in the Community College STEM Transfer Pathway," *NACADA Journal* 33, no. 2 (2013): 65–76.

CHAPTER 5

1. Christopher Chaves, "Involvement, Development, and Retention: Theoretical Foundations and Potential Extensions for Adult Community College Students," *Community College Review* 34, no. 2 (2006): 139–52; Carol Kasworm, "Adult Student Identity in an Intergenerational Community College Classroom," *Adult Education Quarterly* 56, no. 1 (2005): 3–20; Karen A. Kim, "ERIC Review: Exploring the Meaning of 'Nontraditional' at the Community College," *Community College Review* 30, no. 1 (2002): 74–89.
2. American Association of Community Colleges, *Students with Disabilities* (Washington, DC: American Association of Community Colleges, 2018).
3. Michelle Van Noy and Matthew Zeidenberg, "Community College Pathways to the STEM Workforce: What Are They, Who Follows Them, and How?" *New Directions for Community Colleges* 2017, no. 178 (2017): 9–21.
4. Arthur Cohen, Florence Brawer, and Carrie Kisker, *The American Community College*, 6th ed. (San Francisco: Jossey-Bass, 2014).
5. Rosemary Capps, "Supporting Adult-Student Persistence in Community Colleges," *Change: The Magazine of Higher Learning* 44, no. 2 (2012): 38–44.
6. Analysis based on the following items on the first wave of the longitudinal survey: How often do you interact with the following individuals for academic purposes? Academic advisors. Response options included never, rarely, sometimes, often, and very often.
7. Xueli Wang et al., "Exploring Sources and Influences of Social Capital on Community College Students' First-Year Success: Does Age Make a Difference?" *Teachers College Record* 120, no. 10 (2018): 1–46.
8. Cohen, Brawer, and Kisker, *The American Community College*.
9. Regina Deil-Amen, "Socio-Academic Integrative Moments: Rethinking Academic and Social Integration Among Two-Year College Students in Career-Related Programs," *Journal of Higher Education* 82, no. 1 (2011): 54–91.
10. Robert Weis, Lauryn Sykes, and Devanshi Unadkat, "Qualitative Differences in Learning Disabilities Across Postsecondary Institutions," *Journal of Learning Disabilities* 45, no. 6 (2012): 491–502.
11. American Association of Community Colleges, *Students with Disabilities*.
12. Daniel Seth Katz and Karen Davison, "Community College Student Mental

Health: A Comparative Analysis," *Community College Review* 42, no. 4 (2014): 307–26.
13. Michael M. Gerber, "Globalization, Human Capital, and Learning Disabilities," *Learning Disabilities Research & Practice* 22, no. 3 (2007): 216–17; Noel Gregg, "Underserved and Unprepared: Postsecondary Learning Disabilities," *Learning Disabilities Research & Practice* 22, no. 4 (2007): 219–28; Noel Gregg, *Adolescents and Adults with Learning Disabilities and ADHD: Assessment and Accommodation* (New York: Guilford Press, 2009).
14. Daniel Eisenberg et al., *Too Distressed to Learn? Mental Health Among Community College Students* (Madison: Wisconsin HOPE Lab, 2016).
15. Katz and Davison, "Community College Student Mental Health."
16. United States Department of Labor, *TAACCCT Program Fact Sheet* (Washington, DC: United States Department of Labor, 2018). This grant program is offered by the United States Department of Labor and provides funding to adults to attend community colleges and obtain industry-aligned skills and qualifications toward family-supporting jobs.
17. American College Counseling Association, "Community College Task Force Survey of Community/2 Year College Counseling Services, 2012–13," https://www.insidehighered.com/sites/default/server_files/files/ACCA%20CCTF%202012-2013%20Survey%20FINAL.PDF.
18. Eisenberg et al., *Too Distressed to Learn?*
19. Brett R. Nachman, and Kirsten R. Brown, "Omission and Othering: Constructing Autism on Community College Websites," *Community College Journal of Research and Practice* (2019): 1–13.

CHAPTER 6

1. Burton Clark, "The 'Cooling-Out' Function in Higher Education," *American Journal of Sociology* 65, no. 6 (1960): 569–76.
2. James Edward Rosenbaum, "College-For-All: Do Students Understand What College Demands?" *Social Psychology of Education* 2, no. 1 (1997): 55–80.
3. Jon Marcus, "More High School Grads Than Ever Are Going to College, But 1 in 5 Will Quit," *Hechinger Report*, July 5, 2018; James Edward Rosenbaum, "Institutional Career Structures and the Social Construction of Ability," in *Handbook of Theory and Research for the Sociology of Education*, ed. John Richardson (New York: Greenwood Press, 1986), 139–72.
4. Jill Barshay, "Wasted Time and Money on Undergraduate Classes," *Hechinger Report*, September 4, 2017.
5. Analysis based on first and third waves of the survey data.
6. Christopher J. Matheny, Hsun-yu Chan, and Xueli Wang, "Assembling a Career: Labor Market Outcomes for Manufacturing Program Students in Two-Year Technical Colleges," *Community College Review* 43, no. 4 (2015): 380–406.
7. Matheny, Chan, and Wang.

8. Mina Dadgar and Madeline Joy Trimble, "Labor Market Returns to Sub-Baccalaureate Credentials: How Much Does a Community College Degree or Certificate Pay?" *Educational Evaluation and Policy Analysis* 37, no. 4 (2015): 399–418.
9. For more details regarding this result, see Xueli Wang, Seo Young Lee, and Amy Prevost, "The Role of Aspirational Experiences and Behaviors in Cultivating Momentum for Transfer Access in STEM: Variations Across Gender and Race," *Community College Review* 45, no. 4 (2017): 311–30.
10. For a detailed examination of how students in our project wrestle with competing directions in the next stages of their education within a multitude of contexts, see Kelly Wickersham, "Where to Go from Here? Toward a Model of Two-Year College Students' Postsecondary Pathway Selection," *Community College Review*, (2019): 1-26.

CHAPTER 7

1. While I approached analysis of the project's qualitative data primarily from an interpretative-constructive framework, in this chapter I included an intersectional lens that examined structures of inequity and inequality in response to the emerging findings and patterns. This approach does not deemphasize students' experiences as they viewed them, but rather offers additional interpretations, especially through structural inferences that I made in social and historical contexts. As Bowleg argues, structural inequality at the macro level may not be known or observed by the participants, and in such cases, it is up to the researcher to "make explicit the often implicit experiences of intersectionality." See Lisa Bowleg, "When Black + Lesbian + Woman ≠ Black Lesbian Woman: The Methodological Challenges of Qualitative and Quantitative Intersectionality Research," *Sex Roles* 59, no. 5-6 (2008): 312–25. For more examples where intersectional analysis is used to complement and enrich qualitative inquiry from a different framework, see Elisa S. Abes, "Constructivist and Intersectional Interpretations of a Lesbian College Student's Multiple Social Identities," *Journal of Higher Education* 83, no. 2 (2012): 186–216; and Lisa M. Diamond and Molly Butterworth, "Questioning Gender and Sexual Identity: Dynamic Links Over Time," *Sex Roles* 59, no. 5-6 (2008): 365–76. For a more detailed discussion of the potential and tension around the application of an intersectional perspective, see Antonio Duran and Susan Jones, "Using Intersectionality in Qualitative Research on College Student Identity Development: Considerations, Tensions, and Possibilities," *Journal of College Student Development* 60, no. 4 (2019): 455–71.
2. Gloria Ladson-Billings, "From the Achievement Gap to the Education Debt: Understanding Achievement in US Schools," *Educational Researcher* 35, no. 7 (2006): 3–12.
3. Ladson-Billings.
4. John B. Diamond, Amanda E. Lewis, and Lamont Gordon, "Race and School

Achievement in a Desegregated Suburb: Reconsidering the Oppositional Culture Explanation," *International Journal of Qualitative Studies in Education* 20, no. 6 (2007): 655–79.
5. Diamond, Lewis, and Gordon.
6. Nancy W. Brickhouse, Patricia Lowery, and Katherine Schultz, "What Kind of a Girl Does Science? The Construction of School Science Identities," *Journal of Research in Science Teaching* 37, no. 5 (2000): 441–58; Gayle A. Buck, Diandra Leslie-Pelecky, and Susan K. Kirby, "Bringing Female Scientists into the Elementary Classroom: Confronting the Strength of Elementary Students' Stereotypical Images of Scientists," *Journal of Elementary Science Education* 14, no. 2 (2002): 1–10; David Wade Chambers, "Stereotypic Images of the Scientist: The Draw-A-Scientist Test," *Science Education* 67, no. 2 (1983): 255–65; Jane Bulter Kahle, "From One Minority to Another," in *Perspectives on Gender and Science*, ed. Jan Harding (New York: Falmer Press, 1987), 63–79.
7. Heidi B. Carlone and Angela Johnson, "Understanding the Science Experiences of Successful Women of Color: Science Identity as an Analytic Lens," *Journal of Research in Science Teaching* 44, no. 8 (2007): 1187–1218; Sarah Rodriguez, Kelly Cunningham, and Alec Jordan, "STEM Identity Development for Latinas: The Role of Self-and Outside Recognition," *Journal of Hispanic Higher Education* 18, no. 3 (2019): 254–72; Sarah Rodriguez and Kathleen Lehman, "Developing the Next Generation of Diverse Computer Scientists: The Need for Enhanced, Intersectional Computing Identity Theory," *Computer Science Education* 27, no. 3-4 (2017): 229–47.
8. Carlone and Johnson, "Understanding the Science Experiences."
9. Kimberlé Crenshaw, "Demarginalizing the Intersection of Race and Sex: A Black Feminist Critique of Antidiscrimination Doctrine, Feminist Theory and Antiracist Politics," *University of Chicago Legal Forum* 1989, issue 1 (1989): 139–67.

CHAPTER 8

1. Xueli Wang, "Toward a Holistic Theoretical Model of Momentum for Community College Student Success," in *Higher Education: Handbook of Theory and Research*, vol. 32, ed. Michael B. Paulsen (Cham, Switzerland: Springer, 2017), 259–308.
2. Wang.
3. Thomas R. Bailey, Shanna Smith Jaggars, and Davis Jenkins, *Redesigning America's Community Colleges* (Cambridge: Harvard University Press, 2015).
4. Paul Davis Jenkins et al., *What We Are Learning About Guided Pathways* (New York: Community College Research Center, 2018).
5. Frontier Set. *Working Together for Equitable Student Outcomes: State of the Frontier Set* (Seattle: Bill and Melinda Gates Foundation, 2018).
6. Columbia University, Community College Research Center, "Evaluating the

Potential of Community College Guided Pathways," https://ccrc.tc.columbia.edu/research-project/guided-pathways-undergraduate-stem-success.html.
7. Arthur Cohen, Florence Brawer, and Carrie Kisker, *The American Community College*, 6th ed. (San Francisco: Jossey-Bass, 2014).
8. Christian Geckeler et al., *Helping Community College Students Cope with Financial Emergencies: Lessons from the Dream Keepers and Angel Fund Emergency Financial Aid Programs* (New York: MDRC, 2008).
9. Daniel Collier and Ceceilia Parnther, "Conversing with Kalamazoo Promise Scholars: An Inquiry into the Beliefs, Motivations, and Experiences of Tuition-Free College Students," *Journal of College Student Retention: Research, Theory & Practice* (2018): 1–25; Mary Rauner, Sara Lundquist, and Amelia Smith, *The College Promise Playbook for California and Beyond* (San Francisco: WestEd, 2019).
10. Xueli Wang et al., "The Road to Becoming a Scientist: A Mixed Methods Investigation of Supports and Barriers Experienced by First-Year Community College Students," *Teachers College Record* 122, no. 3 (2020).
11. Stephen J. Handel and Ronald A. Williams, *The Promise of the Transfer Pathway: Opportunity and Challenge for Community College Students Seeking the Baccalaureate Degree* (New York: The College Board, 2012); National Academies of Sciences, Engineering, and Medicine, *Barriers and Opportunities for 2-Year and 4-Year STEM Degrees: Systemic Change to Support Students' Diverse Pathways* (Washington, DC: National Academies Press, 2016).
12. Descriptive analysis based on the survey item repeated across all three waves: "How well do you understand which courses at your college are transferable to a four-year college or university?" Response options were not at all, a little, somewhat, very, and extremely. Percentages were calculated combining "very" and "extremely" among students who indicated intent to transfer in a given wave.
13. Edna Martinez, "'The Rules Change': Exploring Faculty Experiences and Work Expectations Within a Drifting Community College Context," *Community College Review* 47, no. 2 (2019): 111–35.
14. Alicia C. Dowd, "Developing Supportive STEM Community College to Four-Year College and University Transfer Ecosystems," in *Community Colleges in the Evolving STEM Education Landscape: Summary of a Summit*, ed. Steve Olson and Jay B. Labov (Washington, DC: National Academies Press, 2012), 107–34.
15. Pamela L. Eddy and Marilyn J. Amey, *Creating Strategic Partnerships: A Guide for Educational Institutions and Their Partners* (Sterling, VA: Stylus Publishing, 2015).
16. Becky Wai-Ling Packard and Kimberly C. Jeffers, "Advising and Progress in the Community College STEM Transfer Pathway," *NACADA Journal* 33, no. 2 (2013): 65–76.
17. Bailey, Jaggars, and Jenkins, *Redesigning America's Community Colleges*.
18. Linda Serra Hagedorn et al., "Transfer Between Community Colleges and 4-Year Colleges: The All-American Game," *Community College Journal of*

Research and Practice 30, no. 3 (2006): 223–42; Becky Wai-Ling Packard, Janelle L. Gagnon, and Arleen J. Senas, "Avoiding Unnecessary Delays: Women and Men Navigating the Community College Transfer Pathway in Science, Technical, Engineering, and Mathematics Fields," *Community College Journal of Research and Practice* 36, no. 9 (2012): 670–83; Packard and Jeffers, "Advising and Progress."

19. There are no official, publicly available reports on student-advisor ratios at the participating institutions. This ratio was estimated based on published headcounts of students enrolled each year and the number of advisors each year since 2014 and was informed by the working knowledge of college staff via personal communication.

20. Shanna Smith Jaggars and Jeffrey Fletcher, "Redesigning the Student Intake and Information Provision Processes at a Large Comprehensive Community College" (Working Paper No. 72, Community College Research Center, New York, NY, 2014), https://ccrc.tc.columbia.edu/media/k2/attachments/redesigning-student-intake-information-provision-processes.pdf.

21. Kelli A. Bird et al., "Nudging at a National Scale: Experimental Evidence from a FAFSA Completion Campaign" (Working Paper No. 55, EdPolicyWorks, University of Virginia, Charlottesville, VA, 2017), https://curry.virginia.edu/uploads/resourceLibrary/55_Nudging_at_a_National_Scale.pdf.; Benjamin L. Castleman and Lindsay C. Page, "Summer Nudging: Can Personalized Text Messages and Peer Mentor Outreach Increase College Going Among Low-Income High School Graduates?" *Journal of Economic Behavior & Organization* 115 (2015): 144–60.

22. Courtney L. Luedke, "Person First, Student Second: Staff and Administrators of Color Supporting Students of Color Authentically in Higher Education," *Journal of College Student Development* 58, no. 1 (2017): 37–52.

23. American Association of Community Colleges, *Faculty and Staff Diversity* (Washington, DC: American Association of Community Colleges, 2018).

24. Di Xu et al., "Collaboratively Clearing the Path to a Baccalaureate Degree: Identifying Effective 2-to 4-Year College Transfer Partnerships," *Community College Review* 46, no. 3 (2018): 231–56.

CHAPTER 9

1. Sophie Quinton, "'Free College' Is Increasingly Popular—and Complicated for States," *Stateline*, March 5, 2019, https://www.pewtrusts.org/en/research-and-analysis/blogs/stateline/2019/03/05/free-college-is-increasingly-popular-and-complicated-for-states.

2. Doug Shapiro et al., *Transfer and Mobility: A National View of Student Movement in Postsecondary Institutions, Fall 2011 Cohort* (Herndon, VA: National Student Clearinghouse Research Center, 2018).

3. Monica L. Heller and Jerrell C. Cassady, "The Impact of Perceived Barriers, Academic Anxiety, and Resource Management Strategies on Achievement in

First-Year Community College Students," *Journal of the First-Year Experience & Students in Transition* 29, no. 1 (2017): 9–32; Margaret W. Sallee and Rebecca D. Cox, "Thinking Beyond Childcare: Supporting Community College Student-Parents," *American Journal of Education* 125, no. 4 (2019): 621–45.
4. City University of New York, "ASAP at a Glance," http://www1.cuny.edu/sites/asap/about/asap-at-a-glance/.
5. New York State Higher Education Services Corporation, "NYS Part-Time Scholarship (PTS) Award Program," https://www.hesc.ny.gov/pay-for-college/financial-aid/types-of-financial-aid/nys-grants-scholarships-awards/new-york-state-part-time-scholarship-pts-award-program.html; College Foundation of West Virginia, "Higher Education Adult Part-Time Student Grant Program," https://secure.cfwv.com/Financial_Aid_Planning/Scholarships/Scholarships_and_Grants/WV_HEAPS_Grant.aspx. The New York State Part-Time Scholarship Award Program may cover up to six credit hours or $1,500 per academic term for students enrolled at CUNY or SUNY community colleges. However, students may only receive the award for up to four semesters in a row. The grant program in West Virginia allows students to apply for the grant either until their program is complete or nine years from the first year students enroll. However, the grant varies by eligible institutions, along with other application and performance restrictions.
6. Josipa Roksa, "Building Bridges for Student Success: Are Higher Education Articulation Policies Effective?" *Teachers College Record* 111, no. 10 (2009): 2444–78; Gregory Anderson, Jeffrey C. Sun, and Mariana Alfonso, "Effectiveness of Statewide Articulation Agreements on the Probability of Transfer: A Preliminary Policy Analysis," *Review of Higher Education* 29, no. 3 (2006): 261–91.
7. Christopher M. Mullin, *When Less Is More: Prioritizing Open Access* (Washington, DC: American Association of Community Colleges, 2017).
8. Joshua Wyner et al., *The Transfer Playbook: Essential Practices for Two-and Four-Year Colleges* (Washington, DC: Aspen Institute, 2016).
9. Richard C. Richardson Jr., "Faculty in the Transfer and Articulation Process: Silent Partners or Missing Link?" *Community College Review* 21, no. 1 (1993): 41–47.
10. Carrie B. Kisker, "Creating and Sustaining Community College–University Transfer Partnerships," *Community College Review* 34, no. 4 (2007): 282–301.
11. Xueli Wang, "Course-Taking Patterns of Community College Students Beginning in STEM: Using Data Mining Techniques to Reveal Viable STEM Transfer Pathways," *Research in Higher Education* 57, no. 5 (2016): 544–69.
12. Geneva Gay, *Culturally Responsive Teaching: Theory, Research, and Practice* (New York: Teachers College Press, 2018).
13. Gloria Ladson-Billings, "Culturally Relevant Pedagogy 2.0: A.K.A. the Remix," *Harvard Educational Review* 84, no. 1 (2014): 74–84; Gloria Ladson-Billings, *The Dreamkeepers: Successful Teachers of African American Children* (San Francisco:

Jossey-Bass, 2009); Gloria Ladson-Billings, "But That's Just Good Teaching! The Case for Culturally Relevant Pedagogy," *Theory into Practice* 34, no. 3 (1995): 159–65.
14. Ladson-Billings, *The Dreamkeepers*.
15. Heidi B. Carlone and Angela Johnson, "Understanding the Science Experiences of Successful Women of Color: Science Identity as an Analytic Lens," *Journal of Research in Science Teaching* 44, no. 8 (2007): 1187–1218.
16. Carlone and Johnson, "Understanding the Science Experiences"; Sarah Rodriguez, Kelly Cunningham, and Alec Jordan, "STEM Identity Development for Latinas: The Role of Self- and Outside Recognition," *Journal of Hispanic Higher Education* 18, no. 3 (2019): 254–72.
17. Serena Klempin et al., *iPASS in Practice: Four Case Studies* (New York: Community College Research Center, 2019).
18. Kelli A. Bird et al., "Nudging at Scale: Experimental Evidence from FAFSA Completion Campaigns" (NBER Working Paper No. 26158, National Bureau of Economic Research, Cambridge, MA), https://www.nber.org/papers/w26158.pdf.
19. University of Southern California, Center for Urban Education, "Equity Mindedness," https://cue.usc.edu/about/equity/equity-mindedness/.
20. University of Southern California, Center for Urban Education, "Developing a Practice of Equity Minded Indicators," https://cue.usc.edu/files/2016/02/Developing-a-Practice-of-Equity-Mindedness.pdf.
21. University of Illinois at Urbana-Champaign, Office of Community College Research and Leadership, "Office of Community College Research and Leadership," https://occrl.illinois.edu.

APPENDIX A: METHODOLOGICAL NOTES

1. R. Burke Johnson, Anthony J. Onwuegbuzie, and Lisa A. Turner, "Toward a Definition of Mixed Methods Research," *Journal of Mixed Methods Research* 1, no. 2 (2007): 129.
2. David L. Morgan, "Paradigms Lost and Pragmatism Regained: Methodological Implications of Combining Qualitative and Quantitative Methods," *Journal of Mixed Methods Research* 1, no. 1 (2007): 48–76.
3. Abbas Tashakkori and Charles Teddlie, eds., *Sage Handbook of Mixed Methods in Social and Behavioral Research*, 2nd ed. (Thousand Oaks, CA: Sage, 2010).
4. Morgan, "Paradigms Lost and Pragmatism Regained"; Peggy Shannon-Baker, "Making Paradigms Meaningful in Mixed Methods Research," *Journal of Mixed Methods Research* 10, no. 4 (2016): 319–34.
5. Morgan, "Paradigms Lost and Pragmatism Regained."
6. Vicki L. Plano Clark and Nataliya V. Ivankova, *Mixed Methods Research: A Guide to the Field* (Thousand Oaks, CA: Sage, 2016).
7. John W. Creswell and Vicki L. Plano Clark, *Designing and Conducting Mixed Methods Research*, 3rd ed. (Thousand Oaks, CA: Sage, 2018); Charles Teddlie

and Abbas Tashakkori, "Major Issues and Controversies in the Use of Mixed Methods in the Social and Behavioral Sciences," in *Handbook of Mixed Methods in Social and Behavioral Research*, ed. Abbas Tashakkori and Charles Teddlie (Thousand Oaks, CA: Sage, 2003), 3–50; Charles Teddlie and Abbas Tashakkori, "Overview of Contemporary Issues in Mixed Methods Research," in *Sage Handbook of Mixed Methods in Social and Behavioral Research*, ed. Abbas Tashakkori and Charles Teddlie, 2nd ed. (Thousand Oaks, CA: Sage, 2010), 1–51.

8. Creswell and Plano Clark, *Designing and Conducting Mixed Methods Research*; Michael Q. Patton, *Qualitative Evaluation and Research Methods*, 2nd ed. (Thousand Oaks, CA: Sage, 1990).

9. National Science Board, *Science and Engineering Indicators 2012* (Alexandria, VA: National Science Foundation, 2012).

10. Michael Q. Patton, *Qualitative Research and Evaluation Methods*, 3rd ed. (Thousand Oaks, CA: Sage, 2002).

11. See Xueli Wang, "Upward Transfer in STEM Fields of Study: A New Conceptual Framework and Survey Instrument for Institutional Research," *New Directions for Institutional Research* 2017, no. 170 (2017): 49–60 for a substantive discussion of the conceptual framework undergirding the survey.

12. F. Michael Connelly and D. Jean Clandinin, "Stories of Experience and Narrative Inquiry," *Educational Researcher* 19, no. 5 (1990): 2–14.

13. Abbas Tashakkori and Charles Teddlie, "Quality of Inferences in Mixed Methods Research: Calling for an Integrative Framework," in *Advances in Mixed Methods Research: Theories and Applications*, ed. Manfred M. Bergman (London: Sage, 2008), 101.

14. The minimum sample size required for conducting EFA depends on various conditions, such as the number of factors, factor loadings, and communalities. While our pilot sample size was not a large one, given its exploratory nature as a pilot, this was not a major concern, as a sample size of fifty is considered a reasonable absolute minimum. Joost de Winter, Dimitra Dodou, and Peter Wieringa, "Exploratory Factor Analysis with Small Sample Sizes," *Multivariate Behavioral Research* 44, no. 2 (2009): 147–81.

15. Stanley Presser et al., "Methods for Testing and Evaluating Survey Questions," *Public Opinion Quarterly* 68, no. 1 (2004): 109–30; Gordon B. Willis, *Analysis of the Cognitive Interview in Questionnaire Design* (New York: Oxford University Press, 2015).

16. Nataliya V. Ivankova, "Implementing Quality Criteria in Designing and Conducting a Sequential QUAN → QUAL Mixed Methods Study of Student Engagement with Learning Applied Research Methods Online," *Journal of Mixed Methods Research* 8, no. 1 (2014): 41–42.

ACKNOWLEDGMENTS

CONTRARY TO THIS BOOK'S TITLE, I certainly was not on my own in completing this book. While its underlying research took off in the fall of 2014, I owe my intellectual debts long before that, to my graduate school years at Ohio State. Barbara Ingling offered me the graduate assistantship that changed my life. It led me to many community college transfer students. They, along with their peers who did not end up transferring, represent the student population that has become the heart and soul of my research career. This opportunity was the genesis of my passion, and the intellectually liberating space that Barbara provided allowed me to fully explore and follow my instincts, being the hugely intuitive learner that I am.

I could not have asked for a better team to work with on the research project that led to this book. Seo Young Lee and Kelly Wickersham were among the earliest and core members of the team. They have both provided incredibly timely and thoughtful assistance to every phase of the project since 2014. It was a remarkable honor to learn and grow with you, witnessing your journeys from budding graduate researchers to doctoral recipients to the amazing scholars in your own rights that you are today. Amy Prevost, who came on board in 2015, is the consummate project manager and researcher in one. Having your able and calm support as the project developed in so many ways allowed me to stay grounded even during the worst days.

Yen Lee took on the role as quantitative data manager following Seo Young's graduation and has equally evolved into a vital asset to the team. Several other graduate students at UW–Madison helped with various facets of qualitative data collection during the project's first year: Ning Sun, Ashley Gaskew, Na Lor, Brit Wagner, and Falon French. Your stellar assistance enhanced our entire team's capacity to gather the rich volume of qualitative data during the project's foundational year. Last but certainly not least, Hsun-yu Chan, Xiwei Zhu, Sara Jimenez Soffa, and Brett Ranon Nachman also contributed to data analysis and interpretation that focused on several key topics that emerged from the larger project. In particular, Hsun-yu Chan led a few highly informative analyses of our participants' transcript records.

All of you are not only my team members; you have all become my coauthors, collaborators, and most importantly, thought partners with a shared commitment to the success of two-year college and transfer students. The journey that led to this book wouldn't have been as fulfilling and thought-provoking without you.

For the writing of this book, I am grateful to Kelly Wickersham and Amy Prevost for support related to literature searches and for editorial assistance. I also thank Yen Lee for assistance with quantitative analysis. Thanks also to Xiwei Zhu for help with formatting tables and figures. To each one of you: your high-quality assistance made it possible for me to focus on my writing and remain in a creative space. The thoughtfulness, kindness, and patience you infused in the process kept me going even when life became a roller coaster during the final years of this project.

A study of this nature and scope requires a considerable amount of financial resources, and I am privileged to have received them to carry out this work. I am thankful for a small seed grant in 2013 from the University of Wisconsin–Madison Graduate School Fall Competition that made possible the pilot work to set up the project. More significantly, I was honored to receive a major award from the National Science Foundation (NSF; DUE-1430642). I would especially like to recognize my program officer at NSF, Connie Della-Piana, for appreciating the importance of transfer as a key function of community colleges. I thank Connie for believing not just in me but, more notably, in work that focuses on transfer in STEM fields. You imposed no restrictions on how I approached this research rather than to always follow where students led us, and I thank you for your guidance around navigating politics in building partnerships. NSF is lucky to have you as such a big advocate and proponent for community colleges.

I would also like to acknowledge the UW–Madison Survey Center, especially Griselle Sanchez-Diettert and John Stevenson. Our survey design, implementation, and eventual high response rates benefited tremendously from your vast expertise. The numerous brainstorming sessions we had together, from visualization of the sampling schemes, to the design of the survey questionnaires, and to implementation, all ensured that our surveys were fielded in a high-quality fashion, did right by the students, and achieved the best possible response rates.

I am also indebted to the many wise and supportive people with whom I discussed this book and its underlying research program. The conversations I shared with or feedback received from all of the following individuals helped inform and enrich my thinking in various ways: Eboni Zamani-Gallaher, Turina Bakken, Linda Sax, Zong Her, Gregg Nettesheim, Yan Wang, Valerie Lundy-Wagner, Martin Rudd, Greg Lampe, Pamela Eddy, Todd Stebbins, Michael Feder, John Fink, Marilyn Amey, Gloria Crisp, Lara Perez-Felkner, Jason Taylor, Debra Bragg, Manuel González Canché, Rachelle Winkle-Wagner, Thai-Huy Nguyen, Peter Miller, Nick Hillman, Clif Conrad, and many others. I especially thank John Fink and Pamela Eddy, who offered thought-provoking feedback on several chapters of the book manuscript.

As this project evolved, my team and I presented our emerging research findings at multiple national conferences and meetings held by professional organizations, including the American Educational Research Association, the Association for the Study of Higher Education, Council for the Study of Community Colleges, and the National Institute for the Study of Transfer Students, among others. In each case, the audience's thoughtful engagement with our work pushed and deepened our thinking. I am also grateful for the opportunity to present an earlier version of the book's key findings as part of the Visiting Faculty Scholars of Color series at the University of Pennsylvania's Graduate School of Education, during which I received insightful feedback.

To Jayne Fargnoli, my editor at Harvard Education Press, I remain grateful for your invested interest in community colleges and issues of inequities in STEM and transfer. Thank you for the care and validation that always accompanied your constructive feedback, for honoring my voice as a researcher and a writer, and for the gentle nudging and unwavering support when I needed it the most. All that you did and how you did it meant the world to me as a first-time book author. I also extend my thanks to Sarah Weaver, my copy editor, and to all the editorial team members at Harvard Education Press who made publication possible.

For this book, I owe my deepest gratitude to the students who participated in this study. Your awe-inspiring agency, resilience, and thoughtfulness continue to move and propel me, and I dedicate this book to you. My thanks also go to the two-year institutions, both in my study and elsewhere, for what you represent, for your genuine will toward always better serving your students, and for the vast promise of what you could become.

Finally, Weijia, for your unconditional support and all the sacrifices you made.

ABOUT THE AUTHOR

XUELI WANG is a professor of higher education in the Department of Educational Leadership and Policy Analysis at the University of Wisconsin–Madison. She studies college students' learning, experiences, pathways, and success, with a particular focus on community colleges and STEM education. Her longitudinal, mixed methods research has addressed inequities in access to transfer, particularly in STEM fields, as well as how faculty development translates into teaching practices that subsequently shape students' experiences and outcomes. Dr. Wang has received multiple awards for her research and teaching. She was selected as a Young Academic Fellow in 2012 by the Institute of Higher Education Policy and the Lumina Foundation. She is a two-time recipient of the Charles F. Elton Best Paper Award by the Association for Institutional Research. In 2015, she was honored with the Barbara K. Townsend Emerging Scholar Award by the Council for the Study of Community Colleges. In her department at UW–Madison, she has been honored with the Teacher of the Year award six times since 2012.

INDEX

access to courses, 7, 34, 47, 146–147, 160–161
active learning, 34–42, 162
adult learners, 22–24, 91–97
advising
  adult learners, 96–97
  bias in, 48
  friction against momentum, 150–153
  gender and, 73
  helpfulness of, 45, 46, 89
  mental health issues, students with, 102–103
  nudging, 152, 164–165
  redesign needed for, 163–165
  reflection about, 168–169
  relationships needed for, 164–165
  systemic issues with, 50–51
advising loads, 51, 151–152
affordability. *See also* financial aid
  deferred trajectory and, 135
  disparate impact of, 7–8
  family income and, 20–21
  limiting people who can transfer, 48–49
  of schools accepting transfer credits, 47–49
  students of color and, 7–8, 84–85
  transfer intent and, 111
  for women, 62
ageism, 95

agency, 44–51
age of students, 22–24, 93
applied learning, 34–42
articulation, 44–45, 146–148, 157–159
aspirations. *See also* transfer intent
  overview of, 107–108, 119
  of Bethany, 108–110
  of Clyde, 110–111
  momentum trajectories and, 163
  transfer process as discouraging, 115–120
  value of transfer versus job, 108–115

Bethany, 41, 108–110, 111–112
bias
  ageism, 95
  alma mater and, 48
  gender and, 66–68
  nontraditional students and, 149–150
  racial, 81–84, 88
  training about, 73, 150, 161
block scheduling, 160
Bubbles, 86

cafeteria-style model, 141
Callan, 23, 94, 99
career pathways, 20, 38–41
caregiver roles, 22–24

237

Center for Urban Equity (CUE), 166–167
Chad, 78, 87
characteristics of transfer students, 18–24
Clark, Burton, 107
Clyde, 84, 110–111, 115–116
collaboration, 158–159
college-educated parents, 22
college-for-all ethos, 107–108
college preparatory courses, 33–34
community, sense of, 162–163
community colleges. *See* two-year colleges
Community Colleges in the Evolving STEM Education Landscape summit, 28–29
confidence, 31–34, 36–38, 118
contextualization, 162
cooling-out concept, 107
"The 'Cooling-Out' Function in Higher Education" (Clark), 107
cost. *See* affordability; financial aid
courses
 access to, 7, 34, 47, 146–147, 160–161
 gender and, 74
 reflection about, 169
course transfer
 difficulty in figuring out, 45–46, 110–111, 147
 first-generation students and, 49
 friction against momentum and, 146–148
 guided pathways and, 140–141, 143
 linearity of STEM and, 46–47, 146–148
 problems with, 45–46, 118
credentials, race and ethnicity and, 81
credits, unneeded, 46
CUE (Center for Urban Equity), 166–167
cultural inclusion, 79–80, 149, 161–163
culturally responsive education, 161–163

daycare issues, 23, 74
deferred trajectory
 defined, 24, 122–123
 financial issues and, 135
 of Kanda, 6–9, 122–123, 130–131, 135
detoured trajectory
 defined, 24, 122
 disadvantaged background and, 134–135
 reasons for, 5–6
 of Seamus, 3–6, 122, 130
diversity, 79–80. *See also* inclusion; students of color

Elizabeth
 active learning and, 41
 diversity and, 81
 math and, 33
 motivation for, 70
 parent education and, 22
employment, 23–24, 108–115
encouragement from parents, 21–22
engagement, 149
equity issues. *See also* friction against momentum
 access to higher-level math in high school and, 34
 guided pathways and, 143
 inclusion and, 79–80, 149, 161–163
 momentum trajectories and, 123–136
 privilege and, 128, 139, 142–143
 reform for, 153
equity-mindedness, 166–170
ethnicity and race. *See* students of color

faculty, 88, 159, 165
failure, impacts of, 9–10
family expectations, 82–83
family income, 20–21, 125–126, 132–133

financial aid
  friction against momentum and, 145–146, 156–157
  grants, 74, 101–102
  at schools accepting transfer credits, 48
first-generation students
  course selection and, 49
  encouragement from parents, 21–22
  intersectionality and, 132–133
  momentum trajectories and, 125–126
  support resources and, 83
fit with program, 5
foundational courses, 160–161
four-year colleges, 20, 93, 152–153. *See also* institutional issues
free tuition, 145
friction against momentum
  causes of, 139–140
  curricular domain, 146–148
  financial domain, 145–146, 156–157
  importance of removing, 139–141, 142
  motivational domain, 150–153
  removal of, 144–153, 165–170
  as systemic, 136
  teaching and learning domain, 149–150
funding, 51

gender. *See* women
gender stereotype threat, 65–68, 149–150
Gertrude, 23–24, 33
grants, 74, 101–102
Greer, 33, 67–68
guaranteed transfer programs, 1–2
guided pathways, 140–141, 143
Gwyneth
  as adult learner, 23
  bias against, 66–67
  drive to achieve, 70–71
  identities of, 65, 66

motivation for, 69–70
on their own, 54–55

Hewitt, Nancy M., 27

implicit bias training, 73, 150, 161
inclusion, 79–80, 149, 161–163
income, 20–21, 125–126, 132–133
initiative. *See* on their own
inspiration, multiple roles and, 69–70
Institute of Medicine (IOM), 11–12
institutional issues
  acknowledgement of, 143
  adult learners and, 93
  advising, 50–51
  articulation and, 44–45, 146–148, 158–159
  friction and, 136
  functionality and impact of, 105–106
  mental health issues, students with, 102–106
  momentum lost due to, 138–139
  transfer information needed, 118–119
  women and, 72–75
intent to transfer. *See* transfer intent
intersectionality, 132–133, 146
introductory courses, 10, 29, 137
isolation. *See* on their own

James, 22, 24
Jasmine
  as adult learner, 23
  identities of, 65–66
  mental health issues and, 98–99, 101, 104
Jennifer, 53–54
Jennipher, 32, 79
Jim, 94–95
"jobbing out," 113, 114

Jordan
- course transfer and, 45–46
- equity-mindedness and, 170
- identities of, 124
- linear upward trajectory of, 1–3, 122, 127–130
- math and, 30
- support resources limited for, 56
- on their own, 43

Kanda
- advocacy for course offerings by, 6–7, 61
- deferred trajectory of, 6–9, 122–123, 130–131, 135
- diversity and, 77–78, 87
- equity-mindedness and, 169–170
- identities of, 61–62, 124
- intersectionality and, 132
- on their own, 44, 47–49

Katy
- as adult learner, 94
- equity-mindedness and, 170
- identities of, 62–65, 124, 131–132
- learning disabilities and, 103, 104
- math and, 31
- taking a break trajectory of, 9–11, 123, 131–132, 137–138
- on their own, 44, 49, 137

Kelly, 98, 100–101
Kevin, 21, 40
Kirsten, 21, 71
Kooks, 36, 88–90

learning disabilities, students with, 91, 97–99, 103–104
learning styles, 162
lecture-based courses, 40–41
life circumstances of students, 22–24
linear upward trajectory
- advantaged background and, 125–130, 142–143
- defined, 24, 122
- of Jordan, 1–3, 122, 127–130
- long-term versus short-term payoffs, 114–115

majors, 72, 108
math education
- developmental classes, 28, 30
- as gatekeeper, 10–11, 29–34, 160
- importance of, 30
- range of majors needing, 17
- self-perceptions and prior experiences with, 31–34
Mathias, 103–104
mental health issues, students with, 91, 97–106
mentorships, 73–74, 162–163
momentum trajectories. *See also* friction against momentum
- overview of, 24–25, 121–122, 127
- deferred trajectory, 6–9, 24, 122–123, 130–131, 135
- detoured trajectory, 3–6, 24, 122, 130, 134–135
- disadvantaged background and, 130–136
- friction removal having domino effect on, 144
- inequities embedded within, 123–136
- linear upward trajectory, 1–3, 24, 122, 125–130, 142–143
- motivation and, 138, 150–153, 163–165
- taking a break trajectory, 9–11, 24–25, 123, 131–134, 137–138
- on their own and, 136–139
- types of, 24–25, 122–123
motivation, 138, 150–153, 163–165

National Academy of Engineering (NAE), 11–12

National Academy of Sciences (NAS), 11–12
Nelkowicz
   active learning and, 36, 38
   changing aspirations of, 112–113
   math and, 32
   parent education and, 21–22
nontraditional students
   adult learners, 22–24, 91–97
   class schedule difficulties and, 47
   financial requirements and, 156–157
   friction against momentum and, 149–150
   support resources limited for, 56–57
   women, 64–68
Norman, 92–93, 95
nudging, 152, 164–165

occupational education, 20, 38–41
Office of Community College Research and Leadership (OCCRL), 167
older students. *See* adult learners
online advising, 151–152
on their own
   overview of, 43–44
   advising and, 151
   momentum trajectories and, 136–139
   prevalence of, 51–55
   student agency and, 44–51
   transfer information needed, 118–119
   variation in available resources, 56–57

parent education, 21–22
parents, factors involving, 21–23, 63–64, 82–83, 125–126, 132–133
passive learning, 40–41
Paul, 116–117
perseverance, 95
President's Council of Advisors on Science and Technology, 14
prior experiences, 31–34

privilege, 128, 139, 142–143
professional development, 73, 150
promise programs, 156

race and ethnicity. *See* students of color
reflection, 165–170
research study
   overview of, 14–18
   generalizability of, 18
   location of, 17–18
   student overview, 18–26
resilience, 86
Rising Above the Gathering Storm (NAS, NAE & IOM), 11–12
role models, 74, 162–163

safety, 98
scholarships. *See* financial aid
science education, 10–11
Seamus
   detoured trajectory of, 3–6, 122, 130
   equity-mindedness and, 169
   identities of, 124
   intersectionality and, 132
   on their own, 43, 46–47
self-efficacy, 36–38, 68
self-initiative, 44–51
self-perceptions, math and, 31–34
Seymour, Elaine, 27
Shinichi, 21, 81–84, 134–135
short-term versus long-term payoffs, 114–115
single parents, 23, 63–64
Stella, 117
STEM
   defined, 16–17
   identity and, 163
   lack of women in, 59–60
   shortage narrative, 11–13
   transfer rate for, 45
   white males as default in, 129–130

STEM education
  classroom experience as central in, 28–29
  cost of, 145–146
  course transfer and linearity of, 46–47, 146–148
  dissatisfaction with classes in, 27
  need for, 12
  students changing away from, 28
stereotype threats, 65–68, 149–150
structural diversity, 79–80
student advisors. *See* advising
student agency, 44–51
students of color
  overview of, 77–79
  access to higher-level math in high school and, 34
  advising and, 151
  affordability and, 7–8, 84–85
  benefits of diversity and, 80
  educational aspirations of, 80
  intersectionality and, 132–133, 146
  multiple barriers for, 84–86
  racial bias and, 81–84, 88
  in STEM fields, 130
  support resources and, 88–90
  systemic inequities and, 129
  taking a break trajectory and, 124–125
  two-year colleges valued by, 86–87
  white students compared, 79–81, 129–130
study. *See* research study
subbaccalaureate options, 20, 38–41, 107
summer bridge programs, 3
support resources
  adult learners and, 96–97
  background and, 128
  first-generation students and, 83
  gender and, 73
  race and ethnicity and, 81–84
  students of color and, 88–90
  for transfer, 51–57

transfer intent and, 67–68, 116–117

taking a break trajectory
  defined, 24–25, 123
  disadvantaged background and, 133–134
  of Katy, 9–11, 123, 131–132, 137–138
Talking About Leaving (Seymour & Hewitt), 27
teachers, 90, 159, 165
teaching strategies, 34–42
Temperance
  active learning and, 40
  as adult learner, 94, 95
  changing aspirations of, 112, 114, 119–120
Tom, 84, 118
trajectories. *See* momentum trajectories
transfer intent. *See also* aspirations
  active learning and, 36–38
  actual transfer and, 108
  affordability and, 111
  Bethany, 108–110
  Clyde, 110–111, 115–116
  confidence and, 117
  gender and, 72
  limits of studying, 15–16
  potential future of, 119–120
  race and ethnicity and, 81
  support resources and, 67–68, 116–117
  with two-to-four-year transfer difficulties and, 117–118
transfer pathways. *See also* on their own
  active learning and, 38–42
  initiatives to expand, 14
  into institutions versus into desired major, 45
  need for clarity with, 57
  problems with, 44–45
  as unfulfilled potential, 13–14
transfer rates, 45, 81, 88

transfer services. *See* support
resources
transfer student characteristics, 18–24
trust, 147–148, 152
two-to-four-year transfer. *See also*
transfer intent; transfer pathways
articulation and, 44–45, 147–148,
157–159
completion rates after, 13
financial aid and, 145–146, 156
gender and, 72
support for, 88–90
transfer intent and difficulties with,
117–118
two-year colleges. *See also* advising;
institutional issues
age of students, 93
bachelor's degree as goal and, 18–19
self-worth increased by attending,
115
STEM shortage narrative and, 12–13
STEM students switching pathways,
28
student differences from four-year
colleges, 20
transfer potential as unfulfilled, 13–
14, 148
underfunding of, 158
valued by students of color, 86–87

Valerie, 84–85
vocational programs, 38–41

white students, 79–81, 129–130
women
overview of, 59–64
addressing diverted dreams of, 72–
75
affordability and, 7–8
coping mechanisms for, 69–72
gendered experiences of, 64–68,
149–150
intersectionality and, 132–133
in STEM fields, 130